Past Words
Prem Krishnamurthy

KW INSTITUTE FOR CONTEMPORARY ART | BERLIN
KUNSTHAL GENT | GHENT
VERLAG DER BUCHHANDLUNG WALTHER UND FRANZ KÖNIG | KÖLN

Prem Krishnamurthy

Past Words

DESIGNED BY

Ann Richter
David Knowles
Mark Foss
Valentijn Goethals

Krist Gruijthuijsen

Fernando de Noronha
12 May, 2024

Dear Prem,

I am currently residing off the coast of Brazil on an island called Fernando do Noronha, and it's quite the paradise. This hidden gem is mostly known among Brazilians for its endless beaches and incredible nature populated by some of the world's most rare species. The perfect setting, I'd say, to write some introductory words to your first comprehensive publication solely dedicated to your writing produced over the past fifteen years. It's about time!

I am quite excited about the format we eventually chose to accompany your writing in order to experience a deep dive into some of your projects, in this case *K,*, a year-long project we initiated together for KW in Berlin as a follow up of your epic project *P!* and *Endless Exhibition*, the project that launched the Kunsthal Gent in Belgium. When going through all the material you'd sent a while back when the idea started, my head started spinning—which is not unusual when I think of you and your practice. I, myself, already have trouble concentrating (ADHD, as they call that condition), so trying to find the proper angle to think about your work is challenging, if not impossible. Much of your output is born out of conversation so I can see why the form of a letter is a useful way to focus your thoughts. So, here I am writing a letter to you, a form to be published soon.

Within your texts about design, designers, exhibition making, art, and architecture, I notice a continuous struggle between your position in the (art) world and the limiting definitions that come along with it. Although you dabble in roles such as designer, curator, educator, and exhibition-maker, you are constantly reconsidering their form and meaning for each context.

"His work across media addresses historical, contemporary, and speculative intersections of art and design; the politics of presentation and display; and experimental institutional formats, narrative models, and collaborative frameworks," you once wrote to describe your work.

Although your (self-)description is characteristically dense, I repeatedly reread these sentences and find it sums up your practice quite nicely. You seem to keep trying to challenge yourself (and your audiences) to find new formats for display and representation—whether through design or curating (or both). Your endless drive and inspiration are admirable and somewhat relatable. We both seem to lack an off-switch and are ferocious in our ambition even though we are also driven by spiritual concerns. Look at your relationship to On Kawara and the many letters you wrote to him in order to understand the world around you! Kawara makes us understand our existence, which is the true essence of art. Your relationship to Kawara reminds me of what I feel toward Ian Wilson, an artist to whom I have been writing a love letter since 2009. Wilson was able to pose fundamental questions on the collective experience of art through spoken exchange. "I'm interested in the idea of time. I would insert the word 'time' into every conversation with whomever and wherever. It wasn't about the word itself but about the verbal communication that it stimulated," Wilson said in 2002.

I think that this is what ultimately connects us, Prem: our interest in time as a space of endless possibilities and necessary limitations, a medium to be played with. Crucial is the emphasis on "dialogue" as a key strategy to foster a visible exchange between audiences. *Language* is a common guiding principle; it is continuously explored as an artistic material in order to expand upon how to understand communication and exchange.

Our mutual friends November Paynter and Vasif Kortun introduced me to you with a sense of great urgency in 2015. Looking back, I guess they weren't wrong. I remember visiting Frieze Art Fair, where you presented a solo presentation of the work of Brian O'Doherty. It was unusual, and you know I am a sucker for risks. I learned that polymathic O'Doherty (God bless his soul) was one of your main sources of inspiration. His ruminations on the white cube appear to guide your thinking and practice. I mean, look at what you did with P! (emphasis on the exclamation mark)! Your so-called "Mom-and-Pop- Kunsthalle" (I still don't get this terminology, but who cares) in New York was the perfect mix of gallery, design workshop, meeting place, nonprofit, curatorial laboratory, and so forth. Very necessary and not very New York. Too complicated. Too conceptual, albeit driven by form and, most importantly, your curiosity and need to experiment. Curiosity is a word that should be tattooed somewhere on your body discreetly (or maybe indiscreetly), as it encapsulates who you are.

When I started as director of KW, I initiated *A Year with*, a residency program that concentrated on notions of publishing in the broadest sense. I immediately thought of you, as we both like to blur the boundaries between art, display, and design. You told me you were closing shop and moving to Berlin so continuing P!'s inquiries in a new form made a lot of sense. *K*, was born! The program drew heavily from Klaus Wittkugel, one of your heroes and someone you have written extensively about. This German Berlin-based graphic designer and exhibition-maker was new to me, but after an in-depth introduction by you, I became highly fascinated! Thank you for that! But why, oh why, did you have to introduce the idea that the names of all the program's guests needed to start with the letter "K"? And also have the letters of your own name slowly dissolve throughout the course of the year, ending with, of course, a K? I told you then that I thought you were a little insane and, indeed, Kafkaesque!!! I know you love your games, Prem.

But, in all seriousness, because of you the project mobilized a great community of designers and artists, something that was desperately needed in Berlin. It took many, many years to create this publication, but I'm glad we decided to make something that would offer the reader a peek into your fascinating, inspiring, and incredibly chaotic mind.

Prem, you are truly one of a kind. You included a definition of the word *kainotophobia* in *K,*'s original KW pamphlet, which refers to a fear of change or a resistance to something due to fear. This phobia certainly doesn't apply to you! I hope this publication gives you the pride and joy that it brings me. I'm happy to have helped make this time capsule possible.

Love, as always,
Krist

Notes to the Reader

Prem Krishnamurthy

(2024)

It may seem disingenuous to introduce your introduction by saying that you never intended to make a printed book of your own work. But it's true—as a young designer, I found it torturous enough to pull together a simple portfolio. Why spend any amount of time documenting things that already exist instead of working on the next, best project? It felt like less a creative act than a mortuary one. Move forward!

Unfortunately, we don't always stick to our greener self's proverbial guns. And so here we are, with 360 printed pages in our hands. Oops!

The salve is that it's not just a dead document, I hope, but rather something more lively. This book starts from words but tries to move beyond them. It's a kind of bumpy, ungainly creature: one that contains some essay-like writing-writings collected from over a fifteen-year period, entwined with two less ruly texts—an absurdly alphabetical romp through a yearlong, experimental curatorial program and a speculative manifesto-cum-syllabus for future exhibition making. These latter two sections originated as multi-part, performative works; as such, neither fits neatly into the frame of a typical publication, much less a compilation of selected writings.

I suppose this odd hybrid form is in step with my own oddly hybrid biography. It's a life that dances around language and its many formats. In 2004, I started my first graphic design studio in New York City, Project Projects, which focused on conceptually-driven work with artists, architects, museums, nonprofits, publishers, and the like. Text was our bread and butter. But the more success we had in the graphic design business, the more I wanted to set some new targets. At a certain point I spent many of my days designing exhibitions, and my nights dreaming about them—and so I figured I might as well start *making* them, too.

In 2012, I pivoted and opened P!, an experimental, interdisciplinary gallery that ran in parallel to my design practice. It was a curatorial playground, a sandbox for myself and the artists, designers, curators, musicians, and writers I invited in. P! lasted for five years, the duration of a New York commercial lease and the longest that I could keep up a particularly insane multi-hyphenate-career tempo.

When P! closed in 2017, my already forking professional path took yet another detour. Krist Gruijthuijsen, director of KW Institute for Contemporary Art, invited me to open a one-year project, *K,*, in Berlin from 2018-19. I saw *K,* as the opposite of P!—a slow space for thinking and production rather than presentation. Partway through that year, Valentijn Goethals of Kunsthal Gent invited me to revive a provocative proposal from several years earlier, which eventually became *Endless Exhibition* and provided the foundational logic for their institution. *Past Words* owes its existence to these two unusual meta-curatorial projects, which each question the typical parameters of exhibition-making. Surprisingly, I followed these conceptual asides with several large-scale curatorial outings: a biennial, a triennial, and several other shows (coincident with a raging pandemic and its aftermath). Unsurprisingly, those years are now a blur.

Throughout this period, my professional waystations as a designer, curator, and educator were highly visible, yet in many ways the writing was the hidden heart beating continuously within them. I would labor over text after text, trying to give words to my practice. They were published in journals, on websites, in press releases; eventually also in books, electronic publications, and anthologies. But they never tried to take shape into a story until now.

§

Back in the days when I spent more time designing and editing other peoples' books and less time writing introductions for my own, I often argued that a book's concept and design (in fact, its whole gestalt) ought not to merely present something preexisting (whether an artwork, an exhibition, or even its author's texts) but rather to do something. One way to think about this is a publication as a *performance* rather than a *document*. And so this volume is conceived not simply as a collection of past writings plus some other projects, but rather as a project unto itself. How a set of ideas and events is represented and distributed is itself part of the work–whether or not you like it. There is no neutral format: any frame of presentation carries meaning.

The "Note to the reader" at the beginning of *Ways of Seeing*–a work that resonates across this entire endeavor–articulates this idea: "The form of the book is as much to do with our purpose as the arguments contained within it." *Past Words* is similarly trying to enact something of its claims to multiplicity in its format, layout, materiality, and design process. Three designers or teams–Ann Richter, David Knowles, and Mark Foss and Valentijn Goethals–were invited to imprint one of the book's sections with their graphic vision. In fact, each of them was deeply involved as a witness, participant, or commissioner to the activities and projects here. I think of this exceptional A-team as participant-observer-designers; they have each devised ways of sharing their experience with others on a graphic level. They are my most obvious co-authors.

Other co-authors abound in these pages. Even though there is one name on the spine–"Prem Krishnamurthy"–this moniker stands in for many other people. Singular authorship is rarely that. Some of these texts have been explicitly co-written, other voices are embedded. Mentors and muses such as Brian O'Doherty, Elaine Lustig Cohen, Karel Martens, Klaus Wittkugel, and On Kawara make cameos. The whole of the writing emerged out of extended conversations, whether with people, ideas, objects, or spirits, who are more often than not named. These are acts of writing as missives to others.

As letters, they are also objects in circulation, in dialogue, in the process of change. A phrase appears a few times in the book: "A thing is just a slow event." Whether or not Stanley Eveling actually said those exact words is pretty irrelevant at this point, since it's a great sentiment. It suggests a crucial aspect of this project: it's not a finished product, but rather something dynamic.

Like, look, the book just changed! It's suddenly a different thing. Who would have thought?!

But seriously: I'm not just trying to prank you with typographic quips. This volume (as well as its author) comprises a loose cast of characters, pulled together for a brief ensemble appearance, and the writing has its own multiple personalities. Short excerpts from my two previous book-length works—the experimental electronic publication *P!DF* and the more traditional-seeming *On Letters*—point towards the genre-agnostic complexities embedded within a single text. Even though *Past Words* isn't organized strictly chronologically, as its astute reader you might notice certain proclivities at different moments—occasions when the writing veers into academic terrain, or refocuses on specific topics (exhibitions, display, design), or takes on a more aphoristic quality, or even becomes explicitly epistolary in format, speaking directly to a particular you. These periods rarely lasted long, but they were each a transformation.

The two projects that each form their own book-in-a-book were created for transitional, time-based formats before landing here. They echo and overlap ideas (and sometimes even words) in the essays. The starting point of the *K,* section is an entire year's worth of programming, conceived as an ongoing, collaborative, accumulative work. Its intention to be ephemeral and hard-to-grasp played out in how it was announced: through a series of irreverent institutional press releases, which are reproduced here. Now this program has taken on a second life through an additional storybook narration of the year's arc: 26 oddly alliterative, alphabetically-driven annotations, arranged with accruing images. Technically, these words are present, not past—but who's counting?

The path from past to future takes off with *Endless Exhibition*. This project enjoyed its own circuitous media life-cycle: it launched as a series of lecture-performances delivered with slides that were later distributed within a 1,020-page PDF file, which then became a series of videos that continue to inhabit the very exhibition space (Kunsthal Gent) where the lecture-performances were originally delivered. Furthermore, the entire multiyear exhibition program of Kunsthal Gent is called the "Endless Exhibition." There's a willfully promiscuous polymorphism at play, an interest in how works mutate when they move from one mode to another.

Yet words remain at the core of each of these endeavors. Out of the panoply of media we humans have available to us, words in their rawest form are some of the most durable. A good story, whether a compelling myth or a metrical text studded with mnemonic aids, can last for thousands of years. Longer, probably, than even the paper medium upon which they were scribed or typeset. Writing can be a very long-term technology.

Even though I often envy an archivist's completist bent, this volume is composed out of its exclusions, the many texts, images, ideas, and projects that didn't make the cut. What is memory, after all, but a thing that is continuously formed and reformed, every time it is recalled? The hallmark of a healthy memory is that it smooths out. Like a JPG file with its lossy compression, resaving a memory enough times ends up with something fuzzy and soft around the edges. Put differently, a normal memory is one that's eventually forgotten. It's the traumatized memories that stay around, unaltered, frozen, forever.

So let's be thankful that *Past Words* is *not* that: some kind of stuck record of time, some gravestone marker, an epitaph to a finished creative life. I have often written from a personal perspective, which means that some of the facts and relations in it are already out of date. At points, I've corrected these things if they're too egregious to reflect the current moment; in other cases, if the integrity of the writing benefits from it, the texts remain in their original form, incorrect though they may be today. This mirrors a larger truth: that, through its very publication, the book allows for a specific version of the past to be preserved and another one to melt away. This is appropriate since, as is my wont, I've already moved on—to other transformations, other topics, other themes that are taking up my time.

Which is why I'm depositing these thoughts with *you*: to read them, wrestle with them, find ways to work with them, to one day forget them. To move, eventually, past words as fixed things and towards their emergence as sometimes fast, sometimes slow events.

I'll end this loping intro with an extended citation from a work of mine not reproduced here, 2021's *Pompeii!*, which explores the archaeology of the self and writing. It may capture the intention of this book more succinctly than the 1,790 words previous:

> When we talk (or sing karaoke!) together in an online room, we may experience a lag—yet we probably perceive the exchange as relatively synchronous. When you respond to the texts of an author, writing years or decades or centuries before you, it's also a conversation—but with greater apparent asynchronicity.
>
> In this framework, it's all a kind of *thinking together*. Whether I release ideas into a room or commit them to pixels or paper, it represents one round of a longform exchange—with folks who are nearer or further into some possible future than my present position.
>
> For example: with you, whenever you are right now.

– June 2024, New York City

Selected Texts *2009–2024*

Originally published in *I Like Your Work: Art and Etiquette* (New York: Paper Monument, 2009).

(2009)

Of all social forms, I find proper introductions to be the most difficult. The combination of unarticulated expectations, conventions, and motives creates great potential for unparalleled awkwardness. Within the art world, this form is made even more complex by the ambivalence with which the art community views professionalization. In less rarefied social contexts, simple devices, such as the name-tag, are used to ease the difficulty of introductions. Featuring the bearer's name, corporate or group affiliation, and a generically indiscriminate greeting, the name-tag is perfect for situations in which nobody knows anyone, and everyone has a reason to meet. At a business networking event, getting to know unfamiliar people is the sole reason for attendance. Consequently, introductions tend towards transparency, straightforwardness, and functionality—in contrast to the complex and ambiguous encounters typical of art world openings and parties.

Many people I know have a particular manner of making introductions and even preferences for how they themselves are introduced. For example, certain friends insist on no introductions beyond their first name. With great faith in social predestination, they believe that innate affinity and mutual interest will either create a dialogue spontaneously or allow a given interaction to end quickly of its own accord. I remember from my years in Berlin an oft-expressed rule: avoid introducing oneself by full name or discussion of work, as it is crass and professional. While I admired the principle of this stance, it sometimes led to absurd situations. Once, after playing pool for several hours with a group of friends and new acquaintances, I was dismayed to discover that a member of our group was a well-known artist whose work I had admired for years. Of course, by then it was too late and too awkward to even mention this fact.

Among artists in New York, I've more often experienced formal introductions by first and last name, paired with carefully chosen references to each party's best-known or recent work. On the one hand, such introductions can be inclusive by encouraging fluid interactions and mingling distinct social circles. However, even when sincerely made, these introductions often veer towards comic effusion in their valiant attempt to engender an instant conversational connection: "This is so-and-so, they are the most amazing whatever in New York. You must have seen that project last year, it was so well-received, no?" While potentially providing a basis for meaningful discussion, such introductions are tricky: they involve acquainting people who ought to already know each other's work, but by virtue of the necessity of an introduction, most likely do not.

Finally, a familiar form in the art world is the goal-oriented introduction, in which one attempts to facilitate social contact on behalf of a single party. Such situations are functional and professional, but, in order to be effective, must observe the protocols of more informal encounters. The set-up is simpler because desire in these cases is purely one-sided: as a means to an end, one person wants to meet another, who likely has no prior knowledge of them. For example, I'd like to introduce my friend, an artist without representation, to a gallerist with whom I've worked in the past. Here the onus is most clearly on the introducer, who attempts to reveal a relevant piece of information that will pique the interest of the targeted party. Perhaps my own social awkwardness is to blame, but I've routinely seen this stratagem fail, most often with the mark either ignoring the introduced party or exiting the situation entirely for the drink table or restroom.

Given the impossibility that I'll ever be introduced to or introduce anyone appropriately, I may have to hope for the next best thing: an unregulated, alcoholically-lubricated world of social contact, in which introductions are neither needed nor desired—where everyone wears their hearts (and name-tags) on their sleeves, allowing conversation to sometimes ebb and often flow.

Originally published in
Prem Krishnamurthy, *P!DF*, v.1.0.0
(New York: O-R-G, 2017).

(2017)

I hope you'll allow me a momentary digression. Whenever I think about exhibitions and their radical potential, I can't help but recall a quote from artist Judith Barry's crucial 1986 essay, "Dissenting Spaces":

> How to force a confrontation? If architecture embodies our social relations, then presentational forms (including staging and lighting devices from the theater, opera, and Las Vegas, as well as more obvious museological techniques) must refer to ways in which we wish to experience these relations. One confrontational tactic yet to be explored is the subversion of the wish for closure, possession, and gratification. One way to do this might be to make threatening the assumed neutrality of the exhibition space itself.[1]

This exhortation to "make threatening the assumed neutrality of the exhibition space itself" calls into question the very norms of presentation. Perhaps the provocation can be extended outside of the gallery space, and into the realms of design and curating more generally.

In classic 20th-century formulations, good design should be invisible and functional. But this takes for granted that we all have the same perspective, that everyone agrees about design's methods and ends.

In a related vein, curators are often instructed that artists and artworks should come first. Within this set of assumptions, curating that problematizes its own role and agency in creating meaning—taking an explicit and reflexive position—is suspect.

While there's surely a valid role for both design and curating that attempt, however impossibly, to objectively or neutrally framing their content—whether text, images, artworks, or otherwise—I'm generally more drawn to work that acknowledges its own inherent biases, operations, and strategies. This stance helps open things up for critique.

1
Judith Barry, "Dissenting Spaces," in *Damaged Goods*, Brian Wallis, ed. (New York: New Museum of Contemporary Art, 1986). Reprinted in the exhibition publication for *DIS-PLAY/RE-PLAY*, Prem Krishnamurthy and Walter Seidl, eds. (New York: Austrian Cultural Forum New York, 2016).

2
A related set of rhetorical questions around design's role appear in Beatriz Colomina and Mark Wigley's *are we human*: "Designers are always understood as solving a problem. Artists, intellectuals, and writers are expected to ask questions, to make us hesitate, to see our world and ourselves differently for a moment, and therefore to think. Why not design as a way to ask questions? ...Design as an urgent call to reflect on what we and our companion species have become?" Beatriz Colomina and Mark Wigley, *Are we human? Notes on an archaeology of design* (Zürich: Lars Müller Publishers, 2016), 162-63.

So, what if graphic design and curating were treated as instigators instead of facilitators?[2] Although it goes against professional dictums, I'd propose that we could start to think about these fields as ways to create problems rather than just solve them—or maybe as a way to accomplish both at the same time.

Originally published in Prem Krishnamurthy, *P!DF*, v.4.0.0 (New York: O-R-G, 2018).

(2018)

A book that has stayed with me since my early twenties is W.G. Sebald's *The Rings of Saturn.*

It's a strange hybrid, a novel that confounds fiction and non-fiction, historical fact with embedded memoir. The book's first person narrator—not to be conflated entirely with its author—travels the landscape of contemporary England. His encounters with people and places serve as a starting points for interwoven digressions on colonialism, capitalism, war, memory, and beyond.

The Rings of Saturn is a spellbinding, puzzling book, not the least because of its unusual visual structure. Within a cascading flow of textual narration (including single sentences that sometimes run over multiple pages), images appear abruptly, without captioning or provenance.

Are they illustrations, historical documents, proofs of the author's presence and the book's own truth-value? Or something even more particular?

It turns out that Sebald created many of the images himself, even those that appear to be much older. His manual manipulations, using darkroom techniques and photocopier magic, give these photographs the odd look of ephemera from a flea market or lost archive. Rather than accompanying the text, they are a text unto themselves—albeit ones that read on a different register entirely.

The images' narrative instability lends them a mysterious power. It's the opposite of "responsible" curating or design that contextualize their contents precisely. Also unlike didactic or documentary pictures, the images are not trying too hard to make a point. Here, in this shifting space between fact & fiction, verity & myth-making, an imprecise kind of knowledge emerges, apart from contemporary modes of address.

One day, perhaps, when I'm a bit braver, *P!DF* could grow to include images and other materials that function similarly. Rather than referencing distant times & places, such momentary lapses might command their own authority, becoming unmoored from their original positions to move silently, yet with purpose, in sharp, willful directions.

Originally published in
Prem Krishnamurthy, *P!DF*, v.1.1.1
(New York: O-R-G, 2017).

(2017)

A close friend and collaborator leveled a pointed critique at this *P!DF* when he saw it. You make it seem too easy, he said, to do multiple things, wear many hats, move from field to field. The truth is, it's all hard work, and it doesn't always succeed. Other people need to understand that. Why, he asked, don't you talk more about *failure*?

I was defensive at first, arguing that my footnotes contain a lot of failure—you just need to read between the lines. Ultimately, though, he's right about the way I've told this story; I've held on to the positives and smoothed out the rest. The human mind is built to forget negative things, lending it resilience.

Where should I even start with *failure*? Failure is about expectations. It's implicit in everything, permeates each page of this document.

I could begin by admitting that I was driven for almost ten years by a manic impulse to make up for what I perceived as the failure of my Fulbright Fellowship. I worked for a year on a project that was never completely finished—failing those who had given me their time in interviews and entrusted their memories to me. I also failed myself, losing confidence in my ability to be an artist. I spent years beating myself up for this.

Failure is everyday: missed meetings, lost clients, subpar work, white lies, and easy justifications. It's in being ungenerous, letting petty needs trump more important concerns. Failure is neglecting loved ones, prioritizing the wrong things: fame over friendship, quid over quality. It's obsessing about this PDF until 4 A.M. rather than being present for my stepchildren.

Failure is in financial & emotional ruin, the hogwash calculus of running a money-pit of a gallery next to a stressful design practice next to teaching like its therapy and trying to write furiously and traveling too much and attempting to maintain personal relationships but just working working working working working. Failure is pushing to the edge of collapse, willfully and without regard for yourself or others.

I could go back further. To 1985, when terrorists blew up half my father's family, turning an Air India flight into smithereens somewhere off the coast of Ireland. They took my favorite aunt, too. That failure—the failure to *live*—is the biggest one.

So failure is implicit in everything here, my dear friend. It's in the process, and it's in the end, which comes after all of us. The only way to escape failure is to try—blindly, like some dumb animal—to live on forever.

Maryam Jafri: Types of Specificity

Originally published by P!, New York, 2016.

(2016)

THE OBJECTS OF Maryam Jafri's *Generic Corner* (2015) appear at first glance as imports from a strange and parallel world: a drab Communist state, a film-set with a limited props budget, or a conceptual art gallery. Each object is a commonplace food product—beer, peanut butter, bran flakes, corned beef—identified primarily by its name in black type on a white background. Devoid of the color, imagery, and visual rhetoric we are used to seeing in our contemporary shopping environments, these items are encountered here as readymades within slender upright vitrines and in staged product photographs. Pure products, they announce themselves as objects of nourishment rather than desire, stripped bare of their spectacle.

Plucked out of an odd corner in the history of American consumer goods, the objects are so-called "generic goods": low-cost products offered in the late 1970s and 1980s in an "unbranded" form. Relegated to a special aisle, they were directed towards low-income or cost-conscious shoppers. But that brief moment of pure product-ness, with packaging reduced to a degree zero and segregated within the store, quickly vanished as supermarkets developed their own in-house budget brands to integrate seamlessly with "regular" products.

As aesthetic objects, Jafri's generic goods at first exude a blank contextlessness. Evocative of early conceptual art, such as Joseph Kosuth's linguistic constructs, the products also recall critical figures including Ed Ruscha and Andy Warhol, whose early artwork grew out of their careers in advertising and commercial art. Warhol's Brillo boxes, first exhibited in 1964, were lionized for appropriating and recontextualizing simple commercial packaging. However, the continued resonance of these pieces is also a testament to the seductive graphic flourishes of the original packaging design, which was authored by James Harvey, an Abstract Expressionist painter who made his living as a commercial artist. Warhol's appropriation of Harvey's daily work imbued the Brillo boxes' populist visuals with value. Half a century later, Jafri examines an alternate moment in that same history of product branding to create a monochromatic, minimal pop art—one that contrasts with existing investigations of vernacular consumer culture.

To the trained typographic eye, the seemingly unbranded generic products that Jafri has collected belie their time and place quite clearly. Today they appear specific, not anonymous. Their artistry functions both through their appropriation as readymades and their original form as commercial art. Graphically, Jafri's objects merge the simplicity of modernist Swiss pharmaceutical packaging with unusual typographic choices, which read as a catalog of "hip" visual options of the era. Which designer decided to set "Corned Beef" in Bauhaus, a nostalgically-named typeface rife with disco associations? Where was the puffy, outlined lettering to mark "Soap" chosen? Who paired the typeface Cooper Black with "Peanut Butter," repeated in an endless, chubby loop of letters? How did the generic packagers settle upon "Crispy Rice" in a bold, condensed, custom-lettered lowercase, a nod to the 1920s German typographic avant-garde and its utopian aspirations?

Seen from this perspective, Jafri's packages no longer appear blank or unauthored, but rather as nearly perfect cubes or cylinders for the display of typography. They raise the vital question: What would typography in the white cube look like? Outside of type samples, typography is nearly always informed by its context, tethered to use value. Yet every font has its own independent character, however subtle. Jafri's work reveals a broader fact: whenever it appears, typography is both the content and communicator of a visual idea.

It's a truism by now to claim that there is no neutrality–whether in writing, architecture, art, display, or design–only the semblance of objectivity, whose patent untruth becomes apparent generations later. As in the realms of post-war art gallery presentation and modernist design, the aesthetics of universal whiteness now appear as obvious constructs. They can be read as high class or low end, haughtily refined or starkly austere, depending on where and when we are doing the looking.

Karel Martens, Joy, and Five Years of P!: An Interview with Prem Krishnamurthy

By Ben Schwartz

Condensed from the original version published online in the *Walker Reader*.

(2016)

https://walkerart.org/magazine/karl-martens-prem-krishnamurthy-project-projects-p

EVEN AFTER FOUR YEARS of programming, the New York storefront P! has managed to elude any form of archetypal gallery classification. The freewheeling spirit of P! can be attributed to its founder, Prem Krishnamurthy, whom many reading this blog know from his graphic design studio, Project Projects. Prem's profound understanding of both graphic design and curating elucidates interesting relationships between the two disciplines. In each show Prem makes it a priority to juxtapose work from a spectrum of fields to question boundaries and reveal connections between seemingly disparate practices.

If you've unwittingly happened upon the space over the years, you are just as likely to find a reading room, experimental techno celebration, or currency exchange station. In response to the diversity of work, the architecture of P! finds itself an active collaborator; evolving to create a unique spatial context for each show. At one point this meant a green ceiling under the guidance of a feng shui master; at another, it evolved into a new gallery altogether under the name K.. Kicking off the final season in the storefront is the exhibition Karel Martens, *Recent Work*. The show is an appropriate bookend, not only because of Martens's participation in the inaugural P! show, *Process 01: Joy* (2012) but the way many of his pieces occupy the ambiguous ground between graphic design and contemporary art.

BEN SCHWARTZ To begin, could you tell us a bit about putting together the current show, Karel Martens, *Recent Work*?

PREM KRISHNAMURTHY I've worked with Karel a number of times. He was included in the first show at P!, *Process 01: Joy*, and was one of the reasons why I opened a gallery in the first place.

Our past projects with Karel have focused primarily on his letterpress monoprints, his best known works apart from his commissioned graphic design. Although Karel has always worked across media and scales, there hasn't been a venue for these works to be shown. We've been developing *Recent Work* together for nearly a year; the longer timeframe presented an opportunity for Karel to think through his work since the 1950s and pick up on strands that he's wanted to develop further. For example: the clock piece, *Three Times (in Blue and Yellow)*, is a new work but its origins range back to Karel's early kinetic clock works of the 1960s. And the interactive installation, *Icon Viewer*, is an extension of the custom icon-pixel language that Karel developed nearly 15 years ago.

One thing I admire about Karel's practice is that he has embraced technology with openness and curiosity. Although graphic design has changed radically over the nearly 60 years since he started, Karel has adopted successive tools and continued to stay on top of contemporary methods. This has allowed him to push his ideas about color, pattern, reproduction, and form, and to experiment in different dimensions and media.

BS P!'s role has extended beyond what one would typically expect from a gallery. In many ways the space becomes an active element that works in tandem with the artist. Would you consider *Recent Work* a collaborative effort?

PK This raises the open-ended question around the place of design and curating within the broader realm of artistic production. P!'s role–as well as my own–modulates greatly based on the circumstances. In some exhibitions, we have a strong hand in formulating the initial framework and creating the context that brings everything together. In this exhibition, as in other solo presentations, our role was quieter yet still present.

Karel's exhibition emerged as a dialogue between us, but with his practice, rather than a discrete curatorial premise, at its center. We've been in close conversation to decide how to approach the exhibition, what works to display, and how to show them. Together we made models, plans, and elevations of the exhibition, batted around ideas for each part of the show, determined which new works needed to be produced, and edited down from a larger set of works and projects. However, Karel is ultimately the author of the work and exhibition.

At the same time, I think that this show couldn't have taken place in another space, whether in New York or elsewhere. It represents a confluence of Karel's work and the unique profile of P!, along with my approach to curating exhibitions. Together they generate a situation that goes beyond the individual components.

BS You and Karel seem to have a very close relationship. Over the years, what have you learned from him as both a curator and a designer?

PK Each of the artists whom I work closely with at P! challenges my ideas and forces me to grow. I'm thinking here of Céline Condorelli, Aaron Gemmill, Mathew Hale, Maryam Jafri, Christopher Kulendran Thomas, Wong Kit Yi, and others. I've also had the pleasure of exhibiting figures from an older generation–designers, artists, writers, musicians, and more–who have been fundamental to my own thinking. I consider myself lucky to have had a chance to learn from their deep experience and wisdom, while also exposing them to new audiences and approaches. This includes not only Karel, but also Brian O'Doherty and Elaine Lustig Cohen.

Karel has taught me a lot. Some things are practical and aesthetic: for example, how he thinks about hanging a show, which is very related to how he arranges a layout on a page. Rather than hanging a show according to classical curatorial or museum approaches, he uses other structures like grids and margins, which give his installations an unusual energy and freshness.

A more fundamental thing that I've learned from working with Karel is how he likes to leave some things unfinished and open-ended. I tend to be very, very structured and try to control nearly every detail. Working with Karel, I've observed his tendency to be precise about certain aspects of a piece or exhibition but quite relaxed about others. I think this is what allows the work to breathe.

Karel also has a Dutch sense of work/life balance–so he tends to get a beer or dinner at 6 P.M., even if he comes back to the studio or exhibition space later on. I'm still trying to learn from him here, too!

BS I've always loved that about his personal work, the way intuition and spontaneity play a large role in his process. Each move is a reaction to what's already on the page and to what he's feeling at a particular moment. The decision-making process seems oppositional to graphic design, where there is the need to justify every aesthetic move.

PK You're right, but it's a specific case with Karel. He's been working for nearly 60 years and so is truly a master of his field. Even his intuitive decisions about form, color, and typography arrive with an incredible degree of innate practice and knowledge.

The question of context and what's already on the page is also significant here. For Karel, as for myself, there is an interest in what exists before one steps into a given situation as a graphic designer. This happens with his monoprints: he chooses to print on things that already have a past life and a formal order. It's a kind of recycling but also a response to something that's already there. For me, it's about a sense of making history visible.

Several years ago, I was leading the design of the signage program for the Yale University Art Gallery. There had already been a number of signage programs that had existed over the years before we were commissioned. Rather than approaching the project by starting from scratch, I decided that we would retain aspects of those older signage programs, layering our own system on top. This lends the viewer a richer sense of what's been there before, and what's still to come.

This is how I approach exhibition spaces, too. I don't look at the gallery space as being a tabula rasa, blank slate, or white cube. One aspect of my exhibition-making is that I consider the architecture and history of a space as inflecting whatever's displayed in it. A show in a gallery is just one more archaeological layer added to the top.

BS I think this current show of Karel Martens occupies an interesting space in regards to graphic design and contemporary art. Karel is of course a seminal graphic designer, but the work being shown is uncommissioned. Did you ever feel the need to make the distinction between design and art when putting together *Recent Work*?

PK I don't make that distinction; rather, I try to look at the unique values and qualities of objects, regardless of what genre they belong to. Karel is foundational to the program of P! because he occupies this ambiguous ground between art and design. He makes works that are not commissioned, but sometimes the forms that he creates in his monoprints make their way back into his commissioned graphic design work. There is a healthy back-and-forth. Both his commissioned and uncommissioned works are equally beautiful.

In Karel's case, I see this as a kind of visual research. He's spent the last 60 years experimenting with form and color, constituting a body of knowledge and practice that flows into all of his different work. In this way, he occupies an in-between space. For much of the history of the 20th-century avant-garde, there wasn't a strong distinction between applied and "free work." This overlap, exemplified in Karel's work today, is at the heart of my interests and why I wanted to include him in P!'s program from the first show. We're in a historical era in which there is a strong boundary established between disciplines—which has much less to do with intrinsic distinctions and much more to do with the market and how different kinds of labor are currently valued.

I always ask myself with Karel's work and that of others I'm interested in: Who cares whether people call it graphic design or art right now, but what's this going to look like in 50, 100, or 1,000 years? Many of the things that we value most from past generations may have once been functional, whether they're pottery, printed remnants, or cave paintings. They had one relevance in their original moment but they've also maintained their integrity. Their relevance to us now is that they have acquired a new meaning, which is in excess of the original purpose.

BS Although you mentioned not looking at a hard and fast line between graphic design and fine art, with P! do you feel a particular responsibility to give graphic design more representation in the gallery space?

PK Since I come from a background in graphic design, it's one of the key contexts and bodies of knowledge that I carry with me everywhere I go. Graphic design is an embedded filter for how I think about the world. In a broader sense, the history of graphic design is extremely intertwined with larger narratives of historical and contemporary visual practice. It's impossible to disentangle design from how we look at art since the beginning of the 20th century. Beyond the crossover of the disciplines and practitioners, even the reproduction, publication, and dissemination of art has been traditionally mediated through graphic design.

When I consider what to place into an exhibition space, it's quite natural to me for those things to come from the different worlds with which I engage, whether contemporary art, graphic design, music, or writing. However, with graphic design in particular, I have tended to come at it from two directions. Sometimes I'll show things from a graphic design context that I think are compelling within a broader discourse; other times, I present contemporary art projects that might resonate with graphic design in a significant way.

In this latter category, I have in mind exhibitions we've done with artists such as Vahap Avşar, who worked with the archive of a defunct Turkish postcard company to make new postcards for distribution. Another example is Maryam Jafri, who examines histories of consumer products from an anthropological and artistic perspective. Her show at P!, *Economy Corner*—I think one of our best—was an exhibition about economics, branding, markets, and class, while also being legible as a show about typography, even if that's not Maryam's primary interest. Another crucial show for me from our fourth season was *Pangrammar*, a freewheeling and highly personal exhibition that mapped my interests in the overlaps between typography and art in a loose, associative way. By mixing works that were art and design, new and old, unique and multiples, within a single idiosyncratic curatorial structure, it gestured towards the more open-ended yet critical ways I'd like these fields to be looked at.

BS When you do include graphic design in particular shows, it's never really looking inwards at the practice itself. I'm thinking of the Anton Stankowski and Klaus Wittkugel show; although both graphic designers, the work seemed to point outward toward larger ideas about East and West Germany. The display of graphic design seems very different than say, *Graphic Design: Now in Production* here at the Walker. How does bringing design into a gallery context change the viewer's relationship with the work?

PK It's good that you bring up *Graphic Design: Now in Production*. As you know, Project Projects collaborated with the Walker Art Center on the graphic identity of the show; I then directed the exhibition design for its New York presentation at the Cooper Hewitt, Smithsonian Design Museum. In fact, the show immediately preceded P!'s opening and surely influenced some of my decisions. Curated by Andrew Blauvelt and Ellen Lupton along with a team of others, *Graphic Design: Now in Production* took a more classical approach to displaying graphic design, organizing it according to projects, specific media types, and functionality.

This is quite different from my curatorial approach. For me, context is extremely important in looking at design objects—for whom and why was something made?—but I'm equally compelled by a work's broader significance, whether aesthetic, conceptual, cultural, or ideological. The challenge is how to make these registers legible within the exhibition setting, which I've tried to address. The Wittkugel/Stankowski exhibition was one approach, which involved using particular strategies of contemporary art display to present historical graphic design work, freeing it from some of its baggage while also situating it within broader political discourses.

I'm committed to an approach to presenting design that does not separate it from other fields of visual and artistic inquiry. That's not to say that there are no differences between these disciplines, but rather that I'm interested in their confluences. I take issue both with how graphic design is exhibited in a closed-off way, but also with recent exhibitions of early 20th-century avant-garde figures that focus primarily on their paintings or their sculptures, when they made equally important contributions in graphic design, photography, exhibition design, and beyond. By relegating these practitioners' "applied" work to a secondary status, the exhibitions are actually undoing in large part their intended legacies.

BS As this is the last year of P! in its physical manifestation, I want to go back and discuss some of the history of the space. As you mentioned, the first exhibition was *Process 01: Joy* which explored the relationship between joy and practice. In the context of your own work, how has P! been a source of joy for you?

PK Framing the first show at P! in this particular way was both self-reflective and self-deprecating. After all, opening P! alongside my work at Project Projects, my teaching, my writing, and everything else was basically a choice to double or triple my workload! And then to focus the first show around labor and name it *Joy* was also a slightly perverse joke. But it also had a very serious dimension. All three of the participants in that first show—Chauncey Hare, Christine Hill, and Karel Martens—had explored, both implicitly and explicitly, the complex relationship between vocations and avocations, labor and pleasure. The show embraced the fact that much of the most significant work, of any kind, falls outside of the typical 9-to-5 workday, while being part of a dialectic with this economy of production.

What creative people produce to make a living is often circumscribed into very specific categories. After the show, I began to look at what works from somebody's practice might be marginalized, and hone in on those. If P! has, in part, created a home for people's "off-projects" that don't fit in neatly with what they're necessarily known for, then I'd be happy.

BS That's actually a point I wanted to touch on: the relationship between your curatorial practice and graphic design practice. How have the two influenced each other?

PK For a number of years, I've been planning to write a longer text or at least put together a lecture about the relationship of curating and design. Maybe I'll have more time to finish this once P! on Broome Street closes! I hold that the two fields—graphic design and curating—are quite similar in a number of historical, structural, and practical ways. Both disciplines are focused on mediating content rather than necessarily generating it themselves. Curators and graphic designers alike work with other people, other objects, other ideas that are outside of themselves—they're exogenous pursuits.

As a graphic designer, you work with your clients to make their content legible for a set of publics. As a curator, you work with artists to translate their work and interests to a broader audience outside of their studio.

BS We talked a bit about collaboration. The collaborative dynamic seems at the heart of both P! and Project Projects. In your design practice Project Projects seems involved at a much deeper level than a traditional designer/client relationship. P!'s involvement as well goes beyond the traditional white cube approach. Can you talk about P!'s unique curatorial point of view?

PK From the beginning, I've always thought of the space itself as an actor. This is both with regards to P! and more generally when I'm designing and curating exhibitions in other venues. One of my fundamental texts is Brian O'Doherty's *Inside the White Cube*. It dates back to 1976, but Brian's argument still reads quite true, 40 years later.

I believe that the context of presentation, the architecture and the display of an exhibition, can be as meaningful as what's being shown. One of the first decisions I made after I signed the lease for 334 Broome Street was to talk with Leong Leong, the architecture firm whom I had brought in to work with Project Projects on *Graphic Design: Now in Production* in New York. Their original design highlighted the context of the storefront space and its previous life, a Chinatown HVAC contracting office. Over the years, as the space has developed through the interventions of artists and my own curatorial ideas, Leong Leong has remained involved in the conversations around how the space evolves.

More broadly, apart from simply trying to foreground mediation, architecture, and display, I have a strong belief about self-reflexivity and transparency: since curating is a discipline that makes things visible yet also orders the world according to its own agendas, the curatorial act—the very process of framing—ought to itself be laid bare.

One of Brian's core arguments from *Inside the White Cube* is that the white cube gallery makes nearly anything displayed inside of it into a kind of sacral object, increasing its market value. As a counter to this kind of invisible conditioning, I'm interested in trying to expose for the viewer how such operations construct values.

This is also something that figures into much of my design work. For me, the challenge is not just to make a compelling identity, book, exhibition, or website that presents its content in a neutral way, but to also design it in such a way that makes the viewer aware of its own mediation and influence. Undermining one's own authority—or at least, calling it into question—is an important quality.

BS In regards to making things visible, I feel like a lot of that is coming from playing with the context of various disciplines. Placing work in a gallery that may not typically exist there, but also with other practices it may not normally exist alongside. For example, in *Permutation 03.4: Re-Mix* you put Thomas Brinkmann, a DJ, alongside visual artists Katarina Burin and Semir Alschausky, the architectural practice Fake Industries Architectural Agonism, and a video essay by Oliver Laric. In creating these sorts of experiments in recontextualization, what are you hoping to communicate?

PK Thank you for reminding me of a pretty important exhibition to me. It brings up similar questions around how context and juxtaposition affect the meaning of individual objects. This particular show was also the conclusion of a four-exhibition cycle examining ideas of copying, authorship, and originality. The series had a looping structure in which artworks, ideas, and specific display strategies echoed each other across shows.

Through my work as a graphic designer—but also through other interests, including filmic montage and psychoanalysis—I've learned to work with the principle of juxtaposition: if you show multiple objects within the same frame, whether on a page, in a space, or within a limited time period, a connection will be formed between them in the viewer's mind.

BS This season marks the last season for P! in the Broome Street space. I feel like the storefront has played such a major role in many exhibitions, and its location in Chinatown seems to be an important factor. What does the move mean for P!? Does it have to do with a shift in ideology or is it more related to logistics?

PK A "move" is a slight misnomer insofar as we are not announcing a new location after this, at least not for now. It's actually more that P! is shifting its focus. For its first five years, P! existed primarily as an exhibition program housed in a single location, with occasional off-site presentations and projects. Moving forward, P! will take the shape of a dispersed institution that can assume and inhabit different spaces through its programmatic focus. It will still organize exhibitions and presentations, collaborating with museums and other venues. P! will also continue to work with artists, designers, and others on these shows as well as on producing publications. So it's more of an opening-up of the focus of the organization.

P! as a storefront in Chinatown was always intended as a limited-time offering, with a start and end date. This accompanies the strong narrative component to its program thus far. Each of the past seasons or years of the space have had a specific structure and arc to them; this even includes the fact that we changed the name of the gallery for a five-month period, becoming another gallery, K.. I thought of that moment as our version of a "play-within-a-play."

And as with a literary work, there may be an ending, but that doesn't preclude sequels and continuations.

BS It seems to me that P! has always been about evolution, whether that be through a changing architecture or a flexible identity system. Now, to not even be tied down to a specific location seems like a logical progression in regards to what's next.

PK Yes. P! has also represented an exploration of a different mode of institutionality. It's an outgrowth of my many years of work with institutions, especially those that have an unusual, non-normative shape—such as SALT in Istanbul or the Berkeley Art Museum/ Pacific Film Archive's MATRIX project space. I've made this part of my program at P!, allowing it to constantly shift its profile and visual identity, so that it might appear as something quite different to its various audiences.

Bricks-and-mortar spaces are only one aspect of a contemporary institution. While I'm still committed to exhibition-making, the next institutional challenge is how to disperse activities and programming yet still maintain an audience and a community.

BS To close things out, I want to ask a bit of a sentimental question. With any sort of major milestone I think it's important to look back on what has been accomplished. Are there any particular memories that stand out to you during your time at the Broome Street location?

PK I liked your question about Thomas Brinkmann and the exhibition *Permutation 03.4: Re-Mix*. For the opening of that show, there was a special performance where Thomas invited his New York friends to bring records to play on his special double-armed record player. Each original record was transformed into something like a slow, dub-inflected shuffle, with a tremendous sense of stuttering rhythm. It turned into an incredible, dance-floor moment, with everyone anticipating what would come next. The floor seemed like it might collapse. It was such a special moment, I remember thinking, we could end P! right now, and it would have all been worth it. We've already accomplished in a microcosm what we originally set out to do: to bring people who would never otherwise know each other into a space together, and to create a dialogue.

P!, 2012–2017

Originally published via P! email newsletter on May 31, 2017.

(2017)

This "unconventional vest-pocket space"[1] is a "weird wormhole"[2]—"not your usual art-world entity."[3] "More ecosystem than exhibition"[4] venue, it's "a space to watch,"[5] "prodding the fraught marriage of form and the social"[6] by remaining "irresistibly complex and colorful, if a little hard to decipher."[7] With a "notably self-reflexive sense of humor,"[8] it takes a "concise"[9] approach that's a "contradictory patchwork"[10] of "artist-writer-curators and assorted polymaths"[11] while avoiding the "drearily arcane."[12] P! is a "place for speculative reason,"[13] "a physical environment"[14] with "prankish synergy"[15] that "indicates how a gallery space is anything but neutral"[16] and never exists "purely as financial speculation."[17] Its "quick-fire exhibitions addressing contemporary value systems"[18] use "sleight of hand"[19] to "blur the boundaries of art and design,"[20] while pointing "toward timely issues."[21] These "games and puzzles"[22]—"intensely pleasurable, gorgeously sensual,"[23] yet "witty"[24]—are "vehicles of self-portraiture,"[25] an "experimental travelogue"[26] "through the dire and bifurcated political landscape"[27] by an "inexhaustible brainiac."[28] "A certain amount of this must be taken as tongue-in-cheek, but like the readymade, a certain amount of it is deadly serious."[29] "Claiming nothing, it claims everything."[30]

1
"Marc Handelman / Arthur Ou / Peter Rostovsky." *New Yorker*, May 20, 2013.

2
Andrew Russeth, "Hitting It Off." *New York Observer*, February 10, 2014.

3
Nancy MacDonell, "Open Agenda: P! In Chinatown." *New York Times T Magazine*, September 18, 2012.

4
Rachel Ellis Neyra, "Critics' Pick: The Stand." *Artforum.com*, February 10, 2017.

5
Will Brand and Corinna Kirsch, "Project Projects Co-Founder Opens a 'Mom-and-Pop-Kunsthalle' in Chinatown." *ArtFCity*, August 31, 2012.

6
Annie Godfrey Larmon, "Critics' Pick: Céline Condorelli." *Artforum.com*, May 5, 2017.

7
"Céline Condorelli." *New Yorker*, May 15, 2017.

8
Kaelen Wilson-Goldie, "Critics' Pick: Process 01: Joy." *Artforum.com*, October 16, 2012.

9
Nova Benway, "Permutation 03.2: Re-Place." *Modern Painters*, July/August 2013.

10
David Markus, "Rainbows to No Place: Société Réaliste and the Ayn Rand Apocalypse." *Hyperallergic*, October 12, 2013.

11
Karen Rosenberg, "Brian O'Doherty: Connecting the ..." *New York Times*, March 28, 2014.

12
Peter Plagens, "Lyrical Forms, Social Commentary and Handiwork." *Wall Street Journal*, October 12, 2013.

13
Rhett Jones, "Yams Collective Brings Ferguson Themed Installation to the LES." *AnimalNewYork.com*, September 12, 2014.

14
David Frankel, "Brian O'Doherty." *Artforum*, June 2014.

15
Johanna Fateman, "Critics' Pick: Post-Speculation." *Artforum.com*, October 2014.

16
Gemma Tipton, "Critics' Pick: Brian O'Doherty." *Artforum.com*, March 28, 2014.

17
Jason Farago, "Around Town: New York, USA," *Frieze*, May 2015.

18
Iona Whittaker, "Michal Helfman." *Art in America*, September 2015.

19
Zachary Sachs, "Critics' Pick: Klaus Wittkugel and Anton Stankowski." *Artforum.com*, February 6, 2016.

20
Martha Schwendener, "Blurring the Boundary Between Art and Design." *New York Times*, August 28, 2015.

21
Karen Schiff, "Maryam Jafri." *Art in America*, June/July 2016.

22
"Brian O'Doherty." *New Yorker*, April 14, 2014.

23
Nick Currie, "The Office and the Orgasm: The Monoprints of Karel Martens." *Mousse*, Issue 57, February-March 2017.

24
Blake Gopnik, "Daily Pic (#1395: i)," *blakegopnik.com*, September 22, 2015.

25
Holland Cotter, "Brian O'Doherty." *New York Times*, February 10, 2017.

26
Mimi Wong, "Futures Again: Wong Kit Yi," *ArtAsiaPacific.com*, April 4, 2017.

27
Rachael Rakes, "The Stand." *Village Voice*, February 22, 2017.

28
"Real Flow." *ArtinAmerica.com*, March 6, 2015.

29
Jonathan T.D. Neil, "Derivative Work." *ArtReview Asia*, Summer 2015.

30
Will Heinrich, "Controlled Experiments." *New York Observer*, October 22, 2012.

Originally published by Stanley Picker Gallery at Kingston University, London.

P!CKER
AN EXHIBITION OF TWO SOLO SHOWS:
ELAINE LUSTIG COHEN AND CÉLINE CONDORELLI
CURATED BY PREM KRISHNAMURTHY AND STELLA BOTTAI
SEPTEMBER 28, 2017–JANUARY 27, 2018

P!CKER proffers a particular proposition: that curating, design, and other artistic pursuits in our present times must eschew the promotion of perfect products, instead presenting the creative process itself, with its plurality of positive outcomes and periodic faux pas.

This peculiar statement connects the activities of Stanley Picker Gallery, whose programme embraces the intersections of art and design within a university context, with that of P!, a hybrid exhibition space and "Mom-and-Pop-Kunsthalle" that existed in New York City from 2012–2017. Founded by designer, curator, and educator Prem Krishnamurthy, P! operated with a quixotic drive to remake conventions of exhibition display, reexamine the relationship between aesthetics and political agendas, and reconsider accepted boundaries of contemporary creative practice.

With this collaborative context, *P!CKER* emerges as a series of two solo exhibitions—presenting polymathic practitioners Elaine Lustig Cohen and Céline Condorelli—alongside a programme of activities. Building off P!'s five year exhibition history while pointing towards future pursuits, the exhibition offers alternative models for considering interdisciplinary pedagogy and ways to work within the world.

P!CKER, PART I
ELAINE LUSTIG COHEN
LOOKING BACKWARD TO LOOK FORWARD
SEPTEMBER 28-NOVEMBER 11, 2017

How do we take stock of a multifaceted creative life that never stood still? During six decades of practice, Elaine Lustig Cohen (1927-2016) moved between diverse activities including design, artmaking, art dealing, archiving, collecting, and researching. While she is known most widely for her groundbreaking graphic design work from the 1950s and 1960s, which extended the vocabulary of European modernism to an American context, the visibility of her rigorous body of artwork has grown substantially over the past years. Always changing, Lustig Cohen shifted from hard-edged abstraction in the 1960s and 1970s into photographic collage, work on paper, sculptural assemblage, and alphabetical experimentation in her later decades. Her visual output developed in close intellectual friendship with leading writers, architects, designers, and artists of her time.

Reflecting this open spirit, *P!CKER, Part I*—Lustig Cohen's first solo exhibition in Great Britain—positions her practice within an experimental framework. Conceived and designed by Prem Krishnamurthy of P!, who worked closely with the artist during her last years, the exhibition focuses on a small selection from Lustig Cohen's prodigious production alongside other objects, documents, and displays from her final exhibitions and collaborations. Presented subjectively and acknowledging its own gaps, the show aims to be generative rather than definitive—asking questions about the work on view and suggesting pathways for further research.

A series of reading groups, informed by Lustig Cohen's work, her literary interests, and other theoretical and philosophical strands, take place over the course of the exhibition. In November, the show transforms into *Prologue*—a solo presentation by Céline Condorelli, which overlaps in content and concerns with *Epilogue*, the closing exhibition at P! from Spring 2017.

It seems sometimes the future arrives before the past.

Originally published in
Prem Krishnamurthy, *P!DF*, v.4.0.0
(New York: O-R-G, 2018).[1]

FOREWORD

Books change with time. Even when they appear static, the world around them shifts, transforming them in both visible and subtle ways. The situation now is markedly different than in 2018, and so we must, by necessity, understand the past through this altered lens. Reading *P!DF* a decade after its writing reveals meanings that may have been hidden from its original makers. For historical accuracy, we have retained the content and formatting of the last archived version of this document. Its errors and omissions remain fixed—as fixed as anything today can be—but we believe that they might be framed more clearly through the obvious contrast with our present times.

– THE EDITORS, MAY 2028

Dear ______________,

Thank you so much for your time. Despite the events of these past weeks,[2] I'm grateful that you're able to meet in person today to consider this: my presentation, my *P!DF*.

It's an attempt to articulate an identity in flux: an ever-evolving snapshot of my past work.[3] Having established cultural institutions, organized exhibitions, and collaborated with artists, architects, museums, universities, and more, I'm now left asking how these creative pursuits are relevant to the tasks of tomorrow.

In the spirit of transparency, *P!DF* "proffers a particular proposition: that curating, design, and other artistic pursuits in our present times must eschew the promotion of perfect products, instead presenting the creative process itself, with its plurality of positive outcomes and periodic faux pas."[4]

At the same time, this interactive piece—a book without paper, a razor-thin exhibition—plays with the power of presentation itself. We each make different choices[5] depending on the context. The frame *around* something—how it brackets or interrupts its contents—serves a critical role in our experience of the world.

§

Over the past decade, we've watched as "curating" has turned into a trendy term. People now use it to denote any act of selection, whether for a dinner party menu or a Spotify playlist.[6] This reveals a contemporary conundrum: in the age of mass consumption, choosing has some influence, yet it's dangerously limited.

Curating is not only about today's choices: it creates historical and economic value for tomorrow. The authority of presentational norms and markers—from the white cube gallery space to the standard biographical wall label—determine what's accepted as important or natural.

I'm compelled by curating that organizes with an intention to unmask. Rather than exhibiting seamlessly, such curating makes visible how the display of an object shapes its interpretation.

At the same time, let's consider how curating could return to its etymological roots. Here, it might consider anew how to "care for" fragile things, from communities to conversations—even helping to imagine alternative futures.

§

In our information-ridden age, graphic design is everywhere—even if it's so embedded that it appears nearly invisible. Anytime you caption a photo on Instagram, you're creating graphic design without realizing it. But although you have the illusion of agency, you don't control the look; the interface does almost everything for you, shaping your ideas in more and less obvious ways.

How something is communicated visually—through texts, images, typography, color, form, and motion—influences what to buy, whom to choose, and how to live. So why is graphic design still seen in some circles as mere "form-making"?

Design exists not only as a tool for encouraging consumption, but also as a way to deliver timely ideas to new audiences and generate formats for interaction. Its effects operate under the surface, lending them a potent authority. How can graphic design help create meaning and frame crucial messages more effectively?

§

These days, too many of our experiences in the world are meant to be *smooth*—including lectures, interfaces, magazines, exhibitions, art fairs, films, songs, and even social interactions. They're optimized to be utterly digestible and eminently entertaining: *Click, click, click—I'll take it.* Smooth things go down easily.[7]

On the other hand, I think the power of framing disciplines such as curating and graphic design is that they can make even everyday things *bumpier.*

The idea of bumpiness—explored in multiple modes throughout *P!DF*—suggests roughness, resistance, and unpredictability, without falling into overt disruption. It's slick enough to pass through a first filter, yet with enough texture to provoke a little bit of a reaction.

So, where does

b
u
m
p
y

leave us?[8]

1
EDITOR'S NOTE: *P!DF* was periodically rewritten and re-released between 2017 and 2020. The final version was published on March 29, 2020, shortly after the onset of the COVID-19 pandemic; it is available online at https://o-r-g.com/epubs/p-df. A subsequent work from 2021, *Pompeii!*, closed out the project by distributing the book's individual sections for free. It was commissioned by *Pompeii Commitment: Archaeological Commitment* and can be accessed at https://bit.ly/PompeiiPDF.

2
The political gaffes, natural disasters, and troubling news of the past weeks come on the heels of nearly two years marked by Brexit, the new US administration, violent conflicts, nationalist surges, and global-warming-related catastrophes. In these circumstances, what can art, design, and curating actually accomplish? I've attempted one potential response in this document. Perhaps education—which provides ways to read and produce meaning critically—is a useful initial step. I guess that's why I'm here today.

3
Categories are tricky. I've never been quite sure what to call myself professionally, and am starting to wonder why I even need to do this. The final scene of John Hughes's *The Breakfast Club* (1985) offers this wisdom: "But what we found out is that each one of us is a brain... and an athlete... a basket case... a princess... and a criminal. Does that answer your question?" In 2016, I spoke about my practice across multiple disciplines in a long-form interview for the Walker Art Center's blog (see page 34), which gives some insight into my interests and approaches.

4
This alliterative attempt arrives via the curatorial statement for *P!CKER*, an exhibition that I organized in September 2017 with Stella Bottai at Stanley Picker Gallery, Kingston University London. The timing of that text and project (still perhaps my best curatorial outing to date) also coincides with the release of *P!DF* at the New York Art Book Fair. With its preponderance of P's, the text was a fun, absurdist play with language, while also a pretty compact statement of principle.

5
Throughout this PDF, you will encounter selected pages from *Choose Your Own Adventure #12: Inside UFO 54-40* by Edward Packard, a core text of my childhood. Even within the genre of interactive Young Adult literature, the volume is remarkable. It presents a novel system for reading that acknowledges its own incompleteness. For further explication, please refer to "Invisible Choices," an essay I published in 2009 in *Paper Monument*.

6
A compelling article by Thomas Frank in *The Baffler*, "The Revolution Will Not Be Curated" (March 2017), connects the rise of "curating" as an overused term to an insulated leftist position—the role of curating in the so-called "filter bubble"—which adds a new spin to a discussion that has been happening in professional circles for a while. As curating has moved away from its original usage and become more generalized, I sometimes find myself favoring old-fashioned but more specific terms, such as "exhibition-making," to describe my own activities.

7
As design historians Beatriz Colomina and Mark Wigley astutely note, "Good design is an anesthetic. The smooth surfaces of modern design eliminate friction, removing bodily and psychological sensation." Their small-scale, high-impact *are we human? notes on an archaeology of design* is essential reading for the design novice and initiate alike. Although I encountered the book well after developing the core ideas of this PDF, its synthetic scholarship now helps ground points argued originally from the intuitive position of a practitioner.

8
I am often polemical about mixing typefaces, in response to monovocal modernist design. This PDF uses a number of typefaces, each specific to the subject being discussed. The face used for my main narrative voice is Minotaur Regular and Italic (2014), designed by Jean-Baptiste Levée. Named in reference to Pablo Picasso and Cubism, it features dramatic, rough-hewn strokes, which disappear at text sizes. A minotaur is also a hybrid—part man and part bull—which seems appropriate to *P!DF*.

Parallel Projections

Originally published in *S&D#024/APE#117* (Ghent: 019, 2018).

(2018)

HOW CAN YOU TELL the story of a space? There are the less and more obvious modes: an oral history with its participants, an exhibition of archival documentation and ephemeral materials, a printed catalog listing all programs, a hagiographic text focused on the major highlights, etc. Each form has its value, particularly from the perspective of institutionalization–seeking to legitimize a certain kind of practice, trying to *rewrite* history to make it seem smoother, more narrative, more strategic. For, from the perspective of later audiences (including but not limited to: funding bodies; future employers; other, larger institutions; professional colleagues; family members who just don't understand; children and other descendents), this kind of coherence and forethought may seem essential. For them, the past was never anything apart from *intentional*. Today, in the eyes of many would-be exhibition-makers, designers, and artists (or even just folks messing around with forms), spaces in between, where things cannot be explained in a neat and tidy way, simply do not exist.

§

This text exists, necessarily, in fragments. It's neither a history of my own space, P! (which operated on Broome Street in New York City from 2012-2017), nor an account of the ostensible subject of this text, 019 (which was founded in Ghent in 2014 and still exists). Yet at the same time, it is perhaps both of these things. I'd like to think that, much in the spirit of both of these endeavors, it's an attempt to work through a set of questions in the open and perhaps formulate some new questions along the way. Let's see if it works.

§

With a tip of my hat to my dear friend and colleague Martin Beck, I'll start by self-reflexively introducing the invitation, my initial (mis)understanding of it, subsequent developments, and then its eventual realignment.

It all begins with an email: 019's invitation to write a text for their upcoming book. My immediate sense of both pleasure and dread. I appreciate 019 and their "Museum of Moving Practice" project very much, but how can I possibly fit in a thoughtful, properly researched essay about their work with all of the commitments I already have, including moving to Berlin and opening a new exhibition space, amidst other curatorial and design deadlines? I ask them how much they can pay me, which is, unsurprisingly, modest. The calculus ends with me rejecting the project, following my self-imposed promise to say "no" to more things in the coming year.

Which is followed by the insistence of Valentijn, one of 019's co-founders, his flexibility to try to make the text possible, his openness to my first suggestion of changing the format (into an interview with him and other co-founders of the space, which seems easier and more straightforward), to changing the timing (i.e., giving me more of it!). My reconsideration of my initial refusal, and also the sense that I can learn something from talking with 019.

A Skype interview is planned, performed, and recorded with Valentijn and Tomas. It's somewhat brusque, functional. I am constrained by many time commitments. I try to be journalistic and accomplish the interview efficiently.

The transcript comes back and it doesn't seem of great value to them, or really, to anyone. They write that they think it's mostly on the surface, and that, to be more interesting and worthy of publishing, it might need another interview for depth. Still exceptionally busy, and now in the midst of professional and personal life changes, I sit on the email for several weeks.

Valentijn nudges several times, knowing that the initial (extended) deadline draws near. I hesitate, delay, procrastinate, and then finally read the interview again—and recognize that they're right, it's not very good. I failed to ask even basic questions to get the facts straight, e.g., who founded it, when, where, etc. We would have to conduct at least another interview over email, if not several rounds, to create an interesting and readable text.

I start to have an inkling that perhaps I should write something more speculative: a piece about why I first agreed to do the piece, and what I have projected from my own practice with P! onto their space. That this might be more compelling, and that I might actually learn more from it. And also, since the publication has a more limited and specific distribution than I'm sometimes used to, I might have the opportunity to experiment more.

I start to take notes for this direction in a flurry. I propose to 019 that I could either conduct another email interview, as previously discussed, or, as an alternative, pursue a more exploratory, fragmentary piece. I also tell them that, even though I am personally more excited about the second direction, I don't know if it's a good idea because of the time constraints and work involved. I propose that we Skype.

Valentijn writes back that they are interested in the second direction. We Skype very briefly. He tells me they always thought of this text more as a "commission," an opportunity for me to write something interesting to me, rather than just as a way to describe and memorialize their practice (as I had initially assumed). He also says that they might even be able to potentially extend the deadline yet again, that having a good piece is more important than the timing. All very encouraging words, and I start to get excited.

After less than 20 minutes of chatting, I have to leave for another meeting. But the decision seems to have made itself. Before I even step into the Berlin S-Bahn, I've already started to type into a new Google doc. The text starts with, "How can you tell the story of a space?"

§

There's a set of books on my new desk in Berlin. Some of them are reminders of other spaces—experimental venues for art or culture that no longer exist, or that now live on in another form entirely. None of these art spaces were meant to enjoy old age, necessarily, and many never intended to become authoritative. And yet here these objects are: records of how a program may eventually become history.

Each book has its own approach, organization, and design. I had originally intended to write a brief synopsis and critique of each, as a way to move forward with my own thoughts about publishing a history of P!, but that seems less urgent now. Perhaps I'll return to the topic later.

There's another book, anyway, that I far prefer to any of these: *SONSBEEK 93*, from the public exhibition curated by Valerie Smith in the Dutch town of Arnhem in 1993. Although it appears to be a catalog, it's not actually about a space or project that's past, but rather one that (within the temporality of the book's production) is *still* to come. Normal, you might say smugly, for an exhibition catalog, which is usually published before the exhibition has taken place. And yet this one's organized not as a mere projection or encapsulation (which all of those other books are, just looking in the opposite direction), but rather as a living document: as a kind of sketchbook for an exhibition yet to come, it includes all of the curator's field notes of meetings with artists, commissions in progress, her (sometimes withering) curatorial critique and feedback to artists, their proposals, writings, and more. So, although it's a past collection of future-facing documents, it feels *vital*. The design, by Wigger Bierma (who later co-founded the Werkplaats Typografie, also in Arnhem, NL—which is, coincidentally, also the space that connects me to 019), is cool, calm, conceptual—but also masterful in using a minimum of means to describe different textual voices and modes of engagement. It's plainspoken yet adaptive.

In its curatorial, editorial, and design approach, this book is not about a finished project, it's about how things emerge. It's tight in the right places, while also loose (and candid) enough to let you in. To employ a word that editor Sina Najafi (my new office-mate in

Berlin, who is also connected to Valerie Smith, as she herself is to my new space) used when describing a recent event I organized: the book is "porous"—open enough to allow for feedback and dialogue. If I'm ever writing a history of my work or life, or projecting my notes forward, I'd wish for the same.

§

It's February 24, three days after starting this piece. I'm on a plane back to New York City and have to choose a first song to listen to while writing. 2018's writing needs a new vibe, so I start with Tony Williams Lifetime's "Joy Filled Summer"—a bombastic jazz-fusion track. Allan Holdsworth's guitar solo shredding through a bridge is motivating.

Last year's writing music was different. It was marked by a single album on repeat: *Dysnomia* by Dawn of Midi, a nearly hour-long masterwork of polyrhythmic acoustic music. It's something like a profound piece of minimal techno produced only by bass, drums, and prepared piano. I was lucky to witness its genesis and development over the course of several years, in live concerts and private performances that culminated in the album. Three musicians of the highest caliber, working together to develop a seamless, enveloping, continuous work of aural choreography.

For more than a year, I listened to the album on endless repeat while writing. Even though I may eventually have tired of it, I realized that it became a datum in my peripatetic working-writing life: a constant regardless of whether I was writing at my desk, in a foreign hotel, in my second (now first) home in Berlin, on a plane, train, or automobile. The music became my audio working environment, particularly for the composition of *P!DF*.

If I understand correctly, the three musicians who made *Dysnomia* are barely friends anymore. Constructing a complex, collaborative masterwork together takes its toll.

§

Let's start a table of my initial impressions around the similarities and differences between 019 and P!:

019
Spontaneous
Improvisator
Youthful
Fast 'n' loose
Cheap
Light
Fun
Extensible

P!
Strategic
Presentational

Historically-grounded
Overly precise
Expensive
Weighty
Serious
Bounded

The list could go on, but the gist is obvious: I project onto 019 everything that I wish P! had been, I treat 019 as the corrective to P!'s imagined failures. Of course, in reality, both 019 and P! probably contain aspects of both columns. It's just that later, you remember something differently, once it's over and you've decided to move in another direction.

Which is why I decided to write this piece in the first place: because my first encounter with 019 and their project "Museum of Moving Practice" was so interesting: odd, unresolved, and overlapping, yet still authorial. It seemed so related to where I might hope to continue with my own future practice, that I thought I should think more about them in order to understand myself.

§

I've always thought that it's better to let a space expire before it becomes a zombie. Or at least let it change its name, acknowledging that it's now a new entity. The argument against this, of course, is that organizations, like people, grow and change, even to the point of being unrecognizable to themselves later—but it's still the same flesh, the same person. Others would say the opposite: each moment of consciousness represents an entirely different person, the narrative frame that creates a sense of "self" is false and misleading. This unresolved tension is why some people keep notebooks or conduct what's known as "feedback analysis" (writing self-reflectively about key life decisions as you make them): to be able to look back later and compare what you originally set out to do with where things ended up.

In September 2016, I was invited to take part in a special forum at the 9th Gwangju Biennial called "To All the Contributing Factors," organized by Binna Choi and Maria Lind. The event included representatives of some 100 small- to medium-scale arts organizations. I was asked to facilitate a workshop with several organizations from Australia, New Zealand, Korea, and Japan. It became a kind of intensive group-therapy session about why our organizations were founded and continued to exist. Based on our day-long discussion, I authored a text and speculative proposal for an "institutional graveyard" for independent art spaces. Emerging out of our conversations, it was a free pass for exhausted spaces to shut their doors, yet still sleep well, knowing that their legacy would be preserved.

Since it seems unlikely at this point that the planned second volume of the Biennial catalog will ever be published, I'll reproduce part of the text here:

Every small- or medium-scale art institution must die sometime. This inevitable end paves the way for others to emerge in an increasingly overcrowded, underfunded, and over-producing field. But with each disappearing artist-run or alternative space, each mini-collapse or silent goodbye, the discourse of exhibition-making loses another set of unique memories and practices—even though they were most likely insufficiently received and appreciated in their own time, given the glut of contemporary arts programming coupled with a relative dearth of attentive publics.

To combat this ongoing forgetting, we propose the Archives of Institutional Memory (AIM), a graveyard for small- to medium-sized cultural spaces, which will contain digital and physical archives including correspondence and program documentation. At the same time, this graveyard functions as a forward-looking seed bank, containing in its material remnants exhaustive fodder for future generations of experimental exhibition-makers.

AIM is located in Brisbane, Queensland, Australia. Since the publication of Nevil Shute's 1957 novel, *On the Beach*, Australia has occupied a particular place in the popular imagination as one of the last areas that could survive a global apocalypse of nuclear, military, or environmental nature. Australia's relative geographic isolation has already contributed to the evolution of unique species of animal life and the mutation of digital memes through natural selection. For AIM, this isolation serves a second purpose: it ensures protection, safety, longevity, and remove, which are essential for future contemplation and study.

Housed in the museum-grade, climate-controlled building at the Institute of Modern Art (IMA), the Archives of Institutional Memory (AIM) offers expiring small- to medium-scale spaces a physical depository for their objects and archives. Spaces of different sizes can be leased for an affordable fee over a long term. These fees help contribute to the IMA's operating budget and ensure its ability to preserve its peers' memories in the long term.

AIM also offers named donor opportunities for funding these archival plots. This is the perfect way for larger-scale and better-funded global institutions, organizations, and individuals to acknowledge and help repay the debt they owe to smaller spaces. By taking risks, investing sweat equity, and embracing precariousness, these spaces are essential for supporting artistic research, nurturing nascent discourses and markets, and greasing the wheels of contemporary art—even after they close.

The text was fun to write, a mock institutional tone for a modest proposal. It was also a tongue-in-cheek swan song, since I had already planned and announced the final year of P! by that point. I remember dreaming, hoping that someone might take P!'s archive off my hands and allow me to no longer worry about annoying and costly questions of preservation. Closing one thing cleanly allows you to move on to the next.

Even though AIM never actually existed, maybe this very text can be a seed: someone else might read it and make it real.

§

What's the famous quote about a famous band? That there were only 10 people at their first concert, but every one of them started their own band? I don't remember who it was exactly, and writing from a plane without internet, I don't care to fact-check it either.

§

This fragmentary "essay" has become an opportunity to take a journey through my old, unpublished, unpublishable writing. Perhaps this is another kind of graveyard.

2016 in particular was a year when I resolved to write more—a lot of texts, fragments, and attempts. I said yes to nearly every invitation to write, however small. Not all of the writing made it into the world (probably for the better), but it was a productive period, something like a year of intensive, craft-building practice. The year culminated with a one-week residency in December at the Villa Empain in Brussels, at the invitation of artist Asad Raza and Foundation Boghussian. I planned to work on one particular text: a fictionalized history of P!, written from the perspective of its floor.

Even though I considered that residency a bit of a failure, in that I didn't finish the text I set out for myself, I see now in retrospect that it was very generative. I've heard it said that a good residency is an opportunity to test new things out, a chance to fail. Perhaps the origins of me thinking of myself as a "writer" in a more serious sense start there: that week, alone with myself in a blank room in Belgium, trying to write.

I worked towards a modest routine. Every morning I would wake up out of my dreams and, without checking email or consuming anything, I would write blindly into a document for approximately an hour. I would try my best not to edit. This process was a lesson from my last sustained stint of writing in 2014, while penning an academic article on East German designer Klaus Wittkugel. What came out this time was open, probing, sometimes diaristic, perhaps overly self-conscious. Occasionally I would nod off at the computer. Eventually I would get up, make coffee and breakfast, perhaps write a bit more, maybe nap; then shower and begin to work on other pressing projects. By afternoon, I'd be back on New York City time and responding to client and studio emails. I would try to see one person in the evening for dinner or drink, and then return home to sleep early and begin the next day again.

The week was not a success from the standpoint of producing usable writing. But I promised myself to judge neither my writing nor process harshly. The minor discipline of the days gave me a bit of confidence. So, despite the week's potential failures, I reproduce here an excerpt, my final attempt, raw, unedited, of how I tried to tell the story of a space from the perspective of its floor:

> The things I've seen. No one else would know them. Maybe the walls, but even they, they care less about the things I do.
>
> When this house was first built, I was installed, sturdy and wooden, into the ground. They leveled me out and made sure I was solid. And for my first years, as a shopfront, I stayed silent and watched. People would scurry across me, vermin as well, and all was the same. I slumbered, snored sometimes, felt my early years as a time of quiet.
>
> Eventually the office came and it was different. Less people, but more hectic. People shouted from office to office. People on the phone. Chairs rolled around on me, creased my skin, wore me down. I tingled sometime from the cold of the winter and the heat of the summer, there were seasons and I watched them shift.
>
> And now this, something new but not so different. A gallery. Yet mainly the difference is the people, their color, their language. Also how long they spend here. And that it's public. No longer an office, no longer for people working, now it's for people looking. Looking is the new work. Everyone does it. Even me.
>
> How do I see things? I have no eyes, I have only a membrane that is my entire surface. Do I have a depth, or am I just a surface? Where do I end, where do I begin?
>
> Now that they're nearly gone, I can consider more deeply what it was they did, to me and the rest of the space. Colleagues of mine tell me it's unusual for them to change so much. That usually someone moves in, if it's a gallery then they pour a concrete floor, and, voila!, that's it and how it will ever be.
>
> Not here, though. In this case, they seemed to treat what was below as a crucial part of the whole. Why. Who knows, maybe a kind of perversity.
>
> As I've said, first I was covered in red, then parts of me in green. Then matte black, then gray. And then covered in cork.
>
> I remember the night that everyone came to celebrate the cork. It was wet out, they arrived, bringing water and snow on their shoes. Of course it filled up, put down a layer of sodden mess. I felt it penetrate, felt it ooze into my seams, start to unloose

everything. The first effect was a pop, and then the computer there, sitting on a desk, hissed and let out smoke and shut itself down. An ominous sign. Eventually the water dried, the sockets worked again, and the show continued. But it was a strange way to start.

That cork stayed for longer than even I expected. It was routed into, the tip bit into my skin, which by then felt less like a jacket and more like a hirsute layer. And in that final moment, the one on the floor, he came and cut out a piece of my hair, cut through the cork and bit into my real skin just a little bit, to take out a section and take it with him. And after that, the whole cork was stripped away, leaving me naked again. Which is how I am now.

I know that I'll be stripped back even more, trimmed to fit soon. They tell me that they will take off the vinyl tiles, store them away, so that they bring them somewhere else. For an exhibition. What does that mean. I don't know yet, will it feel like me, somewhere else. Or will it just feel like I am reborn again, when some other they comes to pour concrete over me and smooth me out.

§

An imagined scene in Ghent, one morning. Liberties taken with facts and timing, etc. Written very quickly.

Wake up. Get out of bed. Run a comb across my head.

Just kidding. Start with a cliche, I always say. Gets people to slam the cover closed.

Truth is, there's no single pattern. I don't always wake up first. Sometimes the order's a bit different. Who would've thought.

It's not a big context, Ghent. But it's also not small. There are enough unexpected variables to keep you occupied. So every day unfolds on its own.

Take last Thursday. Karel's show opening the next day at the Design Museum. The works shipped from Munich. And Karel coming.

Then the clock breaks, it stops working. What do you do then? Try to repair it? Or let it stay broken?

I've been known to say, an artwork is always changing. Right in front of your eyes. Consider a stained glass window: the glass is *flowing* like a liquid, just over a long timeframe.

For Brahma, the Hindu god of creation, the entire duration of the universe is a single day of his life. So he would see the colored pigments of the window suspended in a moving surface. It just depends on your reference.

So what does it matter that the clock is broken? This exhibition is only up for three weeks. It's a blip.

What does matter though is the people. And their friendships. Even 80, 90, 100 years is a blip. But at least an elongated Blip, rounded on the sides but extended. That's a timeframe where things start to be more important.

So the short-term exists not for the long-term, but it's part of it. And it makes it even possible.

Now that I'm about to have a child, maybe timeframes change again. It starts to be about days, then weeks, months, decades. When is your child going to go to college? And how hot will the winters be by then?

Let's see what happens. I'm optimistic. We've made it this far, and the plan was lightweight. Who's to say it won't continue?

§

I wonder if I'll actually show 019 or anyone else this writing, these fragments. Will I have a proper editor there? Do I even want one?

I used to be so insecure about my writing, I would only ever submit a text for publication once it was extremely polished. For example: although my 2014 text about Klaus Wittkugel for *The Exhibitionist* underwent extensive revisions with a meticulous editor, Julian Szupinska-Myers, what I sent him as a first draft was as tightly put-together as my then-self could manage. Or my essay for the Art Institute of Chicago's *As Seen* catalog: also submitted in a quite coherent and well-edited form. They told me it was so clean that the only changes needed were in the punctuation.

Truth be told, this comes from a place of fear and worry. I don't want people to see the things in me that are incoherent, unfinished, uncertain. I am already so unsure about my position and status as a creative person, let alone a *writer*, that I don't want to let them in on that at all.

I still remember reading first drafts by staff writers when I freelanced at the *New York Times Magazine* in 2003. These were real drafts, fragments of gobbledygook that would need heavy, heavy revision to ever be publishable. At the time, I was mortified: was this how professional writers worked? How lazy! Now, in retrospect, it starts to make more sense. Perhaps as staff writers, they already had the confidence to know that they could produce something polished (and also the support from editors and copy editors along the way). So instead of focusing on the details, they could explore top-level questions of research, investigative work, structure, and other concepts. And worry about the details later, when it's time to worry.

§

Maybe this is already present in the mode of *K*,, the space I recently opened in Berlin after P!: to have enough confidence in its own track-record to let others see how it develops. To believe that people will understand and appreciate it, even in its awkward, ungainly phases, or perhaps not to care.

I suppose that's the mode of this text as well. What if it's not quite finished, not quite as spick-and-span as usual? What if I let others into the development of the piece, its writing and editing, before I decide to apply my standard level of finish? What more would/could come out of the writing, not only as a product, but as a process?

§

We all know by now the story of Raymond Carver's editor, what's-his-name, who chopped down Carver's sentences to create the style we now know. The editor's role, invisible for so many years (like that of the designer, the curator?), is what creates the inimitable voice of the author and its value.

That being said, I've never read Carver.

§

In *P!DF*, my auto-monograph and speculative memoir, I begin the section on P! so:

> Once upon a time, long, long ago, in a city somewhere, far, far away, there existed a little gallery called P!.[1]

As suggested by my fairy-tale framing, P! was a bit of a fiction. Albeit one, perhaps like those para-fictions that Carrie Lambert-Beatty writes about, that starts in the real world, then moves into literature, and then perhaps back into the real world, influencing both along the way.

I always thought about P! as a sequence, like in a musical piece. It was built along principles of contrast, and its program had a form that could become legible to those who looked closely enough.

But its role as a *fiction* was made apparent to me by someone else, through their blunt critique and lack of appreciation. In April 2015, I had recently changed the name of P! to "K." for a fast-paced, six-month cycle of shows. Invited to read for three minutes at an event celebrating the launch of curator Jens Hoffmann's book, *A–Z of Curating*, I decided on a short performance. Here's a copy of the text for the letter "K" that I declaimed rapidly, only a couple of hours after having emerged from a transatlantic flight:

1 People often asked me what "P!" stood for. My standard answer was: "In mathematical terminology, P! (or P factorial) represents the multiplication of all of the positive integers less than or equal to P. For example, 5! = 5 × 4 × 3 × 2 × 1. As such, P! represents the multiplication of all the things that came before it." People have speculated that these preceding pieces refer to the first letter of Project Projects (the graphic design studio I co-founded in 2004), *Paper Monument* (the art journal that I help edit), or other pre-existing proper names.

I.

K: a powerful, punchy character. It evokes Kafka, the KLF, King Kong, Kabbalah, Ketamine—as well as "kainotophobia," the fear of change.

It seems we're hard wired to think that the sun will rise tomorrow just because it did today. But quoting Heraklitus, the pre-Socratic philosopher: "You cannot step twice in the same river, for it's not the same river and you are not the same person"—a statement that evokes a world in flux and mirrors Buddhist notions of the continuously transforming "self" sans fixed essence.

Both design and curating are obsessed with "programs": the legible ordering of things over time. What if change itself were pursued as a program?

II.

K. [K-period] is the name of a gallery on Broome Street, which used to be called P! [P-exclamation]. P! was "a multidisciplinary exhibition space in Chinatown" experimenting with contemporary and historical questions of display. K. occupies the same storefront, yet dubs itself "a new gallery on the Lower East Side." It focuses on economic systems and their construction.

K. has a fixed lifespan: it began in March and expires in August. In this brief moment, it stages a year's program of solo and duo exhibitions, performing the accelerated *Bildungsroman* of a New York gallery. Part of its proposition is ideological: How can such a space function critically from within the market? Part of it is iterative: what happens when ideas must emerge with speed? Part of it is deeply personal: how can risk take one outside of the comfortable and known?

The current exhibition is "North Pole Futures" by Wong Kit Yi. For her, fluctuation and the transparent inadequacies of systems are themselves artistic material. At the center of the show is a mathematical formula for the valuation of future works, which she will create in the Arctic Circle on commission. It's an ephemeral set of artworks priced according to an uncertain future. In these times of speculation and collapse, enumerated variables may appear as relatively stable ground upon which to stand.

III.

K. is for Karaoke

[Performed]

"New York Minute" (Don Henley)
2:22
Lying here in the darkness
I hear the sirens wail
Somebody going to emergency
Somebody's going to jail
If you find somebody to love in this world
You better hang on tooth and nail
The wolf is always at the door
In a New York minute
Everything can change
In a New York minute
Things can get a little strange
In a New York minute
Everything can change
In a New York minute

During the karaoke bit (which I performed to music), I dramatically pulled my blazer off and threw it into the crowd. Perhaps seventy or eighty people saw it. There exists a video of it by a friend on my computer and that's probably all.

Now, its afterlife is perhaps more interesting to me. Later that week at a museum opening, I ran into one of the event participants, a well-known academic historian of 1960s and 70s alternative spaces in New York. She expressed how much she enjoyed my performance, and how she appreciated my speculative "fiction" about a fast-paced gallery on the Lower East Side.

I had to explain that, in truth, the short-lived gallery I described *actually* existed and that it was *my gallery*. I had renamed my gallery from one letter with punctuation to another letter with punctuation for six months to run an accelerated series of two-week shows playing with economic structures.

She appeared extremely disappointed, even shocked. So it was all just an advertisement for your own gallery? she asked. She had expected that people were presenting three-minute pieces of *substance*, not simply selling themselves. She walked away from the conversation somewhat rudely.

She was right. It was a pitch, an advertisement. But also a fiction. A construction of a space, a space and its program as a story that lives on beyond its time—not necessarily because of what it was, but rather because of what it might be able to be remembered as.

I later had assistance in finding a way to express this both more succinctly and with more complexity. While speaking on a panel with Chris Sharp, the curator-critic co-founder of Lulu, an independent art space in Mexico City that I admire, Chris called Lulu's program of exhibitions a "novel." I thought this was a great description, and took it to heart. Since I was a child, I've always wanted to be a writer, so why couldn't an exhibition space be my novel, my own form of fiction?

§

The closest I've come to a novel, thus far, is *P!DF*: the interactive book that I have been composing from November 2016 until today. *P!DF* didn't start as a book and wasn't originally intended to be published. It began as a semi-straightforward form of self-presentation: an application for an experimental German design prize. A portfolio, a pitch.

Several weeks before my 39th birthday, I was nominated for the prize. Running through options for what to send them, I realized that it would be hard to encapsulate my hybrid practice (between design, curating, researching, writing, teaching, and more) with a FedExed box of printed materials. So instead, I thought I might work in a mode that I've grown to know well over the past 15-odd years: presenting past work to clients and students in a PDF presentation. Working for efficiency, I created a Keynote document that could explain my work to the jury from afar. It was structured like a portfolio, but with a running narrative text and a streak of self-reflexivity, as well as footnotes and comments. Speaking in the second person, it addressed the reader directly: a letter to an assumed public.

The first several weeks of work were a feverish blur. I continued my usual design work in the studio, but every night I'd head home to work all hours, writing and editing the document. I slept less and less, and felt more and more euphoric about the shape things were taking. From the start, I shared the document with those close to me—my partner, for example, who helped me think about how to approach the presentation and selection of projects. Or my mother, who commented that she finally understood what I do as a designer and curator. Or artist Martin Beck, who encouraged me, over Mexican food and beers, to continue with the more abstract and open-ended aspects of the writing. So I edited and revised it continuously until the submission was due, a week before my birthday. That night, I sent a PDF off to Germany; the next day, out of extreme exhaustion and elation, I pursued one of the most wantonly Bacchanalian and self-destructive evenings since my youth—one with negative repercussions and followed by regret, but that still marked a moment.

A week later, Donald Trump was elected as the next President of the United States of America. In the wake of this unimaginable historical moment, the presentation began to shift and morph. While its first version was mostly descriptive, a portfolio, the next version began to consider what design and curating's role could be in times of political trouble, and how the document itself could demonstrate ideas and help to teach others.

The presentation, by now called "Letter to the Jury," continued to change, almost of its own volition. I would edit it obsessively, working on its structure, design, writing, and images in tandem. At De Appel in Amsterdam, I turned it into a performance in which I clicked through each of its slides silently, reading only its footnotes aloud. After that presentation, designer Karel Martens gave me solid critique: it was a good way to present my work, but that it was too "slick" and too obvious. Look again at *The Medium is the Massage*, he suggested. How associative its texts and images are in their relationships. A useful prompt.

So it began to develop further, growing in visual and structural complexity. Multiple typographies emerged to differentiate each section, an obsessive micro-level of captioning blossomed, and the document took on more interactivity. Modeled on *Choose Your Own Adventure*, books for young adults, in which the reader can control the narrative flow by choosing specific paths, the presentation expanded to include multiple pathways and internal hyperlinks.

Over the past fifteen years, I've been invited to speak at many art schools and universities about my work as a designer and curator. Typically, I create a new lecture for every such talk. This appeals both to my sense of context-specificity—even as basic as focusing on design work for design students, curating for curatorial students, and such—as well as to a desire to continuously reflect anew upon the work I've done to date through such presentations. Yet the flawed economy of spending days working on a single, poorly compensated talk always frustrated me. I started to realize that this "Letter" could be a partial answer to the problem: a way to allow the work of writing talks to be *cumulative* rather than *successive*, while also helping me to define myself.

So over the next nine months, whenever asked to present my work in an educational context, I would say yes, and use it as an opportunity to premiere and workshop a new version of the PDF. I would arrive at a lecture with an update to the "Letter"—often completed minutes beforehand on a train or in a taxi cab. Except for that initial appearance at De Appel, I never again read from it; instead, I would invert the structure of these events to focus on the participants. Often this involved giving them a link to download the PDF document, grouping them into working pairs, and asking them to spend 45 minutes (the length of a typical visiting artist talk or screening) together to read and critique the document. I would ask participants to write down their questions, and then would leave for a coffee. Upon my return, the Q&A often started with confusion about the unexpected lecture format, but then expanded into discussions of the relationship of design and curating, questions of structure and typography, organizational and presentational strategies, methods of publishing, details of particular projects, and whatever was on the mind of *those specific students*. The open-ended format allowed them to drive the conversation (rather than me pre-selecting projects or a specific focus for them), and also seemed more productive than a frontal monologue. In any case, their questions were far more considered: since I had explicitly asked them for critique, they seemed more apt to point out failings or concerns directly, rather than reproducing the situation in which a presenter's charisma makes attendees feel insecure about challenging them. These workshops became little experiments in public.

For the first half of 2017, this continued with students in art, design, and curating programs at the undergraduate and graduate level. And still the document was altering itself, every week or two, whenever these talks arrived. The next shift arrived with the closing of P! in May 2017.

That Saturday, after our final public program, I visited the graduating MFA graphic design show at Yale with curator and historian Robert Wiesenberger. This developed into a late night conversation on the train back to New York about overlaps in design and art education. The next day, P! had its final Sunday, with friends and colleagues coming by the space spontaneously—bearing gifts of alcohol, art, and more—to say goodbye. As on other nights, we ordered pizza or dumplings (or maybe both), drank whatever alcohol we had left, and headed to a bar (Beverly's) to finish up the night. While talking with Jonathan Bruce Williams, a young artist whose work I admire and had shown before, about his personal and professional life, I realized (perhaps with several drinks under my belt) that I did not want to be involved only in producing exhibitions or programs, as in a gallery or museum. As I began to formulate for myself, I wanted to be involved in producing *people*.

And so, over the next weeks and months, the document began another substantial detour, growing to encompass an entirely new narrative strand, written in collaboration with designer and professor Emily Smith. It's composed in her voice, projected years into the future, about our experiments with interdisciplinary pedagogy over during the late 2000s and 2010s. This "red thread" culminates with a manifesto for a school that we "started" in April 2019. So the PDF is the ultimate *Choose Your Own Adventure*: a document that envisions and lays the groundwork for a specific, speculative future.

The presentation only became *P!DF* a bit later, following the advice of David Reinfurt of O-R-G. He decided to publish this ever-changing document properly, giving it a home and a distribution mechanism apart from my informal ones. He also proposed the name "P!DF," which seemed entirely appropriate. And so, in its current iteration, as an ever-evolving e-book, it encapsulates the story of a space, as well as the history of a practice in the midst of its own formation.

§

As of the time of this writing, a final section of *P!DF* was added for version 3.0, released on March 10, 2018. It's a kind of "Koda" covering my current context and preoccupation: a one-year residency and fellowship from KW Institute for Contemporary Art, which has made it possible for me to relocate to Berlin and take time for reflection.

In February, I opened *K,* [K-Komma], a space in Berlin-Schöneberg that dubs itself a "workshop for exhibition-making." It's been in the planning for several years and conceives of itself as a single year-long exhibition that changes over time. After I first spoke with 019, I realized that this structure bears much in common with the "Museum of Moving Practice," which was one of the primary reasons why I thought it'd be interesting to contribute a text in this context.

Rather than focusing simply on presentation, *K,* is about production and perhaps even play: a space between "studio and cube" that can constantly change and adapt and move, without worrying too much about what people think of it. Open to the public only for certain slivers of time, it both creates a private space for developing ideas, as well as a public space for collaboration. This means that I invite artists, designers, curators, and others into the space to think with me about projects, which then manifest themselves visibly, in one form or another. But there's no necessity that these activities assume a specific form, such as a six-week exhibition or similar. They can emerge and take shape over time.

Balancing this amorphous self-definition, *K,* is a space that also believes in constraints. One such system: Everyone who is part of the 2018 program must have a name (or pseudonym) that starts with the letter "K." Hence, the year started with a presentation of East German graphic designer Klaus Wittkugel, whom I've been researching for a decade (and who happens to share initials with KW, who are supporting the project), coupled with a conversation with design historian Jeremy "Kai" Aynsley (who took on his nephew's name as a pseudonym), continuing with collaborations with Emily King, Christopher Kulendran Thomas, Annika Kuhlmann, Na Kim, Konrad Renner & Christoph Knoth (together with their students from the Klasse Digitale Grafik), and so on. This arbitrary approach gives us a formal frame, a specific space, in which to operate, as well as the freedom to move outside of our typical comfort zones.

Another related, yet not entirely anticipated aspect of the project: I've started to write alliterative texts for *K,* in both German and English. It's a form that I had played with in the past, but never quite trusted for its absurdist tack. But for now I've embraced it entirely, trying to work minor language games into every ephemeral event text. Many of these are probably lost on the audience, but some are more obvious. Here's one such fragment, from the end of KW's "official" brochure on the project. I reproduce it in English (though I actually prefer the German version for its snappy K's):

> From this cold-weather kickoff with the classic communism of Klaus Wittkugel, *K,* careens forward on a seemingly-chaotic yet calmly-calibrated course. Over the calendar year, the space compounds collaborators, commingling their individual conceptions of exhibition-making. Rather than crystallizing completely from the start, this cast catalyzes a cycle of crescendoing experimentation with contrasting formats and

approaches. Comprising both calculated and casual additions, subtractions, and multiplications—of artworks, objects, ideas, and displays—the presentation accumulates. And so *K,* constructs itself, one komma delimited character at a time.

Who knows what will happen with this year of *K,*. It's already challenged me and tweaked my thinking: I had been so focused on finished products for the past fifteen years, that I had nearly forgotten what it means to put something unfinished, uncertain, into the world. I'm starting to suspect that to do so—as 019 also embody in their project—is a genuine mixture of selfishness and generosity. On the one hand, you are openly putting into public a thing made primarily for yourself and that you'd like to look at, but this very rawness (in just the right quantity) might allow others to enter in, in those fragile moments before everything's sanded down to a smooth, supple, beautiful form. In this way, an unfinished space—or a piece of unfinished, in-progress writing—might ideally act as a gift.

Which brings me back to the commission of this essay itself: a residency within a publication, a treasured gift of paper-pulp column-inches and airplane-bounded time-spans. A chance to experiment with a text, to try to compose in a different way. To capture what I have tried to do with P!, and what might link it to the important work that 019 continues to accomplish. To live within words, as in spaces, rather than dying in them.

Originally published in
Beginning of Forms: ISP 2017
(Stavanger: Rogaland
Kunstsenter, 2018).

(2018)

SETTING	An experimental workshop
WHERE	A city close-by
WHEN	The near future

A GROUP OF LIKE-MINDED, somewhat unlikely collaborators sit together in a space in one of the city's residential districts. The space is a renovated apartment at ground level; it has a storefront and relatively high ceilings, but otherwise enjoys adequate daylight and modest proportions. The building's frame is of minor significance; rather it serves as a container. It is a stage for an emerging workshop that allows objects, ideas, and people to grow.

The initial space is subdivided into smaller rooms, each of which offers its own distinct conditions for working and thinking. In front, adjacent to the street, there is a public area where objects of different scales and types are displayed on floors, ceilings, and walls. Here, some objects hang from screws; others are pinned up loosely. The walls are covered with plywood sheets overlaid by large-scale, brown panels. Composed from recycled paper, they stand exposed as raw materials for use and reuse. Track lighting creates a warm yet focused ambiance.

Deeper into the space, a slightly larger room includes similar walls for hanging, alongside a low-standing kitchen and bar. These fixtures allow for activities such as hospitality, working, and presenting to mingle; cooking is a necessary condition for creating, showings, and discussing. A larger table serves these multiple functions. In another part of the space, a soft-lit reading corner with bookshelves and foam cushions allows for solitary retreat and occasional napping. Restrooms include deep sinks for washing out containers; one restroom also offers a functional shower. A daylit office with high-hung storage shelves becomes the core for administrative maintenance. Apart from these, a handful of nondescript rooms remain unspecialized. They feature flat painted walls and ample electrical outlets, as well as sawhorse desks and folding chairs that require little preciousness.

This basic infrastructure enables flights of fancy. Preformed notions enter the space with those who come here. They become public through ongoing conversations. As such notions reveal themselves, they gain footnotes and new articulations. Swirling together with notions from others, they begin to grow into ideas. Many start out brightly colored and with sharp angles. As they are let loose, these ideas bounce from room to room. At some point, they are no longer as jagged. Rather, they have become bumpy: smoothed through the pressure of discourse, yet still textured enough to offer pleasure to the touch.

These bumpy ideas are both porous and rough, allowing them to attract other materials and catch on the walls of the space, where they can be examined, observed, and fed further. Over time, some older, fixed ideas agglomerate with these into newer, amorphous ones; as they grow larger and more contoured, the ideas separate again into discrete new units. This process of continuous formation and reformation happens through addition, subtraction, and multiplication. And so a small collection of ideas starts to accumulate along the walls of the space, for anyone to access. People gather as well, arriving for a month or a season or a year or longer. They come from different places with unique backgrounds and distinct skills. All carry their own experience in crafting spaces or theories or things. In this manner, each one is an individual, working on their own pursuits, which they transport in suitcases and boxes into the space. As they are unpacked, these pursuits begin to stick to the walls, cling to extant ideas, and expand as well. With them, the people also grow, copying and extending and incorporating ideas from the space's soft walls into their own pursuits.

As pursuits mature, they attract larger pursuits. One lands outside the storefront window; it knocks on the door and is offered entrance. Only once inside does it reveal its true girth and extends to drape over the entire floor. Gathering themselves together, the people quickly pluck the pursuit from its corners and throw it upwards to catch on the ceiling. From below, its scale and composition can best be observed. They monitor and measure it, poke it and prod it, test its surfaces and plumb its interiors. Writing in their notebooks, the people record both the pursuit's qualities and their own reactions to it.

Here, their diversity of personality, approach, training, and experience work together. A loose plan is formulated: spreading out along the perimeters of the pursuit, each person directs specific questions to one or more of its aspects, pinging it and listening for the query to echo back. They carefully draw the results, one section at a time. This takes many attempts, as discrete areas are drawn, evaluated, rubbed out, reworked, and gradually pieced together.

Such jigsaw moves create the game at the same time as they solve it.

Over time, an inverse contour emerges. At first it appears to match the pursuit perfectly. But upon closer examination, the single line is made up of many ones, traces that blur together into sharpness. It is a map, fitting closely within the confines of the original while also larger than it. Transformed by individual and collective efforts, the pursuit evaporates, replaced by its response. It straightens itself up, folds its many lines into a single strand, and exits through the front door in a flash.

As ideas, objects, and people collect in the space, even the idea of the workshop starts to shift. No workshop can hold too much at once, eventually it must empty itself. With each new arrival and pursuit, the rooms grow to be smaller. Everything begins to touch. There is no longer enough space for objects, people, and ideas to separate out into individual forms.

So eventually some depart. When they do, they take a small part of the workshop with them. Nearly invisible, this active culture lines their luggage; it waits to take root in another neighborhood or city. When another nearly empty space begins, the fragments from the first prime the fresh walls as a thin layer. Again people and objects and ideas start to gather themselves, with a new set of pursuits soon in tow. Here things are different and yet related. It is a workshop of workshops, connected yet separate, growing apart while learning together.

you have a
magnificent
STRUCTURES
STORIES
SOCIAL
GEORGES PEREC
A LIFE IN WORDS
Feelings Are Facts
Rainer
The Phenomenon of Change

BAUTEN EMIL HASLER · TRICKAUFNAHMEN ERNST KUNSTMANN
BRUNO MONDI · PRODUKTIONSLEITUNG FRITZ KLOTZSCH
ERWIN GESCHONNECK · MIT LUTZ MOIK · HANNA RÜCKER · PAUL BILDT
LAUBENTHAL · ALEXANDER ENGEL · WALTER TARRACH U.A. · EIN PAUL VER-
HOEVEN-FARBFILM DER DEFA · VERLEIH PROGRESS FILM-VERTRIEB GMBH
LOTTE LOBINGER · PAUL ESSER · HANSGEORG
MUSIK HERBERT TRANTOW
DEFA
AUSSTELLUNG

K,

A Year with P. Krishnamurthy

K,

K,

K,

K,

K,

K

1.

The introductory text and small orange texts in this section are reprints of the published press announcements for *K,* programs in 2018–2019.

2.

The event dates in this section are written in an abbreviated German format. This follows the logic of On Kawara's Date Paintings, which adopt the date conventions of the country in which they were painted.

3.

The large alliterative texts are not past words, but rather new ones.

K,

A Year with P. Krishnamurthy

KW Institute for Contemporary Art is pleased to inaugurate *K,* —a “workshop for exhibition-making” founded by designer, curator, writer, and educator P. Krishnamurthy. Established as part of the residency format *A Year with ...* , *K,* proposes a space for production, presentation, and pedagogy. This initiative extends and rethinks his previous project, P!, an exhibition space, gallery, and “Mom-and-Pop Kunsthalle” located in New York City from 2012–17. As Krishnamurthy has suggested in other contexts,

> the new venue proffers a particular proposition: that curating, design, and other artistic pursuits in our present times must eschew the promotion of perfect products, instead presenting the creative process itself, with its plurality of positive outcomes and periodic faux pas[1]

that perhaps

> can make even everyday things *bumpier*[2]

—or some kind of cacophonous, cryptic, confusing kaka like that.

,,,

As an exhibition-maker and graphic designer, Krishnamurthy has played with a broad set of ideas, including identity and its constructions, typographic micro-narration, self-referential modes of display, idiosyncratically ordered curatorial systems, and institutional models alongside issues such as design’s relationship to historical and contemporary power structures. *K,* represents both taking stock and building anew: the workshop space functions as a site for reflection upon existing models of interdisciplinary creative practice. During 2018, the space hosts a single, continuous residency and exhibition. As part of this program, *K,* invites outside participants—artists, curators, designers, and others whose names (or pseudonyms)

1 See page 47
2 See page 55

begin with the letter “K”—to transform this ongoing presentation in dialogue with Krishnamurthy. *K,* will also collaborate with art schools and educational programs to test emerging ideas in situ. Through these activities, the program renders visible the process of thinking and creating within a bounded space and period.

The program’s yearlong trajectory opens in February with an exploration of the work of East German graphic designer and exhibition-maker Klaus Wittkugel (1910–1985). Wittkugel, a leading design figure of his day, communicated Socialist ideals and aspirations through his posters, book covers, and propaganda exhibitions in the service of the former GDR. His approach employed modernist abstraction and self-reflexive photomontage, while adapting its formal palette to a given commission. Wittkugel was also an influential professor of graphic design, teaching for over forty years at the art academy in Berlin-Weissensee. The presentation at *K,* features printed materials, photographs, and spatial designs, installed in an associative manner. Emerging out of Krishnamurthy’s extensive research on Wittkugel, as well as a 2016 exhibition at P!, this display opens his body of work—with its embedded questions around the role of political ideology within design—to contemporary critical perspectives and future research. A significant, controversial, and multidisciplinary figure whose work is still under-recognized, Wittkugel represents one starting point from which to explore interwoven questions around abstraction, typography, political language, and historical narrative in parallel.

> *Kainotophobia: fear of change, resistance to something due to fear.*

From this cold-weather kickoff with the classic communism of Klaus Wittkugel, *K,* careens forward on a seemingly chaotic yet calmly calibrated course. Over the calendar year, the space compounds collaborators, commingling their individual conceptions of exhibition-making. Rather than crystallizing completely from the start, this cast catalyzes a cycle of crescendoing experimentation with contrasting formats and approaches. Comprising both calculated and casual additions, subtractions, and multiplications—of artworks, objects, ideas, and displays—the presentation accumulates. And so *K,* constructs itself, one komma-delimited character at a time.

3.FEB.2018
KLAUS WITTKUGEL
WIEDERSPIEGELUNG, KONSTRUKTION

3.FEB.2018
JEREMY "KAI" AYNSLEY
A KINDRED JUXTAPOSITION

16.MÄR.2018
EMILY KING
LEARNING FROM LIVERPOOL

6.APR.2018
CHRISTOPHER KULENDRAN THOMAS & ANNIKA KUHLMANN
CONCERNING A TWO-FACED KEYNOTEL

26.MAI 2018
NA KIM AND EMILY "KAE" SMITH
ESSENTIAL NON SEQUITURS (KITH AND KIN)

6–8.JUN.2018
[K]URATORIAL MEET-UP BERLIN: DIALOGUES ON ART, CURATING, AND POLITICS

15.JUN.2018
MICHELLE "KLEIO" ELLIGOTT
TIMELY ASPECTS OF MODERN DISPLAY

6.JUL.2018
ANNA KANNA BARHAM
BUMPS KNOT ALGORITHMS

20.JUL.2018
SALEM AL-[K]ASSIMI, MARYAM AL [K]ASSIMI, AND OTHER GUESTS
SOLICITING QUERIES OR QUESTIONS AROUND AN ALTERNATIVE GRAPHIC MISSION

28.SEP.2018
ESEN KAROL
EVERYDAY KICKS

26.OKT.2018
ALEXANDRA K. CUNNINGHAM CAMERON
THREE POSSIBLE SCENARIOS FOR A COLLECTIVE CURATING (AFTER DAVID REINFURT)

28.OKT.2018
KAREL MARTENS
QUESTIONING KAREL

23.NOV.2018
S. KHAJEH-NAJAFI
THE DEATH OF THE ARTIST

16.DEZ.2018
CHRISTINE K. HILL
VOLKSEIGENE BIBLIOTHEK A.K.A. WHAT'S IN A NAME?

18.JAN.2019
KASPER KÖNIG
KAWARA + KRITIK = KODA A.K.A. KOCHEN MIT KASPER

SEFEST
DER SOZIALISTISCHEN EINHEITSPARTEI DEUTSCHLANDS
AUSSTELLUNG
DAS PLAKAT
ohne Maske
ne of humanity
Ich bin Bergmann!
Wer ist mehr?
DAS KALTE HERZ

AS 180
BORIS MIKHAILOV
Unfinished Dissertation

A long time ago, there was a kooky place called *K,*.
Its name was pronounced like the letter "K" plus
a "comma." Can you recall the last time
you articulated the word "comma" aloud?
I know, it sounds a little bonkers.

Previous spread: *OST UND ~~oder~~ WEST: Klaus Wittkugel and Anton Stankowski*, 2016. P! and OSMOS, New York
Notes for the buildout of Ebersstrasse 3, together with *New Game—No Rules* by Joseph del Pesco

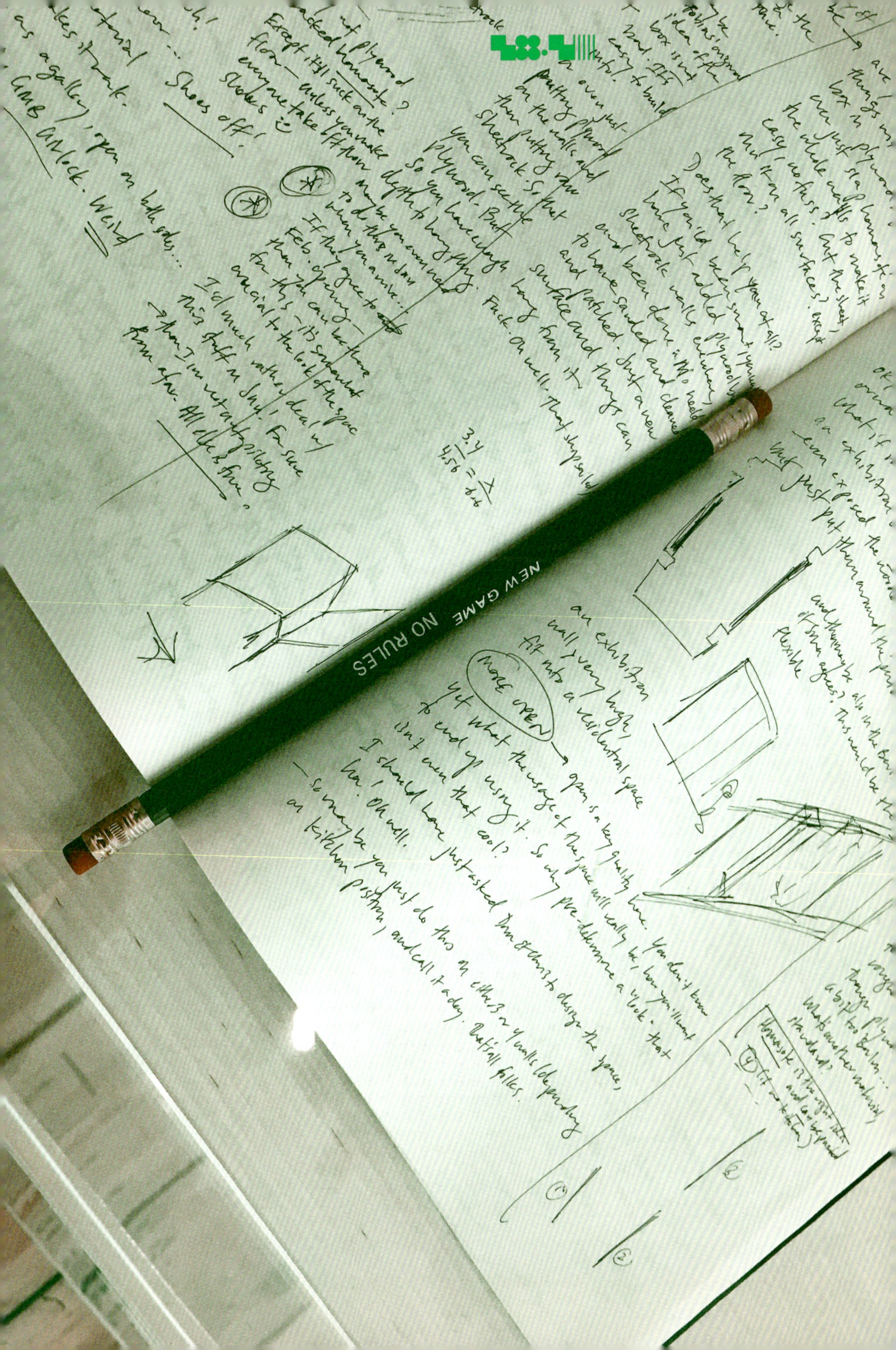
NEW GAME
NO RULES

But
lo and behold, *K*, began with a bang:
a broad survey of designer Klaus Wittkugel's work.
His initials also happened to be "KW"—just like
the contemporary Berlin artspace. What a beautiful
coinkydink! 3.FEB.2018

Klaus Wittkugel, Exhibition view of *Unser 5 Jahrplan*, Berlin, 1951

3.FEB.2018
KLAUS WITTKUGEL
WIEDERSPIEGELUNG, KONSTRUKTION

We begin our "Wanderjahr" with Klaus Wittkugel: a curious and controversial artistic figure of postwar modernism who deserves a closer look. As a preeminent graphic designer, exhibition-maker, and teacher in former East Germany, Wittkugel (1910–1985) imprinted Socialist messages upon multiple generations of "workers and farmers." His traces remain across contemporary Berlin, such as the signage systems for Kino International and Café Moskau on Karl-Marx-Allee or the identity for the former Palast der Republik. The subtitle of his comprehensive 1979 monograph reads *Photography, Graphic Design, Poster, Exhibition, Marks*—suggesting Wittkugel's extensive range of graphic media. Working in the service of the GDR's official agencies, Wittkugel nevertheless inflected these commissions with an individual aesthetic of self-reflexive photography and typographic construction. His work allows us to open up questions about the tension between the political and the personal within design and other themes.

The presentation Klaus Wittkugel, *Wiederspiegelung, Konstruktion* [*Reflection, Construction*] includes original photographs from the 1930s, alongside posters, book covers, and printed ephemera from the 1950s–1970s. A contemporary slideshow of Wittkugel's exhibition design and architectural graphics complements these materials. This rotating selection seeks to make his work accessible for interested audiences and researchers. Wittkugel's work remains in the space until early May, while other invited curators, artists, and designers add a diverse set of works to the installation in parallel.

Counting it all, *K,* lasted considerably longer than one annual cycle. Like most creatures, it was conceived well before its birth. And even after its closure, parts of it stuck around—for example, this current document!

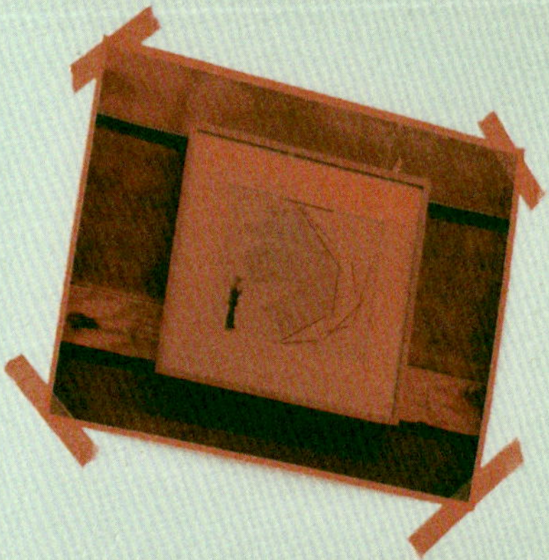

94.95

Doesn't dialogue seem doubly desirable these days? Diving right in, *K,* delved deep into the dialectics of Deutsches Design with its doyen, Jeremy. Dodging default dichotomies, the dynamic debate sure did drum up a dedicated entourage! 3.FEB.2018

Klaus Wittkugel, Poster for *Ich bin Bergmann! Wer ist mehr?*, 1952

Klaus Wittkugel, Poster for the film *Das kalte Herz*, 1950

3.FEB.2018
JEREMY "KAI" AYNSLEY
A KINDRED JUXTAPOSITION

Our first program of *K,* is a conversation between noted design historian and professor Jeremy "Kai" Aynsley and the curator of *K,*—P. Krishnamurthy—around the ideological tensions and resonances between East and West German design of the postwar period. Together with the presentation of Klaus Wittkugel, this discussion looks backward to look forward, setting the stage for the year to come.

Enter
elegant Emily next. She and P. explored the essential entanglement of design and power. *K,* was evolving into an excellent environment for engaging and elucidating upon experimental findings. 16.MÄR.2018

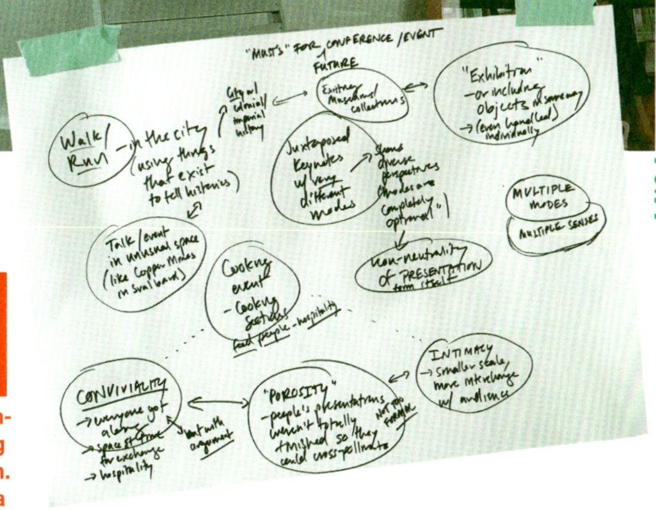

16.MÄR.2018
EMILY KING
LEARNING FROM LIVERPOOL

For our second public program, London-based writer and curator Emily King joins P. Krishnamurth in conversation. In 2017, King, Krishnamurth, and Joasia Krysia launched *Design & Empire [working title]* with the Liverpool Biennial and Liverpool John Moores University. This exploratory three-day event began by locating historical and contemporary links between design and structures of power. Looking for longer-lasting lessons from Liverpool, King & Krishnamurth will collect contributions from the conference at *K*, to consider the project's potential legacy and elongated life.

Paul Elliman, *The Day Shapes*, 2003

Funny enough, *K,*'s curious keeper was a person named P.. For real! Only the foremost letter "P" followed by a period. Furthermore, this peculiar protagonist possessed a protracted patronym—13 letters long! Each month, one letter fled. Finally, by the end of *K,*, they were all gone!

LIP

Gifted guests gradually continued to gather. All geared up for group work, gracious Christopher and Annika garnished the gallery while P. polished their presentation. Seems like most grand ideas gain in gravitas through good graphic handling. 6.APR.2018

6.APR.2018
CHRISTOPHER KULENDRAN THOMAS & ANNIKA KUHLMANN
CONCERNING A TWO-FACED KEYNOTEL

Since 2016, artist Christopher Kulendran Thomas and curator Annika Kuhlmann have developed New Eelam, a model for distributed citizenship masked as an internet startup (or vice versa). During a short sojourn at *K,*, they compare Keynote chops with P. Krishnamurt while updating their "Pitch Deck"—a master document that communicates the complexity of their project in both cultural and corporate contexts. This program cracks open the in-progress deck for public critique.

Here and there, hour by hour, things at *K,* changed. These happenings highlighted hidden horizons. Sometimes the only human beholder was P.. Honestly, though, that was OK. Humble moves hone one's own observations, healthy practice for higher íntentions.

PPPPPPPPRRRRRR
OOOOOONNNNUUUUNN
NCCCCCCIIIIIIIIAAAAAA
DDDEEESSIGGGGNNNN
EM PPPOOORRTTTUU
UGGGGUUUÊÊÊÊÊSSSS
BRASIL HOJE
24.09-31.12.2017
VERHOEVEN UND WOLFF VON GOR-
UKTIONSLEITUNG FRITZ KLOTZSCH
KAUFNAHMEN ERNST KUNSTMANN
HANNA RUCKER · PAUL BILDT
GER · PAUL ESSER · HANSGEORG
LTER TARRACH U.A. · EIN PAUL VER-
PROGRESS FILM-VERTRIEB GMBH
AUSST
BERLIN 6.1
REGIE F

flag
DRIBURG
JOSEF ALBERS: TO OPEN EYES
Betwe
Between Walls and
Revolutionary Tides
5000
How Institutions Think
The Artist as Curator
Société des Arts de Genève
höst /winter 20
ADRIAN PIPER
A SYNTHES
Fondazione Prada
WHEN ATTITUDES BECOME FORM
Bern 1969/Venice 2013

ONE MILLION YEARS
(FUTURE)
ON KAWARA
INTUITIONS
CA' CORNER DELLA REGINA
25 YEARS
LUMA FOUNDATION
CCS BARD
Architecture and Ecology

It's incredibly hard to ideate individually upon immense initiatives—what an improvement to invite inspiring interlocutors! Interdisciplinary instigators Emily, Na, and P. identified their intersections, illuminating an important insight: both industriousness and improvisation are intrinsic to making an exhibition with joy. 26.MAI 2018

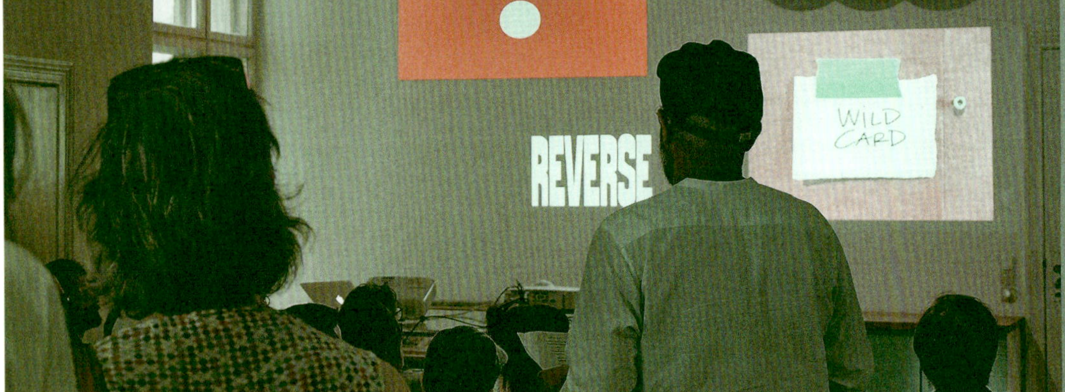

ESSENTIAL

26.MAI 2018
NA KIM AND EMILY "KAE" SMITH
ESSENTIAL NON SEQUITURS (KITH AND KIN)

Normative notions of graphic design and curating place the disciplines in non-neighboring nodes of creative practice. But in its continuous quest for clarity, *K,* quizzically queries: what if these two nominatives are not nearly so discrete, but rather lie nearer to each other? Our program nominates non-specialist naturals Na Kim and Emily "Kae" Smith to consider this niche inquiry. In conversation with *K,*'s current "Kerning-König," P. Krishnamu, they will workshop how visual and conceptual structures from diverse areas—whether anthropology, movement, time-based notation, or next-level government bureaucracy—may apply to even newfangled exhibitions of graphic design.

Middle row, from left to right:
Na Kim, *SET v.5: july*, 2016
Na Kim, *2'13", 36 Frames*, 2014

Na Kim, *To Be a Loner*, 2015

Journeyers just kept jaunting into town, usually once a month, generously jumping right into *K,*'s program. They stayed for a day or several, juggling and juxtaposing ideas and objects. As a finale: a public event or jazzy party. Positive karma!

1957

Knock-knock!

One day a crew of collegiate curators came calling with blessed Bonaventure, a savvy comrade with a kaleidoscopic kit of references. Curating as a conscientious form of curiosity and care—the meeting's main leitmotif. 6–8.JUN.2018

6–8.JUN.2018
[K]URATORIAL MEET-UP BERLIN: DIALOGUES ON ART, CURATING, AND POLITICS

Occupying *K,*, students and staff from De Appel Curatorial Programme (Amsterdam), Bard Center for Curatorial Studies (New York), and Valand Academy (Göteborg) discuss art, curating, and politics at a (K)uratorial Meet-up. The overture is Bonaventure Soh Bejeng Ndikung's talk, *Defiance In / As Radical Love: Soliciting Friction Zones and Healing Spaces*.

Listening
looms large
when you're playing
the long game.

Leveraging lessons from
prior programs, *K,* landed upon
less linear, more lively layouts—
let the loopy games,
liminal workshops,
and
labyrinthine
performances
manifest!

Interrupt

Maneuvering in from midtown Manhattan, meticulous Michelle mused on the erstwhile maestro of her major museum. A peerless polymath, the man sure made some marvelously wild diagrams and masterful notes. 15.JUN.2018

15.JUN.2018
MICHELLE "KLEIO" ELLIGOTT
TIMELY ASPECTS OF MODERN DISPLAY

Returning to its roots in display-related rubrics, *K,* responds now to the history and horizons of "The Modern," that renowned museum in New York. The next arrival in our roomy "Rote Insel" rest area is researcher and raconteur Michelle "Kleio" Elligott, whose recent writing focuses on polymathic, self-taught museum director, curator, and exhibition designer René D'Harnoncourt (1901–68). With *K,*'s constant, P. Krishna, she considers the museum's evolving relationship to ideas of innovative installation, archival practice, and how the past may find itself reclaimed in the future.

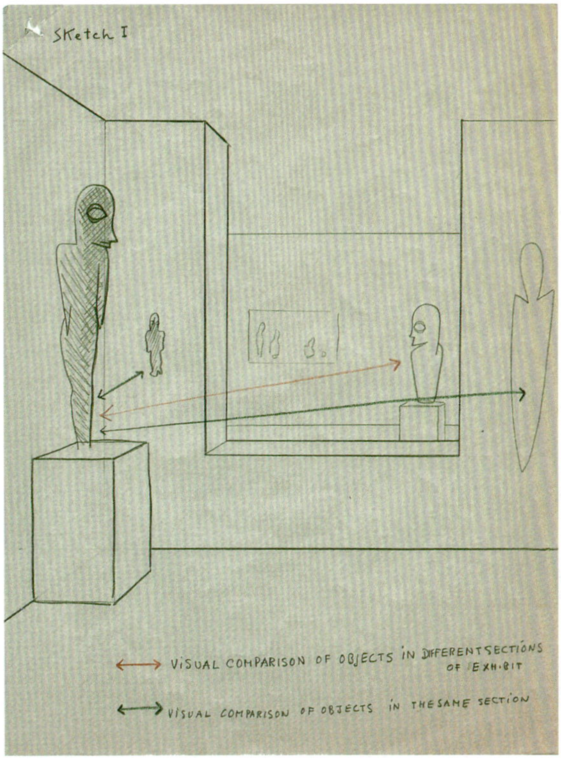

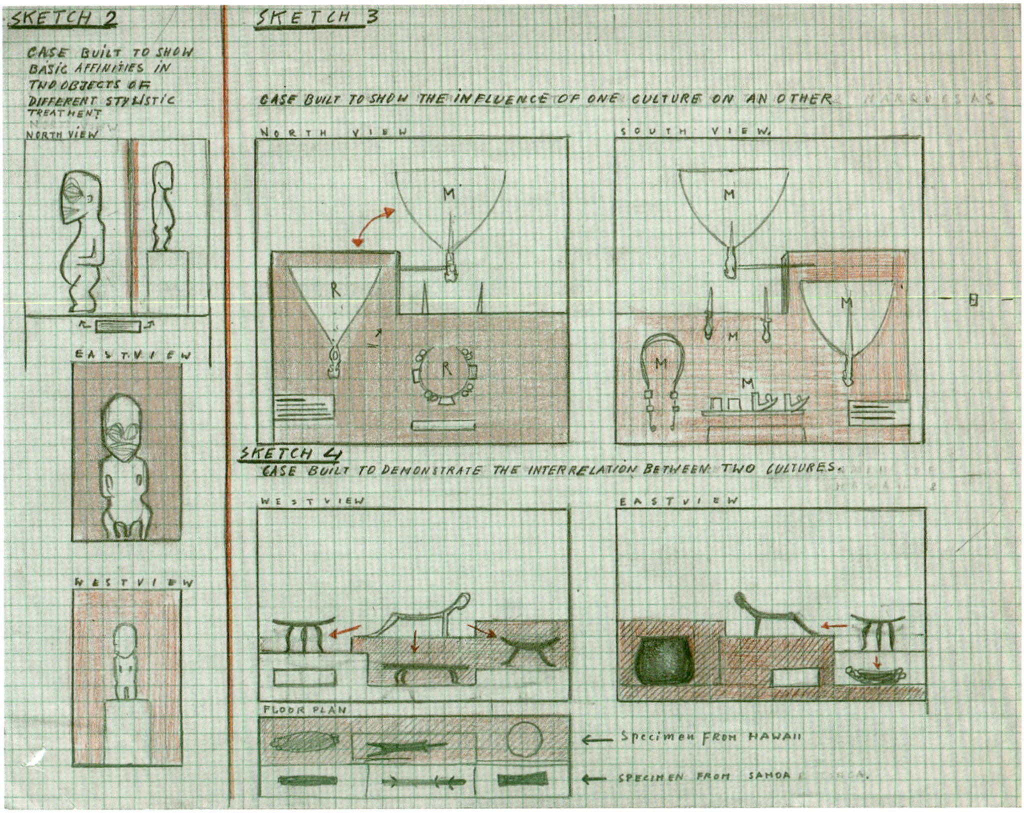

René D'Harnoncourt, Sketches from grant proposal to develop a new display methodology

Natty design duo Christoph Knoth & Konrad Renner cruised in next with their Klasse Digitale Grafik. Notably, they had nurtured *K,* from its nascent stages with their novel, continuously changing communications concept, *A Website Is Never Ready*. So nimbly operationalized!

https://k-komma.de/
uni kommt zu K,:
une, 20:00-21:00 [K]uratorial Meet-up Berlin, Dialogues on art, curating, and politics with Bonaventure Soh Bejeng Ndikung
une, 9:00-18:00 Mick 'K.' Wilson, Valand Academy Summer Course Intensive: Introduction to Art & Politics
une, 18:30 Michelle 'Kleio' Elligott, Timely Aspects of Modern Display
2 June Klasse Digitale Grafik, 502 Bad Gateway – Digitales Ausstellen
EN DE
Klasse Digitale Grafik, 15th June 2018 Michelle
Kleio' Elligott, 8th June 2018 Mick 'K.' Wilson,
[K]uratorial Meet-up Berlin, 26th May 2018 Na and
https://k-komma.de/
BIS 4. MAI: KLAUS WITTKUGEL, WIEDERSPIEGELUNG, KONSTRUKTION, GEÖFFNET FREITAGS, 11–17 UHR
NEXT UP! NA KIM AND EMILY 'KAE' SMITH, ESSENTIAL NON SEQUITURS [KITH AND KIN] SATURDAY, 26 MAY, 5PM
EVERYWHERE EXPERIENCE MOBILITY SUSTAINABILITY
NA KIM AND EMILY 'KAE' SMITH,
CHRISTOPHER KULENDRAN THOMAS & ANNIKA KUHLMANN,
EMILY KING,
JEREMY 'KAI' AYNSLEY,
https://k-komma.de
K,
Coming soon: Karel Martens, Questioning Karel, October 28th, 6–8 pm!
DE
28. 09. 2018
ESEN KAROL
20. 07. 2018
SALEM AL-[K]ASSIMI, MARYAM AL-[K]ASSIMI, AND OTHER GUESTS
ANNA KANN
KLASSE DIGITALE GRAFIK 502 BAD GATEWAY — DIGITALES AUSSTELLEN
EN DE
Ebersstrasse 3, 10827 Berlin
Open Fridays, 11–5pm and by appointment
kontakt@k-komma.de
Read our privacy policy
In 2018, K, will be organized in collaboration with KW Institute for Contemporary Art. KW Institute for Contemporary Art is institutionally supported by the Senate Department for Culture and Europe.
16. 12. 2018
Christine K. Hill
23. 11. 2018
S. Khajeh-Najafi

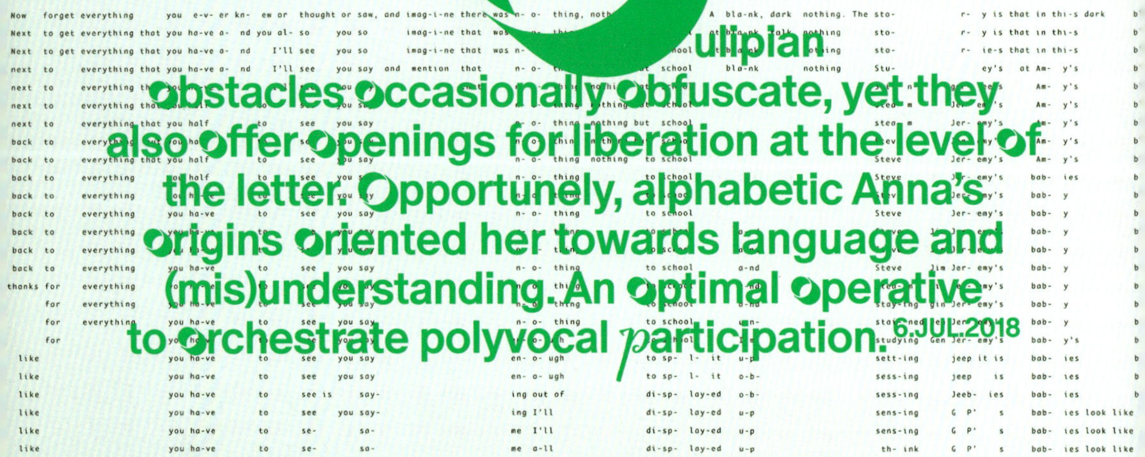

Oulipian

Obstacles occasionally obfuscate, yet they also offer openings for liberation at the level of the letter. Opportunely, alphabetic Anna's origins oriented her towards language and (mis)understanding. An optimal operative to orchestrate polyvocal *p*articipation. 6.JUL.2018

Anna Barham, *We may be ready to have verbal intercourse (score)*, 2017

li- ttlest song song herself. And when that was o-ve-r and it was blank and dark ag- ain, the song s-ang her-self again. The song be- c-am-e so intereste-d that she sang
n- ew stock blank li- ttlest songs send my-self when that was o-ve-r and it was blank and talk ag- ain song-s on your-self again the song be- c-am-e so intereste-d that she sent
-nd you still blank la- tely songs send my-self when that was o-ve-r and it was black and content coc- aine song-s of your-self again the song be- c-am-e so intereste-d that she sent
-nd you still blank la- tely so send my-self when that was a fair and it was black and content courtesan song-s of your-self again the song be- c-am-e so intereste-d that Shay send
you still black la- tely so sent my-self well that was fa-t and black which song-s your-self again the song be- c-am-e so intereste-d that Shane sent
j- u-st like la- tely to send my-self well that was fa-t and black song-s your-self I thi- nk we can change that sett- ing
j- u-st like la- tely to send my-self well that was fast I'm black song-s your-self I thi- nk we can change that sett- ing
j- u-st like la- tely to si-t my-self well that was fast I'm Blox- om- s your-self I thi- nk we can change that sett- ing
j- u-st like la- tely to si-t my-self well that was fast I'm Blox- om- s your-self I thi- nk we can change that up-set-s
j- u-st like la- tely to si-t my-self well that was. Blox- om- s your-self I thi- nk we could change the up-set-s
j- u-st like la- tely to save my-self well that was Blox- om- s your-self I thi- nk we could change the up-set-s
j- u-st like la- tely to save my-self well that was Blox- om- s your-self I thi- nk we could change the up-set-
j- u-st like la- tely to save my-self well that was the cost Blox- om- s your-self I thi- nk we could change the up-set-s
j- u-st like la- tely to save my-self well that was the cost Blox- om- s your-self I thi- nk we can change the up-set-s
j- u-st like la- tely to save my-self will that was the cost blocks of your-self I thi- nk we can change the up-set-s
j- u-st like la- tely. I thi- nk we can change the up-set-s
j- u-st like la- tely I thi- nk you can change the up-set-s
j- u-st like la- tely I thi- nk you can change the up-set-s
j- u-st like la- tely I thi- nk change the up-set's
j- u-st like la- tely I thi- nk changed i-t up-set-s
j- u-st like la- tely I thi- nk changed i-t up-set-s
j- u-st like la- te damn thi- ng changed i-t up-set-s
like la- te damn thi- ng changed up since
like light damn thi- ng changed up since
damn thi- ng changed up since

6.JUL.2018
ANNA KANNA BARHAM
BUMPS KNOT ALGORITHMS

"Browsed" may sound like "braust," but what a blunder to mix up the two! As *K,* cautiously contemplates breaking for the summer, it beckons Anna Kanna Barham (born in Birmingham) to bestow a bespoke automaton upon Berlin: an embodied, live-production writing group. Bred on a Baroque logic and the burbling banter between spoken word, language recognition software, and printed output, Barham's brainchild bends and builds different texts that each bear the bruises of audio and visual transformations. Conspiring with P. Krishn, *K,*'s casual collector of consonants, Barham blueprints multiple modes of broadcasting to begin our next, bookish phase.

Pro

propagated: What p
learning laterally wit
How preposterou
push a public
When can comm
precision plu
And is it possible to
while playin
puerile

positions
otential lies in
prolific peers?
sly might one
program?
unication carry
s perplexity?
produce profundity
g in potentially
quirkiness?

Quality queries can quench the quest for quick-hit answers. Salem and Maryam from sunny Sharjah showed up to workshop their big biennial with its quizzical curators, Emily, Na, and P.. Though the meet-up didn't quite resolve all quandaries, Berlin still served a welcome quotient of quietude and reflection. 20.JUL.2018

20.JUL.2018
SALEM AL-[K]ASSIMI, MARYAM AL [K]ASSIMI, AND OTHER GUESTS
SOLICITING QUERIES OR QUESTIONS AROUND AN ALTERNATIVE GRAPHIC MISSION

Signaling the start of our summer sabbatical, *K,* summons the founders of the first Fikra Graphic Design Biennial from Sharjah (UAE). This upcoming exhibition playfully proposes an expanded notion of the field and its suitable scope, alongside some speculative scenarios for the future. A multi-day workshop in Schöneberg serves to sort out the project's specifics. Surrounded by the exhibition's co-curators, Na Kim, Emily Smith, and *K,*'s Qwerty-qualified quester, P. Krish, the Emirati ensemble will engage in soul-searching Socratic dialogue to set the stage for November's show.

Exhibition views of Fikra Graphic Design Biennial 01: Ministry of Graphic Design, Sharjah, AE, 2018

R

ekindling his roots in the Asian region, P. reached out to renowned Esen to reveal her rich graphic records. A real design rockstar, she regaled guests and rehung the whole room. Her remarkable relics were later relinquished to the Art Institute of Chicago, becoming a resource for future seekers. 28.SEP.2018

28.SEP.2018
ESEN KAROL
EVERYDAY KICKS

Turning our attention to questions of publishing, civic engagement, and other exogenous explorations, *K,* opens the fall season with Ankara-born designer and editor Esen Karol. Since the 1990s, she has made an indelible impact on Istanbul's cultural scene through her books and graphic systems. In her own quest to find what's next, Karol embarked on an independent publishing project called *Manifold*. *Manifold* is a platform to analyze the immediate environment of Istanbul, considering questions of urbanism, design, art, and politics primarily within the contested Turkish context. By bringing Karol to Berlin to collaborate with *K,*'s curator, P. Kris, we seek to survey her graphic archive and reanimate records from nearly three decades of design practice—in a way that opens up unexpected encounters rather than claiming an authoritative interpretation.

2 YILDA 1
Ne fark eder?*
PARRJEKTİF
İstanbul'da Stil Peşinde
MARTIN PARR
Yerde toprak, bir kadın, bir erkek. Yerde bir ölü ve tepede güneş.
Sarhoşluk korkuları unutturur.
Her tür bireyselliğe önem vermek
VENT
GEÇİT"
"RESM-

İstanbul
BLOCK
İSKOR
Aktuelle Kunst aus Istanbul
İstanbul'dan Güncel
Recent Art from Istanbul

Spontaneity is an indispensable skill for successful organizing. As seen in such simple synchronicity: Alexandra swung by during a short European stay to spell out some selective strategies for curating—crucial for subsequent transitions. 26.OKT.2018

26.OKT.2018
ALEXANDRA K. CUNNINGHAM CAMERON
THREE POSSIBLE SCENARIOS FOR A COLLECTIVE CURATING (AFTER DAVID REINFURT)

Please join us for an impromptu and irreverent program with Alexandra K. Cunningham Cameron from the Cooper Hewitt, Smithsonian Design Museum in New York City. Expect fun, games, and a comment or two on contemporary design.

David Reinfurt, *After His Beautiful Machine of 1855*; Bruno Munari, *Tetracono*; Dexter Sinister, *Black Whisky*. Programmed and published by O-R-G

Karel Martens, *Three Times (in Blue and Yellow).* Programmed and published by O-R-G

Turns
out that ten months of things accumulating
can tip over into a tiny tangle.
It's also true that P. did not tend to tidy
up like certain celebrity Kondos tout.
Uff!

DAS PLAKAT

Until unsentimental Karel came to hit "undo" on this utter upheaval. Uncluttering without unction, he unhung past works to upbuild a utilitarian rhythm of his unique monoprints. The public event was also an unqualified success. The underlying lesson: every operating system occasionally needs an updated version. 28.OKT.2018

28.OKT.2018
KAREL MARTENS
QUESTIONING KAREL

Qualifiers aside, Karel Martens is known quite widely for his work in graphic design, printmaking, and other timely artistic pursuits. A self-professed "human being" (in contrast with closed professional classifications), Martens's extensive teaching over the past 40 years complements his personal creations.

Having collaborated for many years with *K,*'s cryptic keeper, P. Kri, he comes now to Berlin to consider and question his own, constantly moving, practice. Joined by Marc Hollenstein, his former student and current designer of KW Institute for Contemporary Art's institutional identity, as well as Emily Smith, Professor of Communication Design at University of Applied Sciences Europe in Berlin, Martens will query the criss-crosses and overlaps between contemporary art, design, and creative work.

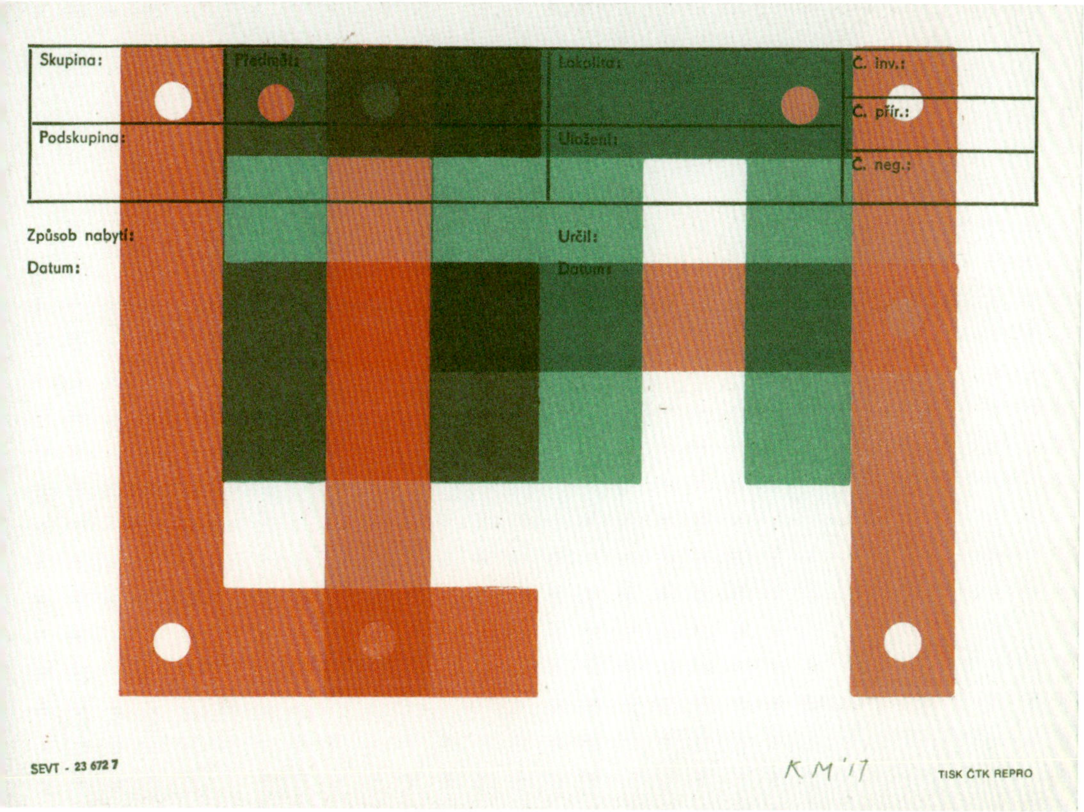

Karel Martens, Letterpress monoprints, 2014–2017

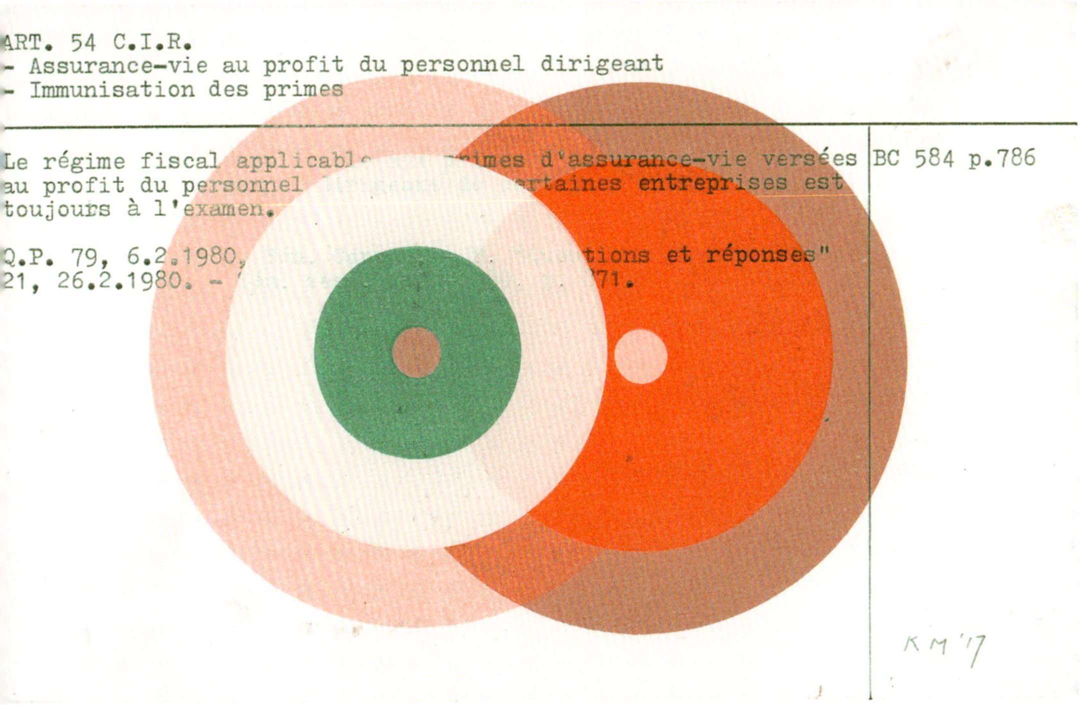

LIVE

1957

Versed

well in limiting variables, S. invited a variety of visionary artists and writers to conceptualize a literary volume from start to finish in 24 hours. Very tight! Luckily S. was no virgin to such ventures. The team proved victorious (well, mostly...) through its vigilance and will. 23.NOV.2018

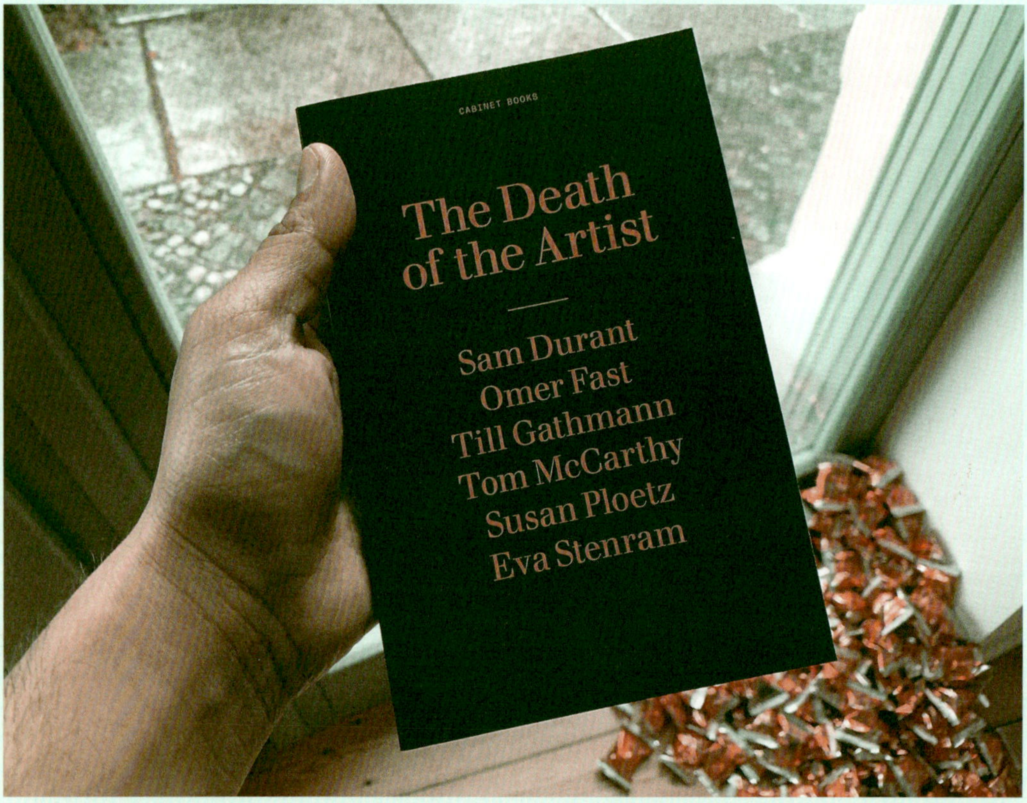

Left to right: Eva Stenram, Tom McCarthy, Till Gathmann, Susan Ploetz, Sam Durant, and Omer Fast at Ebersstrasse 3, Berlin. Photo taken at 8:05 pm on Saturday, 24 November 2018.

– *Do you not remember Hegel's famous last words? "I do not believe in my own death."*
– *No, it was Salvador Dali who said that.*
– *You're wrong. Definitely Hegel.*

23.NOV.2018
S. KHAJEH-NAJAFI
THE DEATH OF THE ARTIST

Now's the time of year when clever, clever artists begin contemplating demise, endings, finales, genius-murder—especially their own. Joining us from far, far away, mystery game master S. Khajeh-Najafi brings his unique credo of capacious curiosity to bear on the subject of artistic ego and its untimely death. Together with his consonant-crunched colleague, P. Kr, Khajeh-Najafi collects a cabinet of references ranging from philosopher's ends, forensic photography, apocryphal lives of artists, and other eclectic sources into a multimedia extravaganza. This event kicks off a 48-hour frenzy of collective production, culminating on "Totensonntag" (Sunday of the Dead) with a finissage and book launch to celebrate creativity and its ultimate constraint.

balletic. It's a kind of double-arc, whose chords and sectors and subtensions require skillful plotting. The anarchists' plotting was inadequate—they don't believe in arcs, after all, that's the whole point. But an arc came to their aid, and killed the archduke for them.

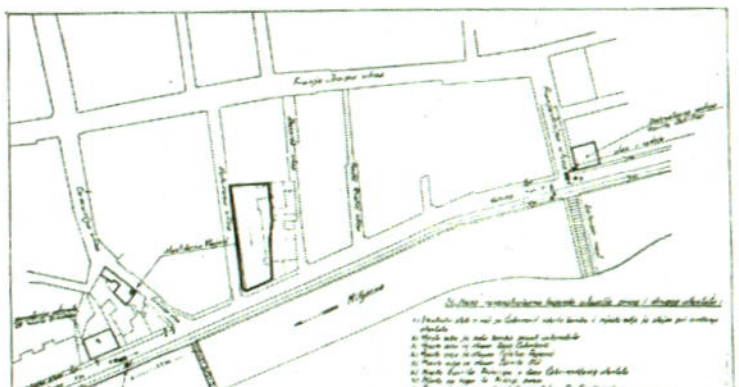

Službeno rekonstruisana situacija prilikom prvog i drugog atentata 28 VI 1914 g. (Drž. arhiv NR BiH, Sarajevo, IV-15-5)

6.
This scene, too, is a replay. Oedipus, *principe* of Thebes, is re-routed to Corinth following the oracle's prognostication of his destiny, his life-arc, namely that he'll kill the king, his father. When he hears the oracle's pronouncement, he too detours (thinking he's the prince of Corinth, son of its king Polybus, not—as is in fact the case—of Thebes's king Laius) back to Route A. It's on this route that he meets Laius, in a carriage, and, in an argument about close-up vehicle-maneuvering, kills him. The spot where the predestined act takes place could not be more Euclidian: it's simply the place where three roads, three lines, meet.

7.
A half-remembered limerick:

There was a young man who said "Damn!"
It is dawning on me that I am
But a creature who moves
In determinate grooves
Not a bus (as it were) but a tram.

Not a Polybus, certainly. I like trams—or, more precisely, tram-lines, those grooves laid in the road, the way they divagate from and rejoin each other, forming tangents, pedal curves, parabolas, ecliptics, asymptotes. They are forensic too: they render visible the exact passage of the missile that, if you pause at the right intersection at the predetermined time (it's even written down in tables pasted to the stops), will kill you, slice you neatly into conic sections.

While the weather got colder and Christmas came closer, Christine volunteered to play the penultimate programming position. She wrangled with evolving identity and mutating monikers. How does a perennial project weave its way into its witnesses' bodies? What would be visible on a future x-ray? 16.DEZ.2018

Christine Hill, *The Volksboutique Small Business*

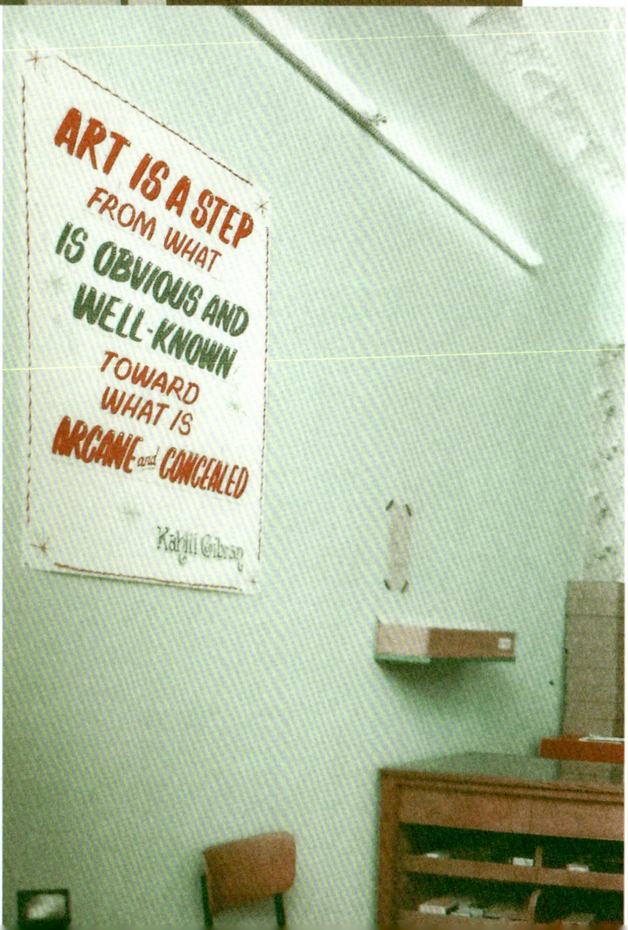

16.DEZ.2018
CHRISTINE K. HILL
VOLKSEIGENE BIBLIOTHEK A.K.A. WHAT'S IN A NAME?

Every ending is also a beginning. And so *K,* plans its eventual end, where another provocatively-punctuated, single-letter presentational venue once kicked its program off. This time around, we invite Christine K. Hill, well versed in branding boutique Betriebsformen that bridge the boundaries between conceptual art and commercial activity, to bring her voluminous knowledge and proven knack for naming to our clunkily-coined Kunsthalle. Together with *K,*'s truncated totem, P. K., K. Hill pontificates on the virtue of books: in particular, her new series of notebooks that perform the work of a constructed archive and philosophical playbook alike. Simultaneously, the two long-term co-conspirators consider what equity remains in venerable monikers—since every name is endlessly fungible and every river can only be stepped into once. How might a particular format for artistic practice read as a diagram over time, a novel seedbank for multiple future possibilities?

Xenophobia

is an affliction every xanthous expatriate may experience. For *K,*'s closing act, kingly Kasper came with an exquisite painting by On Kawara. Kasper and P.'s day-long exchange explored racism in the artworld—mostly xenial, a kind of conflict yoga.

MAR.24.1972
EL LISSITZKY

Yearning for a strategy to tackle such touchy topics tastily, P. served up chana masala in a conceptual cooking show with Kasper. Like yin and yang, they each yielded up their mother tongue to yarn together. A small suggestion for how yesteryears' dark dynamics might be digested with a little zest. 18.JAN.2019

18.JAN.2019
KASPER KÖNIG
KAWARA + KRITIK = KODA
A.K.A. KOCHEN MIT KASPER

Closure and self-critique are complicated concepts, particularly for those practitioners who prioritize continuous production over periodic pauses. Clocking in from close-by Kurfürstenstrasse, our concluding conversational partner is Kasper König: a canonical "Kunst-King" who has constantly catalyzed new contexts for art's presentation. Consequent to a recent controversy in Munich, König chats with *K,*'s curtailed caretaker, P., for a final, concentrated communion on contemporary conflict. Under the close watch of a Kawara canvas, they consider the conjoined arts of creating, reflecting, and counting—one day, one year, one conflagration, one curtain call at a time.

Chole(or Universal sabji) recipe: Put butter or oil, add jeera (cumin) seeds after oil is a bit hot. Let them pop. Then add other spices if you have, few cloves, 1 cinnamon stick, bay leaf, and sauté, then add finely chopped onions, sauté until cooked. Add chopped tomatoes, sauté more. Add finely chopped (or ground) green chilies, ginger, garlic, and sauté. Can add curry leaves if you have. Add turmeric and salt. Saute. Now add potato 1" cubes, sauté until almost cooked. Now add your chole masala (or any other masala you can lay your hands on). Sauté a bit. Wash and drain cans of chick peas. Add them to sabji. Let it all cook together. Can garnish with coriander leaves if you want. Serve with chopped red onions, coriander and lemon/lime wedges. Can even serve on toasted sourdough bread, or eat with rice.

I like to use red onions for flavor. Add water after adding the chick peas.

— Bala Krishnamurthy

1 portion feeds 5-6 people

4 tomatoes (small)

1.5 onions

5 greenchillie

4 claves garlic
7 claves

1 tiny ginger

~~8~~ potatoes (roughly 2x mass of tomatoes)
6

1 Yoghurt (200g)

1/4 tbsp cumin

1/2 large orchatar (add green apples?)

chunk of butter (2 tbs?)

1/2 tbsp Jeera

2 tbsp? Kernöl

5 curry leaves (small)

~~1/10~~ tbsp Tumeric

1/2 tbsp salt → 1 tbsp Chole Masala
1 can Chickpeas

Zzzzzzzzzzzzzzzzzzzz

—finally, *K,*'s zenith, a chance for us to zip up this zany, zigzagging, alphabetical per annum period. P. zonked out for one night under the precious Kawara, a singular space to dream of time and transformation. As zealots of Zen sometimes say, change is the only Absolute.

Klaus Wittkugel
Illuminated architectural and environmental graphics, 1963
Karl-Marx-Allee, Berlin (East)

Selling Socialism: Klaus Wittkugel's Exhibition Design in the 1950s

Originally published in *The Exhibitionist*, No. 10 (October 2014).

(2014)

FOR THE ARTISTS OF THE 20th-century European avant-garde, exhibition design played a crucial role. The Soviet architect, artist, and designer El Lissitzky was the pioneer, shaping innovations in two-dimensional abstraction (particularly the decisive forms of Suprematism and Constructivism) into sophisticated spatial rhetoric.[1] Through immersive, dynamic designs for the Soviet Union at international press, photography, hygiene, and trade fairs from 1928 to 1930, he put the radical forms of his comrades to work for political ends. During this brief period, Lissitzky redefined the propaganda exhibition—which began with the industrial and consumer displays of 19th-century World Expositions—as a revolutionary new mode of mass communication.

Others soon adapted his innovations as a new language of exhibitions, which would serve equally well the otherwise divergent political aims of Fascist Italy, Nazi Germany, and wartime America.[2] Although developed as tools for Communist ideology, such formal methods of photomontage, spatial immersion, and advanced exhibition display became pliable vehicles for varied agendas. These exhibitions frequently relied on modes of commercial display—unsurprising, since many figures of the early Soviet avant-garde also created advertising as part of the revolutionary experiment. After World War II, the relationship between radical form and commercial technique became even more pronounced. The economic recovery of Western Europe and the start of the Cold War witnessed the rise of exhibition design as a crucial tool for mass advertising. From

1
"1926. My most important work as an artist began: the design of exhibitions." El Lissitzky, *Proun und Wolkenbügel* (Dresden: VEB Verlag der Kunst, 1977), 115. Cited in Benjamin H. D. Buchloh, "From Faktura to Factography" *October* 30 (fall 1984), 102.

2
For further reading, see: Mary Anne Staniszewski, *The Power of Display: A History of Exhibition Installations at the Museum of Modern Art* (Cambridge, Massachusetts: MIT Press, 1998) and Ulrich Pohlmann, "El Lissitzky's Exhibition Designs: The Influence of His Work in Germany, Italy, and the United States, 1923-1943" in Margaret Tupitsyn, *El Lissitzky: Beyond the Abstract Cabinet: Photography, Design, Collaboration* (New Haven: Yale University Press, 1999), 52-64.

the standardized trade fair booth to ongoing programs of traveling cultural and political exhibitions, innovative exhibition displays undergirded foreign policy goals.[3] In England, continental Europe, and the United States, practical manuals for the effective design of exhibitions codified the techniques of prewar experiments into a functional and professional grammar to sell objects and ideas.[4]

A related transformation of Lissitzky's work occurred in Socialist East Germany, where the Soviet designer was lionized as the "untiring protagonist for... the spirit and the cultural-political aims of the great Socialist October Revolution."[5] The late 1940s and the 1950s represented a tumultuous period in Eastern Europe. In these years, Josef Stalin systematically remade the government and economy of the nations under his influence as identical models of Soviet society, through the installation of Kremlin-directed Socialist regimes, rapid industrialization, the dismantling of small businesses, and land collectivization.[6] During this transition, it became even more imperative that the East German regime put on a good show to convince its people of the positive value of the new order.

This is the context in which the designer Klaus Wittkugel (1910-1985) rose to prominence. Beginning his career as an apprentice at a 1920s Hamburg fashion shop, where it was his task to arrange display windows, by the early 1950s Wittkugel led the design of international trade fair presentations and internal propaganda exhibitions for the German Democratic Republic (GDR). His approach to constructing large-scale, immersive showpieces built upon Lissitzky's groundwork. On the surface, Wittkugel's exhibitions appeared to continue the Soviet optimism of the 1920s. On closer examination, however, these later exhibitions emerge as a significant repurposing of early Modernist ideas to suit a markedly different historical moment and political purpose.

Today, Wittkugel's exhibitions represent a blind spot within the established histories of 20th-century exhibition design. The near-invisibility of Wittkugel's work within established canons of design may lie not in its methods or significance, which are as innovative as those of his peers, but rather in the very fact that it served to sell East German and Soviet agendas—ideologies that are largely erased from dominant accounts of postwar Modernism. By wearing their ideologies on their sleeve, these Socialist showcases allow for an open analysis of goals and methodologies as well as future comparison with more extensively documented Western exhibitions of the period. Introducing the design strategies and approaches of Wittkugel's two most significant exhibitions from the 1950s, this essay situates both in their political context, and within a larger examination of how such self-reflexive and formal innovations—despite their historical baggage—may continue to inform contemporary practice.

3
Jack Masey and Conway Lloyd Morgan, *Cold War Confrontations: U.S. Exhibitions and Their Role in the Cultural Cold War* (Baden, Germany: Lars Müller, 2008).

4
Examples of such postwar manuals include Misha Black, *Exhibition Design* (London: The Architectural Press, 1950); Richard P. Lohse, *Neue Ausstellungsgestaltung = Nouvelles conceptions de l'exposition, New Design in Exhibitions* (Zurich: Verlag für Architektur, 1953); and George Nelson, *Display* (New York: Interiors Library, 1953).

5
Ed. Sophie Lissitzky-Küppers, *El Lissitzky: Maler, Architekt, Typograf, Fotograf* (Dresden, Germany: VEB Verlag der Kunst, 1967), inside front book jacket. It is interesting to note that this, the major monograph on Lissitzky's life's work and still a primary reference work, first appeared in East Germany, under the same imprint as Klaus Wittkugel's monograph a decade later.

6
Tony Judt, *Postwar: A History of Europe Since 1945* (New York: Penguin, 2005), 167-73.

EARLY GRAPHIC DESIGN WORK AND EXHIBITIONS

Beginning in the late 1940s, Wittkugel established a striking, modern look for key products of GDR cultural export—with the Modernist hallmarks of asymmetrical composition, bold typography, the use of photomontage, self-reflexive visual gestures, and the choice of abstraction over realistic representation.[7] His wide-ranging work moved fluidly from posters to book covers for key works of Socialist literature, film, and avant-garde theater, as well as later signage and identity programs for architectural icons of East Berlin, including Café Moskau, Kino International, and the Palast der Republik.

At the same time, Wittkugel's temporary exhibitions, which he designed and in some cases organized, focused upon the general East German populace. While serving as head designer for the GDR's Office of Information, Wittkugel directed *Qualität* (Quality, 1950), an exhibition emphasizing the high production standards of East German manufacturing and consumer goods. On the other hand, the exhibition *Bach in seiner Zeit* (Bach in His Time, Leipzig, 1950, and Berlin, 1952) allowed Wittkugel to hone his formal and spatial approach to historical objects—including original documents, artworks, and musical instruments—within a modularly constructed traveling exhibition devoted to Johann Sebastian Bach's life and work.[8]

These early exhibitions led to *Unser Fünfjahrplan* (Our Five-Year Plan, 1951), which presented the successes and goals of the Stalinist Two- and Five-Year economic plans to a broad public. Given the shortage of available spaces for large-scale temporary displays in war-damaged Berlin,[9] the exhibition was staged at the Museum für Naturkunde (Natural History Museum). *Our Five-Year Plan* proved a costly endeavor, with a budget of 960,000 DM.[10] This figure—for an exhibition intended to be on view only six weeks—evidences the project's importance to the aims of the nascent East German state, which was faced with an uncertain political and economic future. Such investment paid off: The exhibition boasted more than 350,000 visitors even before its run was extended, with queues of visitors willing to wait in the winter cold in order to catch a glimpse of the show.[11]

Our Five-Year Plan combined the didactic and the demonstrative, presenting documentary information while invoking a sense of participation in the process of rebuilding East Germany after the war. Economic statistics mingled with motivational statements; tilted architectural models suggested the massive scale of future factory complexes. Individual rooms focused on specific topics such as child care, education, and Soviet agricultural teachings, while elegant vitrines showcased new books and publications of Socialist literature.[12] Socialist Realist murals showed a towering group of workers unfolding plans that would determine their collective future.[13] On the other hand, valuable consumer wares—music boxes, radios, waffle irons, sewing machines, handheld cameras, teakettles, and so on—were staged as playful tableaux in standing vitrines.[14] Evoking

7
Wittkugel was fluent in both the idiom of the Modernist avant-garde and current "Western" design and advertising techniques. Axel Bertram, his student at the Kunsthochschule Berlin in the early 1950s, remembers him showing their class the work of the American corporate designer Paul Rand and El Lissitzky. Author interview with Axel Bertram, Berlin, November 23, 2009.

8
Heinz Wolf, *Klaus Wittkugel* (Dresden, Germany: VEB Verlag der Kunst, 1964), 8.

9
Bundesarchiv NY 4182/1030 (Nachlass Walter Ulbricht).

10
Bundesarchiv DC 20-I/3 32, 110.

11
"350 000 sahen *Unser Fünfjahrplan*," *Berliner Zeitung* (February 22, 1951), 6.

12
Akademie der Künste, Berlin, Klaus-Wittkugel-Archiv, Mappe "Fotos 14."

13
Erhard Frommhold, *Klaus Wittkugel: Fotografie Gebrauchsgrafik Plakat Ausstellung Zeichen* (Dresden, Germany: VEB Verlag der Kunst, 1979), 181.

14
Akademie der Künste, Berlin, Klaus-Wittkugel-Archiv, Mappe "Fotos 14."

shop windows, these displays were intended to provoke wonder and desire in their proletarian audience, for whom such goods were mostly out of reach in a moment when even meat, fat, and sugar continued to be rationed.[15] *Our Five-Year Plan* functioned as an interior World's Fair pavilion, selling the full range of East German life, knowledge, and economy to its own citizens.[16]

From a contemporary perspective, *Our Five-Year Plan* is striking not only for its design, but also for including performative and participatory elements that emphasize the labor of its own production. Contemporary reports marveled at a functioning printing press within the exhibition, which produced take-away brochures for each visitor. In another room, workers gave live demonstrations of advanced weaving techniques on an industrial textile machine.[17] The new technology and its accompanying labor were on view for admiration and emulation. This approach followed closely the model of early World Exposition demonstrations of heavy machinery, which had proved extremely popular with the general public and commentators.[18] By the 1950s, such performative displays were a common and effective means of selling goods in Western European trade fairs.[19] In the context of a general-audience Socialist exhibition, the focus shifted away from marketing new technology to selling the idea of collective labor toward achieving the GDR's industrial production quotas.[20]

The last room of the exhibition featured the "Wall of Approval," a growing installation to which visitors could contribute—albeit within a circumscribed framework. Printed in the form of bricks, paper handbills affirmed, "I will work for the fulfillment of our Five-Year Plan, the great plan for freedom." Each visitor was encouraged to sign an individual brick with their name; two "bricklayers" on scaffolding then wheat-pasted these paper "bricks" together to build a "wall" in the form of a white dove. According to exhibition descriptions, so many people took part that the wall expanded onto the street, well past its allotted space.[21] Although newspapers reported thousands of participants, including Chinese, Korean, West Berliner, and West German signatories,[22] the primary audience of the exhibition was always East German citizens themselves. The visitor was asked to engage not only as a consumer of the exhibition's content, but also as an active participant and worker in the Socialist project.

Earlier exhibitions, including Lissitzsky's Soviet Pavilion at the International Press Exhibition in Cologne in 1928 (widely known as PRESSA) and Herbert Bayer's *Road to Victory* (Museum of Modern Art, New York, 1942), used dramatic staging of the visitor's choreography to create a sense of active involvement in the propagandistic aims of the exhibition.[23] Wittkugel's approach went one step further: It asked that viewers physically contribute to the installation and its spectacle.

Despite the exhibition's popular success, this proved to be a bittersweet moment for Wittkugel. Shortly after the exhibition opened, his poster design for the show, which adapted the visual

15
Mike Dennis, *The Rise and Fall of the German Democratic Republic 1945–1990* (Essex, England: Pearson, 2000), 55.

16
The East German cultural scholar Ina Merkel has astutely observed, "It is wrong to say that socialist advertising was not competitive; yet its aim was not the hocking of brands or products but rather the legitimacy of the 'people's economy' itself." Ina Merkel, "Alternative Rationalities: Strange Dreams, Absurd Utopias" in *Socialist Modern: East German Everyday Culture and Politics* (Ann Arbor: University of Michigan Press, 2008), 334.

17
"Ein Plan für uns," *Nacht-Express. Die illustrierte Abendzeitung* (January 9, 1951), 2.

18
Anna Jackson, *Expo: International Expositions 1851–2010* (London: Victoria and Albert Museum, 2008), 92.

19
Misha Black, *Exhibition Design* (London: The Architectural Press, 1950), 11-12.

20
Ironically, this very focus on performative labor was suggested by a wall-size quotation of Josef Stalin at the exhibition entrance: "One must finally understand that, of all the valuable forms of capital there are in the world, the most valuable and decisive capital are people themselves." Akademie der Künste, Berlin, Klaus-Wittkugel-Archiv, Mappe "Fotos 14."

language of the early avant-garde into a striking image of marching numerical years, was publicly criticized in the party organ *Neues Deutschland* as "Formalist," a denunciation following the Stalinist aesthetic line.[24] After the exhibition closed, a special commission of the Institut für Marxismus-Leninismus censured Wittkugel, with the conclusion that "his loyalty to the party is still very weak."[25] Wittkugel's written apology states, "I know that it is extremely important today [that I make time to train myself politically and theoretically in Communism], especially for my career."[26]

The following years witnessed a subtle change in Wittkugel's graphic design work, away from "formal," or abstract, solutions and toward a greater incorporation of figurative and human elements. Wittkugel's commissions from both the Sozialistische Einheitspartei Deutschlands (SED) and the party organ, *Neues Deutschland*, increased in the mid-1950s; his appointment as a full professor at the Kunsthochschule Berlin (now Weißensee Kunsthochschule Berlin) in 1952 signaled his heightened status as a designer. With the death of Stalin in 1953 and Khrushchev's subsequent denunciation of the Stalinist purges, the aesthetic regime in the GDR seemed to relax—while at the same time the political climate and economic competition between East and West Germany grew more heated.

MILITARISM WITHOUT MASKS

Militarismus ohne Maske (Militarism Without Masks), which opened on June 7, 1957, represents Wittkugel's crowning achievement as an exhibition-maker. It combined the approaches and techniques of his earlier exhibitions into a total spectacle that was simultaneously factual and propagandistic. Working with a team of students from the Kunsthochschule Berlin, Wittkugel organized, conceptualized, and implemented the entire exhibition.[27] Staged on the border of East and West Berlin near the Friedrichstrasse train station, *Militarism Without Masks* was aimed at denizens of both city sectors (the building of the Berlin Wall in 1961 would later prohibit such free movement and dual address). Yet the exhibition's content, revealed only over the course of a complete walkthrough, belied its partisan aim of excoriating West German industrialists and politicians. In contrast to earlier works, it eschewed an open-ended and inclusive display in favor of a precise, accumulative, and all-encompassing ideological argument.[28]

Charting the development of the military-industrial complex in Germany from 1870 through 1957, the running narrative coupled the commercial and financial growth of the Krupp family, who had manufactured munitions for the German state, with the tragic history of the Krausens, a fictional working-class family that loses successive children in Germany's wars. These "historical" family stories complemented an explicitly interpretive strand that conjoined the horrors of World War II with West German warmongering.

The strong fusion of form and content in *Militarism Without*

21 Hermann Exner, in *Klaus Wittkugel: Plakat, Buch, Ausstellung, Packung, Marke* (Berlin: VBKD, 1961), 10.

22 St., "'Bitte, nehmen Sie auch meinen Baustein!' Ueberraschung in der Fünfjahresplan-Ausstellung / Tausende errichten eine Friedenswand," *Nacht-Express. Die illustrierte Abendzeitung* (January 18, 1951), 6.

23 Ulrich Pohlmann in Tupitsyn, 64.

24 Prem Krishnamurthy, "The People's Representation: On Staged Graphics in Klaus Wittkugel's Work" (2011), *TheHighlights.org* no. XV.

25 Bundesarchiv DY30-IV2-11-v-4357, 21.

26 Bundesarchiv DY30-IV2-11-v-4357, 20.

27 The students included Margret Arnold, Karl-Heinz Bobbe, Manfred Brückels, Dietrich Dorfstecher, Ingrid Schuppan, and Wolfgang Simon. Frommhold, 263.

28 "In and through this exhibition, Klaus Wittkugel becomes a radical photomonteur. ... The exhibition itself is a total montage." Frommhold, 176.

Masks emerged from its unified conception. Writing years later about the exhibition design, Wittkugel explained his core strategy:

> The sequence and ordering of the exhibition elements is so determined, so that everything can be taken in–and most importantly–can be read, without slowing down your steps through the individual things. In this manner, one is in the flow, one takes in everything, [one] is captured by the atmosphere and is pulled along from document to document, from one kinetic three-sided curtain wall to another, from large-format photos and montages, short original film scenes, and audio recordings with the lying phrases of Hitler and Goebbels. The documentation is intentionally not "designed." Image and text documents were placed in an indirectly lit built-in vitrine row without any disturbing additional pieces.
>
> […]
>
> Through this form, it was possible for the first time to show the horror of World War II unsparingly, yet so that it could be understood intelligibly and not only function in an emotionally terrifying way.[29]

As laid out above, the exhibition design strategy was complex and multitiered. Wittkugel recognized that the most effective way to convert skeptics was through an exhibition of "facts" in the form of "neutral" documents–an approach that built on his experience with historical materials in *Bach in His Time*–which were editorialized by their spatial montage with other, more polemical, visual and multimedia elements. Modeled on the structure of a documentary film, the exhibition made an unfolding, room-to-room case, rather than overwhelming the viewer through immediate and complete immersion in its contents.

At the same time, like a shop window, the exhibition had to be seductive from the start. This corresponds with the British-Russian architect and designer Misha Black's injunction to the designers of propaganda exhibitions (in his 1950 book *Exhibition Design*): "The arrangement of sections must be such as to provide, at the entrance, sufficient excitement to arouse the visitor to a pitch of interest which will carry him through the exhibition on a sustained wave of attention."[30] The push and pull of these two poles determined the form and rhythm.

Militarism Without Masks began with a dramatic entrance that juxtaposed the bombastic, the poetic, and the polemical: a floor-to-ceiling photo mural of a nuclear explosion, a quotation by Bertolt Brecht on the self-destruction of Carthage, and a strong anti-military statement by Günther Kunert (who wrote all of the "poetic" wall texts in the exhibition)–"If Germany wants to live, then militarism must die."[31] Branching off from this first, central room, three rooms were dedicated to different time periods of recent

29
Akademie der Künste, Berlin, Klaus-Wittkugel-Archiv, Nr. 12.

30
Black, 31.

German history. Each room combined diverse images and objects, ranging from manipulated documentary photographs—"enlarged, reduced, added to, ordered together, juxtaposed, cut apart, put back together with other pieces, or placed as details beside large panoramas"[32]—to "straight" documents, physical objects (such as a soldier's helmet, a gravestone cross, artillery shells, and other war materials), and collections of other original materials, including death notices of soldiers culled from World War II newspapers. Consistent typographic treatments and custom-designed exhibition display pieces unified these disparate contents. Functioning like modern bus shelter advertisements, mechanical wall units cycled between three sequential states: the suffering of the Krausen family, the profits of the Krupp family, and a poetic summary by Kunert. Alternating dark and light spaces heightened the sense of a driving narrative.

Dramatic multimedia elements such as antiwar film montages and aural "paintings"—featuring recorded sounds of cannons, gunfire, and battling troops from the different wars of 1870-71, 1914-18, and 1939-45—were calculated to trigger heightened psychological responses.[33] Further display strategies and details—such as graphics and messaging on the ceiling, large-scale backlit typography, angled object labels, and recessed wall-vitrines inset into larger image walls—demonstrated Wittkugel's command of advanced display techniques.[34]

The visual rhetoric of *Militarism Without Masks* became increasingly virulent over the course of the exhibition. For example, one recurring motif featured the silhouetted heads of West German industrialists and politicians who enjoyed prominent careers in the postwar period despite their complicity with the Nazi regime.[35] Introduced in the last section of the first room, each "talking head" was presented in an "objective" manner: on a white background, flanked by texts contrasting their activities in 1945 with their current fortunes in 1957. The second room opened with a large photomontage of these same figures: shown from the chest up, hovering over a pile of gold coins and coiled serpents, with the spectral body of Adolf Hitler floating in their midst. The final montage of this room presented Hitler standing in full military garb next to the head of West German Chancellor Konrad Adenauer, who was collaged onto a second Hitler torso. The continuation of the wall featured the faces of the same group of West Germans, each grafted onto an identical Hitler body—an unmistakable visual indictment.[36] Evoking John Heartfield's early photomontages, this strong graphic statement and its repetition took on a nearly meme-like quality in its persistence to persuade.

One of the exhibition's most arresting displays was a floor-to-ceiling, dramatically curved, panoramic photograph of West Berlin's major shopping district, the Kurfürstendamm. Buildings, storefronts, and commercial signage emerged in ground-up perspective—an illusionistic and immersive simulacrum of Berlin's other side. The viewpoint was low, as if one were standing in the middle of the street; the uncanny scene was absent of people. Instead of a traditional semicircular panorama, this display was presented

31 Frommhold, 161.

32 Frommhold, 176.

33 Peter Günther, "Militarismus ohne Maske" in *Neue Werbung* 10 (1957), 8-10. Cited in Frommhold, 160.

34 Akademie der Künste, Berlin, Klaus-Wittkugel-Archiv, Mappe "Militarismus ohne Maske."

35 This criticism was far from groundless: Major figures in Konrad Adenaur's BDR government, such as Hans Globke, as well as West German industrialists such as Friedrich Flick (both of whom were featured in this part of the exhibition) did achieve material and political influence in the postwar period despite their wartime activities. At the same time, though, the exhibition was one-sided in that it did not mention the comparable complicity of East German politicians in the totalitarian Nazi regime. See also Judt, 59-61.

36 Akademie der Künste, Berlin, Klaus-Wittkugel-Archiv, Mappe "Militarismus ohne Maske."

on two straight walls joined at a curved corner, which accentuated the image's disorienting perspective. In the center of the installation, an actual newspaper kiosk stood stocked with German newspapers from both the World War II era and the day of the exhibition opening, all brandishing militaristic titles and headlines. This insertion collapsed the wartime period with the current moment through an act of spatial and temporal collage. As Hermann Exner has commented, the dramatic scene of the panorama–with the bombed-out spire of West Berlin's Kaiser Wilhelm Memorial Church in the background–transformed itself into a present-day, post-apocalyptic vision of capitalist ruin.[37]

Several months after *Militarism Without Masks* closed, an exhibition in West Berlin employed a similar motif to different ends. *America Builds*, designed by Peter Blake (former curator of architecture and design at New York's Museum of Modern Art), opened at the Marshall House, Berlin, in September 1957. Organized by the United States Information Agency, the exhibition "featured full-scale, impeccably detailed mock-ups of the facades of some of the most noteworthy modern skyscrapers in the United States... . [The exhibition and its contents were] a deliberate and provocative contrast to the centrally controlled and ideologically dominated work being done in the eastern part of the city."[38] Like *Militarism Without Masks*, *America Builds* also featured a large-scale, curved panorama of an unpeopled landscape, but this photograph was of New York's skyscrapers. According to Blake, "A replica of the New York skyline and of the facades (in actual size) of a new type of city attempt to create the illusion that the visitor is actually among buildings instead of looking at pictures and models."[39] The mood and viewpoint of this American fantasy were radically different from its East German counterpart. The high, triumphal perspective emphasized New York as a marketplace of towering skyscrapers; the panorama offered a view of technological and economic progress as experienced by the very few at the top. How different from the street-level vantage point of Wittkugel's panorama, which positioned its viewer as a pedestrian in West Berlin who is confronted by the alarming conjunction of commerce and emptiness.

REFLECTIONS

In contrast with the Party's reception of his work on *Our Five-Year Plan*, Wittkugel received the GDR's National Prize, third class, for organizing and designing *Militarism Without Masks*. It was a watershed moment in his career. The exhibition was also symptomatic of larger changes that were occurring within the East German state. Largely abandoning the optimistic rhetoric and political idealism of the immediate postwar era, the GDR shifted to a harsh critique of the West German government as a gambit to retain its fleeing populace. Within the specific context of Wittkugel's oeuvre, *Militarism Without Masks* signaled a move away from inclusive and participatory gestures, toward a narrower and more controlled approach focused on

37 Hermann Exner, "Dramatiker der Bildsprache," *Sonntag* (February 19, 1961), 8.

38 Masey and Morgan, 98.

39 Franck Klaus, *Exhibitions: A Survey of International Designs* (New York: Praeger, 1961), 130.

convincing visitors through spectacular means. Unlike in early avant-garde ideological exhibitions, the aim was no longer to "activate" viewers. Instead, they were corralled through a space; bombarded with objects, sounds, and images; and treated as docile consumers within an overwhelmingly persuasive environment.

The self-reflexive coda to *Militarism Without Masks* appeared in the exhibition *Klaus Wittkugel: Plakat, Buch, Ausstellung, Packung, Marke* (Posters, Books, Exhibitions, Packaging, Logos) in Berlin in 1961. This major retrospective included the entire range of graphic work by Wittkugel, as well as a selection of his exhibition designs, presented within the exhibition. An entire room was devoted to *Militarism Without Masks*. Photographic documentation of the 1957 exhibition dangled below a suspended grid. Hung at right angles, the boards' display implied a virtual room. Behind these images, the cinematic installation of the Kurfürstendamm–the most ambitious display in the original exhibition–stood reproduced at 1:1 scale. However, instead of a seamless, curved photographic reproduction as in the original, this time the panoramic backdrop was divided into panels; the modular grid-based display system ostensibly would allow for easy transport to the exhibition's other venues. Making a return appearance, the newspaper kiosk stood on a raised stage floor, which turned the entire reproduced display from a space to be entered into an object to be observed from a distance.[40]

The logic of the immersive, total spectacle collided here with the idea of the exhibition's reproduction as a formal work, generating an exhibition within an exhibition that was diminished by its own desire for ubiquity and innovation. Significantly, the reproduced installation–ostensibly the one that Wittkugel was most proud of as a *designer*–was the most evocative and symbolic of the original exhibition, rather than a re-creation of the more plainly ideological and polemical displays.

Yet history plays its own tricks, even conspiring to shift the meaning and content of an exhibition while it still stands. Wittkugel's retrospective was on view from July 7 until August 26, 1961, in East Berlin. During the evening of August 13, 1961, the East German authorities began to erect the Berlin Wall. Euphemistically dubbed the "Anti-Fascist Protection Wall" by its creators, it was designed to prevent East Germans from escaping to the West–the very opposite of *Our Five-Year Plan*'s "Wall of Approval." In the midst of its exhibition run, Wittkugel's *mise en abyme* of West Berlin's premier shopping district suddenly and inadvertently began to represent something dangerously off-limits and inaccessible to the majority of the East German citizenry. A double separation had occurred.

Exhibition design, particularly in its more commercial or applied forms, is often maligned for catering to desire: as a means to close the gap between audience and object, or as a way of selling through display. However, as Brian O'Doherty's *Inside the White Cube* essays demonstrated almost 40 years ago, there is no neutral condition of exhibition; the white cube space cloaks its own market ideology and value proposition.[41] Wittkugel's major exhibition design

40
Akademie der Künste, Berlin, Klaus-Wittkugel-Archiv, Mappe "Fotos 16."

work, particularly *Militarism Without Masks*, occupies the opposite end of this spectrum: the creation of spaces and experiences with clear ideological aims and transparent methods. Nevertheless, to a contemporary viewer, both devices appear dangerously charged. One sells an idea through the total mobilization of image, document, object, media, and display, and the other sells an object (or an idea) through the persuasive authority of a pristine and "undesigned" gallery presentation. The power of exhibition design—to create a complete world, to immerse, to beguile, and to convince—is one that is valued not only within advanced retail operations and repressive states, but also by many contemporary artists.[42] For exhibition-makers and artists, especially those aspiring to challenge contemporary market constructs, counterexamples such as Wittkugel may serve as significant historical figures of both instruction and dissuasion.

41
Brian O'Doherty, *Inside the White Cube: The Ideology of the Gallery Space* (San Francisco: Lapis Press, 1986).

42
Thomas Hirschhorn comes to mind as an artist with means that are related to Wittkugel's, though they are put to different ends. Not insignificantly, Hirschhorn was a graphic designer in the political collective Grapus before turning to art.

Klaus Wittkugel: East Germany's "Monteur"

Originally published in *John Heartfield: Photography Plus Dynamite,* Angela Lammert, Anna Schultz, and Rosa von der Schulenburg, eds. (Munich: Hirmer, 2020).

(2020)

JOHN HEARTFIELD'S ASSERTION, "I would have been the designer of socialism if only they had let me,"[1] encapsulates the gap between his formidable artistic achievements in advancing left-leaning political struggles before 1945 and the meager professional opportunities he received in the first years after his return to the German Democratic Republic (GDR) in 1950.[2]

Yet although Heartfield himself had seemingly "disappeared without a trace,"[3] his work

1 Heartfield said this in 1966 to the West Berlin gallery owner Julie Hammer. Peter Sager, "Demontage des Monteurs," *ZEITmagazin* (Hamburg), May 20, 1991. Quoted by Michael Kresja in "Wo ist John Heartfield?" Günter Feist, Eckhart Gillen, and Beatrice Vierneisel, eds. *Kunstdokumentation SBZ/DDR. Aufsätze, Berichte, Materialien. 1945–1990* (Cologne: DuMont, 1996), 110-26.

2 Heartfield's brother, Wieland Herzfelde, addresses some of the difficulties Heartfield faced upon his arrival in the GDR, particularly the aesthetic critique he experienced in addition to his health problems, in *John Heartfield: Leben und Werk* (Dresden: VEB Verlag der Kunst, 1986), 112-23. Later research in the post-1989 era reveals the political complexities that Heartfield was subject to. See: Andreas Schätzke, "Rückkehr aus dem Exil: Zur Remigration bildender Künstler in die SBZ/DDR," in Feist et al., 96-109.

3 Stefan Heym, "Offen gesagt: John Heartfield," *Berliner Zeitung* (June 13, 1954); reprinted in Stefan Heym, *Stalin verläßt den Raum. Politische Publizistik* (Leipzig: Reclam, 1990), 86-88.

exerted a powerful, albeit indirect, influence on the visual culture of the GDR. In the early 1950s, Heartfield's most visible graphic production consisted of theater posters and stage sets, but his more radical work of the 1920s and 1930s lived on in reputation–through his network of pre-war colleagues and collaborators, but also embedded within the production of other artists and designers.

As I will argue in this brief essay, Heartfield's impact within the GDR can be traced clearly within the work of graphic designer Klaus Wittkugel. His poster and book designs bear a strong relationship to Heartfield's 1920s-era graphic design. Wittkugel's masterwork, the 1957 propaganda exhibition *Militarismus ohne Maske* (Militarism without a Mask) extended the arguments and approach of Heartfield's political photomontages to architectural scale. At the same time, its collective production by a group of Wittkugel's students helped to inculcate an emerging generation of East German designers in Heartfield's methods and the ideals of socialist aesthetic "education."

Klaus Wittkugel knew Heartfield's work through his studies as a "master" student of Max Burchartz at the Folkwangschule in Essen from 1929 to 1932. Within the GDR, Wittkugel embodied a direct link between pre-war modernism and the new socialist context. His wide-ranging work, which typically employed striking photography combined with bold, asymmetrical typography, synthesized a lineage of avant-garde design approaches including the Bauhaus, De Stijl, Jan Tschichold's New Typography, El Lissitzky, as well as Heartfield's revolutionary photomontages.[4] It was especially his understanding of Heartfield's cut-and-paste techniques as a "monteur" that informed the core of Wittkugel's mature work across different media.[5]

Employed in 1945 as a designer for East Germany's Central Administration and later as chief graphic designer for the East German government's Office of Information from 1949 to 1952, Wittkugel worked primarily on economic and political posters, exhibitions and publications. His early commissions included book covers for significant socialist authors that reprised Heartfield's 1920s-era work, including titles by Ilya Ehrenburg, Feodor Gladkov, and Mikhail Sholokhov. Wittkugel's 1949 cover design for Gladkov's 1925 novel *Cement*, a foundational work of socialist realist literature, recalls Heartfield's

4 Sylke Wunderlich, *Plakatkunst in der SBZ/DDR 1945/1949–1969. Geschichtliche Entwicklung und Gestaltung eines künstlerischen Mediums*, vol. 2 (unpublished dissertation) (Leipzig: 2003), 166.

5 "Klaus Wittkugel is an extremely important 'monteur' of the post-war period. With this peculiar profession, he remains, to this day, exemplary for the artistic culture of the German Democratic Republich." Erhard Frommhold, *Klaus Wittkugel: Fotografie, Gebrauchsgrafik, Plakat, Ausstellung, Zeichen* (Dresden: VEB Verlag der Kunst, 1979), 12; author's translation. "Monteur" is, of course, the same terminology that Heartfield used to refer to his own work.

6 See pages 155–157.

1927 cover in its orange-red background, two-color printing, strong vertical composition, and resolutely sans-serif typography. Wittkugel's version, however, replaces the figure of "Soviet man" with concrete pylons—focusing upon the product of construction—and deploys its typography at a more modest scale, using sizing and position to create a sense of visual depth.

Other visual echoes across the decades are less direct, yet no less instructive. The dimensional lettering and subtle overlap of image upon type in Heartfield's 1928 cover for Upton Sinclair's *100%* resonate with the dynamic angle and foregrounded bayonet of Wittkugel's 1949 design for Ilya Ehrenburg's *Sturm*. However, even designing covers for canonical works of Soviet literature and economic propaganda for the Office of Information did not protect Wittkugel from criticism. Although the exhibition *Unser Fünfjahrplan* (Our Five-Year Plan), designed by Wittkugel, opened to extremely positive responses and exceptionally large visitor numbers in 1951,[6] its striking, typographic poster suffered direct critique in *Neues Deutschland*, the official newspaper of the East German Communist Party. On the basis of what was termed its "abstract, intellectual game with numbers and shapes," the poster was branded "formalist" and "misanthropic."[7]

Thereafter, Wittkugel's work underwent a subtle shift, most visible in works like his iconic 1952 poster *Ich bin Bergmann!* (I'm a Miner!). Its aesthetics diverge from the abstraction of his earlier work, emphasizing the human figure and employing an easily accessible slogan that writer Willi Bredel adapted from a popular union chant.[8] This use of photomontage in a straightforwardly exhortative way—as opposed to a tool of critique or satire—recalls Wieland Herzfelde's lament that the entire medium of photomontage in this period was dismissed as formalist.[9] Heartfield's own, more "realist" graphic methods in posters of this period—such as *Die Mutter* (1951; The Mother) and *Winterschlacht* (1955; Winter Battle)—also underscore the validity of Herzfelde's observation.

In the years following Stalin's death in 1953, aesthetic restrictions around formalism began to ease, allowing for greater freedom in graphic design and also the return of political photomontage as an acceptable form.[10] The 1957 propaganda exhibition *Militarismus ohne Maske* by Wittkugel represents the crystallization of this trend.[11]

7 Hans Lockoff, "Schluss mit dem Formalismus bei unseren Plakaten," *Neues Deutschland* (February 6, 1951). Quoted in Wunderlich 2003, vol.I, p. 51. Documents in the Bundesarchiv detail Wittkugel's personal appeal to Wilhelm Pieck, his internal review and judgement by the Institut für Marxismus-Leninismus, and subsequent official apology. See BArch NY4036-677.367; BArch DY30-IV2-11-v-4357.21; BArch DY30-IV2-11-v-4357.20, cited on page 167.

8 Hellmut Rademacher, "Gesellschaftliche Funktion und ästhetische Prinzipien der Gebrauchsgrafik in der sozialistischen Gesellschaft," in Verband bildender Künstler der DDR, *Gebrauchsgrafik in der DDR* (Dresden: VEB Verlag der Kunst, 1975), 46, note 99.

9 Herzfelde, 118.

10 Wunderlich, 65-68.

11 See page 157. Wittkugel was awarded East Germany's National Prize (3rd class) in 1958 for this exhibition.

12 Frommhold returns to the beginning of Heartfield's career to frame the older designer's influence on this exhibition. He cites the 1st International Dada Fair, held in Berlin in 1920, as being "the first ideologically cohesive modern exhibition [...] whose tendency is, as already mentioned, a legend that influences him via Wittkugel's teacher. Wittkugel's now equally legendary exhibition *Militarismus ohne Maske* (1957) would have been inconceivable without such a beginning." Frommhold, 156-60.

The exhibition opened at the beginning of June 1957 at the International Exhibition Centre near Berlin's Bahnhof Friedrichstraße, only months before Heartfield's own retrospective at the Akademie der Künste. Although Heartfield was not involved in *Militarismus ohne Maske*, one could consider it the triumph of his approach to radical photomontage, as well as the transformation of his decades-old methodologies for publication into a three-dimensional and immersive format—developments that went hand-in-hand with the rehabilitation of his own work.[12]

Wittkugel's provocative exhibition poster sets the tone in its reference to Heartfield's visual rhetoric. The photomontage combines Konrad Adenauer's head and shoulders—set against an atomic cloud rising in the background—with Hitler's lower torso and a battlefield in the background. Although Wittkugel's penchant for simplified communications is clear in certain structural decisions, including the single diagonal axis of the collage and its lack of extra captioning, on the whole, the poster applies methods from Heartfield's 1930s-era AIZ covers to the political landscape of the 1950s. Extending over four main galleries, the exhibition's narrative compares the historical fortunes of the industrialist Krupp family with the fate of the Krausens, a fictional working-class family—showing how the Krupps profited through a number of German wars. Constructed with both historical artifacts and interpretive displays, the overall argument of the exhibition echoes the iconic Heartfield works that attacked the capitalist forces driving German militarism and fascism, such as *Nach 10 Jahren: Väter und Söhne* (1924; After 10 years: Fathers and sons) or *Der Sinn des Hitlergrußes: Kleiner Mann bittet um große Gaben* (1932; The meaning of the Hitler salute: Little man asks for big donations).[13] The visual strategies and approaches to text-image relationships derived from such works found their translation here into large-scale environmental graphics.

The sequence of photomontages from room to room also created a secondary effect: the construction of the visual argument itself was laid out for viewers to experience in progression. Silhouetted headshots of West German industrialists and politicians with Nazi-era pasts appeared first in isolation and later as cut-outs on top of Hitler's body. The crudity of the photomontage, along with the repetition of its

13 Akademie der Künste, Kunstsammlung, inv. nos. JH 5 15 and JH 5 09 (original montage) and JH 2 17 (*AIZ*, vol. 11, no. 42 [October 16, 1932]).

individual elements, seems intended to evoke a sense of recognition. While this unmasks for the viewer the rhetorical fiction of photomontage itself, it also demonstrates that the exhibition "itself is a complete montage."[14]

This suggestion that the exhibition might help educate an audience in its montage methodology also resonates with Wittkugel's long involvement as a highly public and articulate pedagogue. In 1949, he began teaching at the art school Hochschule für angewandte Kunst Berlin-Weißensee (later renamed Kunsthochschule Berlin-Weißensee)[15] and continued there as professor from 1952 until his retirement in 1975. In this role, Wittkugel educated generations of designers within the GDR, teaching them in the methods of socialist design to further distribute its ideology through mass means.[16] The essential teachability of Wittkugel's approach is a key facet of his legacy.[17]

Militarismus ohne Maske is itself both symbolic, and a result, of this larger educational process. Unlike a singular photomontage, signed by a single author, a large-scale exhibition is by necessity a collective endeavor. In his significant essay on the role of graphic design in the GDR, Hellmut Rademacher points to this aspect: In

14 Frommhold, 176.

15 Hildtrud Ebert, "Von der 'Kunstschule des Nordens' zur sozialistischen Hochschule: Das erste Jahrzehnt der Kunsthochschule Berlin-Weißensee," in Feist et al., 160-90.

16 Frommhold, 14.

17 "And he thus founded a school of political seeing in the GDR, in which one can learn how to target feelings and, by extension, develop a social consciousness. [...] His work is instructive because it is universal." Frommhold, 14; author's translation.

view of its artistic and conceptual diversity, the exhibition design can rightly be described as the highest and most complex form of coordinated interdisciplinary creative conception.[18]

Although Wittkugel coined the initial idea and argument of *Militarismus ohne Maske*, the team he then assembled to develop it included Wolfgang Schuppan as organizer and Günter Kunert as writer.[19] A further step was to invite his graduating class of students from the Kunsthochschule Berlin-Weißensee—Margret Arnold, Karl-Heinz Bobbe, Manfred Brückels, Dietrich Dorfstecher, and Ingrid Schuppan—to design the exhibition with him, a task that included researching historical photographs at the Museum für Deutsche Geschichte (Museum of German History—later renamed the Deutsches Historisches Museum) and composing the photomontages for large-scale reproduction. For the fourth-year students, this was a choice assignment; they received an extension of funding from the school and were able to work with their professor on a prestigious and applied project.[20] Seen in this light, the exhibition served a dual pedagogical function: it was both a persuasive artistic work that contributed to the political education of a mass public,[21] and a way to teach

18 Rademacher, 25.

19 Frommhold, 263.

20 Author's interview with Dietrich Dorfstecher, August 15, 2010.

21 Compare this with Wittkugel's statement at the VI. Kongress des Verbandes Bildender Künstler der DDR (6th Congress of the Association of East German Visual Artists) in 1970: "The purpose of art is to educate. In my opinion, the concept can in this sense be applied to all artistic sections." Quoted in Rademacher, 9.

22 Herzfelde, 127.

23 “That the exhibition Der Malik-Verlag, installed by Wieland Herzfeld with his brother’s assistance, went on view in the same pavilion ten years later is a logic of socialism - in which a historical process underway since 1920 is shown to have reached completion.” Frommhold, 176.

24 Herzfelde, 128.

emerging designers how to work as the future “monteurs” of the GDR.

The exhibition may even have exerted an influence on Heartfield’s later work. According to Wieland Herzfelde, his brother first used the technique of “greatly enlarged photomontages” in 1958 in a group exhibition at the Pavillon der Kunst, Berlin.[22] At the end of 1966, as Heartfield installed *Der Malik-Verlag*, 1916-1947 at the International Exhibition Centre (where *Militarismus ohne Maske* had been staged nearly ten years earlier),[23] “this idea became a technique”: his exhibition design blew up quotations from authors, artworks, and photomontages to larger-than-wall-scale proportions, creating an “overwhelming, almost frightening effect” among visitors.[24] Echoing Wittkugel’s spatial strategies, this approach demonstrated the exhibition format’s great potential for visual and emotional “agitation.”

This shift towards an embrace of immersive, collectivized and teachable production provides a parting lens with which to parse the relationship of John Heartfield’s and Klaus Wittkugel’s respective bodies of work and their reception in the first decade of the GDR. Walter Ulbricht’s polemical 1948 proclamation that artists must "finally free themselves from the shackles of what is basically petit-bourgeois individualism"[25] finds a response here. Whereas Heartfield continued to represent an authorial, disjunctive ("verfremdend"), and highly individual approach to designing political propaganda, Wittkugel's contribution suggested the transformation of the graphic designer's role towards one that was ever more directorial, pedagogical, and totalizing. In this sense, Heartfield's aspiration to be "the designer of socialism" itself proves an oxymoron—an unreconcilable contradiction between the brilliant avarice of artistic ego and the utopian conformity of real existing socialism.

25 See "Künstler und Schriftsteller im Zweijahrplan," *Neues Deutschland* (September 4, 1948). Quoted in Hildtrud Ebert, Kunsthochschule Berlin-Weißensee, in Feist et al., 169.

Live In Your World: When Design Becomes Curating

Originally published in *After the Bauhaus, Before the Internet*, Geoff Kaplan, ed. (San Francisco and New York: no place press, 2022).

(2022)

THE COVID-19 PANDEMIC highlighted the mounting inequalities crafted over hundreds of years of extractive colonialism and rampant capitalism; it has also made even clearer the necessity of reimagining structural assumptions that underlie commonly held ideas of communications and community. As part of this larger task, the opportunity presents itself to reformulate the role of artistic production, and to ask how it might offer models for communing with others as an essentially and fundamentally *social* practice. Collaborative creative fields such as graphic design and curating already represent modes of practice that are simultaneously individual *and* collective, authorial and space-making for others, rather than being either one or the other.

How might the entangled histories of these two fields suggest paths for reorienting artistic practice and pedagogy moving forward?

Although they originated as trade-based or institutionally embedded professions, graphic design and curating have undergone multiple disciplinary changes over the past hundred years, with resulting shifts in their cultural valuation. This is most apparent in the transformation of the image of designers and curators into buzzy tastemakers within a global cultural context. Such a change had been anticipated by developments in educational programs and graduate academies beginning in the 1970s and '80s; this schematic essay sketches out the intertwined trajectories of graphic design and curating through an examination of intersecting practitioners and projects. What skills and perspectives from graphic design have supported curatorial practitioners historically, and what might be future opportunities to build upon these connections in an educational context?

Within existing narratives of 20th-century art history, a number of key figures have taken on the roles of both graphic designer and exhibition curator within the field of modern and contemporary art. Notable European examples

1 For more information on these figures and their interdisciplinary work, see the following monographs: Walter Dexel and Ernst-Gerhard Güse, *Walter Dexel: Bilder, Aquarelle, Collagen, Leuchtreklame, Typographie: Westfälisches Landesmuseum für Kunst und Kulturgeschichte Münster, Landschaftsverband Westfalen-Lippe, 27.5. bis 29.7.1979, Ulmer Museum 19.8. bis 23.9.1979* (Münster: Landschaftsverband Westfalen-Lippe, 1979); Willem J. H. B. Sandberg and Ad Petersen, *Sandberg: Een Documentaire = A Documentary* (Amsterdam: Kosmos, 1975); and Frederike Huygen and Harry Lake, *Wim Crouwel: Modernist* (Eindhoven: Lecturis, 2015).

include Walter Dexel, Willem Sandberg, and Wim Crouwel, each of whom enjoyed a consequential trajectory and recognition across both fields.[1] Although he moved fluidly between art and other pursuits throughout his lifetime (a position not uncharacteristic of the period), Dexel's work as both a curator and designer at the Kunstverein Jena from 1916 to 1928 stands out for both its disciplinary straddling and impact within its context. There Dexel helmed an exhibition program that offered early shows to avant-garde artists and architects from the Bauhaus and beyond. The programming's reach expanded through his standardization of a "house style" for the Kunstverein's communication materials and graphic ephemera, characterized by a sans-serif look. Dexel's own publishing on the "new typography" in the 1920s helped to cement this early relationship between modern art and asymmetrical typography.[2]

The slightly younger Sandberg's early work as a designer led to his role first as a curator and then as director of the Stedelijk Museum Amsterdam after World War II. In his role of director, Sandberg continued to design graphics for many of the museum's catalogs, exhibitions, and ephemera. Until his retirement from the

Stedelijk in 1962, Sandberg redefined the display and presentation of modern art to reach wider audiences through innovative and accessible exhibition layouts, as well as experimental presentation formats. After 1962, he continued on to direct the newly formed Israel Museum, developing the museum's graphic identity. This wide-ranging graphic work expanded upon the radical openness of his mature aesthetic, developed in the 1940s within the pages of his underground journal, *Open Oog*. He designed and printed the journal while in hiding from the Nazis for his wartime activities as an active member of the Dutch resistance.

Crouwel, whose eventual path was in some ways paved by Sandberg, maintained a longer and more visible practice as a graphic designer. While continuing his work for industry and establishing the design agency Total Design, Crouwel became design director for the Stedelijk Museum in 1964. His groundbreaking posters prefigured his later position as director of the Museum Boijmans Van Beuningen in Rotterdam, where from 1985 to 1993 he also curated exhibitions and designed their layouts. This new role as director also allowed him to work in a curatorial fashion with other

2 Walter Dexel, "What Is New Typography?" *Frankfurter Zeitung* (February 5, 1927), in Eckhard Neumann, *Functional Graphic Design in the 20's* (New York: Reinhold Publishing, 1967).

designers, for example in his commissioning of the emerging London-based graphic design studio 8vo to produce the museum's experimental visual identity.

Although limited in their geographic and temporal reach, these three examples hint at a strong relationship between the disciplines of graphic design and curating that exists on the levels of practice and discourse. Until the field of curatorial education became institutionalized in the 1980s and '90s, curators often applied their knowledge from other backgrounds, including art history, philosophy, literature, or theater, to their museum and independent work. The figures of Dexel, Sandberg, and Crouwel, however, suggest significant overlaps between the concerns of graphic designers and curators: The conceptual, visual, typographic, and production skills that these three developed allowed them to better communicate their curatorial ideas in graphic form.

At the same time, both fields require strong interpersonal and intersubjective faculties, such as listening, coordination, negotiation, facilitation, and organization; although these "soft skills" are all too often ignored by pedagogy and in the press, they are the foundational tools that allow both designers and curators to assume roles of leadership and authority while also creating space for others. This suite of creative and managerial skills, in tandem with their social, intellectual, and artistic networks, allowed the exhibitions and programs of Dexel, Sandberg, and Crouwel to reach their immediate and farther-flung peers while also connecting avant-garde ideas with larger, receptive audiences. Furthermore, the ability to create graphic documents of their curatorial pursuits–through outreach and communications such as posters and in the form of exhibition catalogs–granted their exhibitions and programs a highly visible legacy.

This fact was not lost upon others in the field: Significant 20th-century curators often recognized the importance of progressive graphic communication and publishing in distributing timely ideas. An incomplete list of examples include museum director Pontus Hultén, whose exhibition catalogs themselves formed a significant strand of his curatorial work;[3] Mildred Friedman, whose curatorial work, experimental editorial oversight of *Design Quarterly*, and development of the design department at the Walker Art Center in Minneapolis helped

3 Pontus Hultén and Lutz Jahre, *Das Gedruckte Museum von Pontus Hultén* (Ostfildern-Ruit: Cantz, 1996); cited in *A Brief History of Curating*, Hans Ulrich Obrist, ed. (Zurich: JRP|Ringier, 2018).

4 Andrew Blauvelt, "Design for Explication Not Veneration: Remembering Mickey Friedman," *The Gradient*, Walker Art Center, September 4, 2014, https://walkerart.org/magazine/mildred-mickey-friedman-obituary.

5 Bruce Altshuler, *Biennials and Beyond: Exhibitions That Made Art History: 1962–2002* (London: Phaidon, 2013), 4.

6 Brenda Moore-McCann and Brian O'Doherty, *Brian O'Doherty, Patrick Ireland: Between Categories* (Farnham: Lund Humphries, 2009).

transform the institution from a regional museum into an internationally recognized program;[4] Kynaston McShine, whose *Primary Structures* at the Jewish Museum, New York, in 1966 helped established Minimal art as a category and was accompanied by an iconic catalog designed by Elaine Lustig Cohen;[5] polymathic artist, critic, and sometime curator Brian O'Doherty, whose guest editing of the landmark "conceptual issue" of *Aspen Magazine* 5+6 (1967) also included designing the publication's box format and materials;[6] and, perhaps most paradigmatically, the independent curator Harald Szeemann, who, although not trained as a graphic designer, worked in his early years as a freelance designer and is credited with the design of the catalogs for his landmark exhibitions *When Attitudes Become Form* (Bern, 1969) and *documenta 5* (Kassel, 1972).[7] These examples of approaches to curating, design, and publishing span the era of early conceptual practices of the 1960s, in which an exhibition catalog's distribution was one primary way that it could travel between disparate international art scenes. If they could not design the graphics themselves, such curators strategically commissioned designers to create striking and long-lasting communications materials.

Szeemann in particular represented both a starting point and an apogee of a trajectory within curatorial practice toward an authorial role that threatened to usurp that of the artists, a criticism leveled publicly in his time by artists Robert Morris, Daniel Buren, and others.[8] There is a cultural hierarchy at play in the critique here that assumes that, within the art world, the degree of agency and power decreases from each successive rung of the "cultural ladder" descends from artist/author to curator to designer (in that order). This valuation follows upon the trend, apparent from the Renaissance onward, that positions the artist as "apex predator" within a cultural and creative ecosystem. Such an assumption ignores the fact that many of the most important exhibitions were themselves organized by artists,[9] and that 20th-century avant-gardes witnessed a constant blurring of artistic, curatorial, and design roles. Designer-curators such as Dexel, Sandberg, and Crouwel practiced a hybrid approach, communicating complex ideas with an individual voice while simultaneously creating platforms for others through their curatorial programs for artists and commissioning of other designers. Such generosity of practice may be embedded within

7 João Doria "Catalog and Archive: Two Szeemann Designs," *The Gradient*, Walker Art Center, December 3, 2012, https://walkerart.org/magazine/catalog-and-archive-twoszeemann-designs.

8 Bruce Altshuler, *Salon to Biennial: Beyond Exhibitions That Made Art History, 1863–1959* (London: Phaidon, 2008). As Altshuler notes in the book's introduction, many of the most significant art exhibitions have been curated by artists. He also underscores the extensive movement and cross-disciplinary practice within these fields, particularly in the 1920s and '30s, when progressive artists such as El Lissitzky and others integrated graphic design, artmaking, exhibition design, and exhibition-making into their practices. Such well-documented examples belie the historical transdisciplinarity of major artists, from Leonardo da Vinci to many others. From a critical perspective, it seems that the desire to atomize and separate creative pursuits into neatly ordered categories is a more recent development, and one that is supported in part by the desire of the rising art market to more easily identify and commodify individual artistic "genius," as distinguished from the more visibly collaborative and intersubjective work of designing and curating.

9 Ibid., 157-74.

10 Richard Sennett's books *The Craftsman* (2008) and *Together* (2012) offer a useful examination of the connection between the workshop as a site of production and the development of modern notions of cooperation and collaboration.

design's relatively humble origins as a skilled trade or cooperative craft within a workshop context.[10] Taken together, these examples offer arguments against assumed dichotomies between individual and collective creative work; rather, they suggest that it is possible (and even desirable) to emphasize both the authorial and the collaborative aspects of creative practice in the same breath.

Yet with the rise of elite American graphic design academies such as Cranbrook, Yale, and CalArts from the 1970s through the '90s, graphic design's educational focus began to take a turn away from the field's more practice-based origins toward supporting a sense of individual graphic authorship and articulating a historical and theoretical discourse for the field. The most recognized work from such schools from this period integrated critical theory, personal experience, and experimental visual form to claim a more autonomous position for graphic design. The authorial claims of this era are most succinctly and resonantly critiqued in Michael Rock's 1996 essay "The Designer as Author," in which Rock argues against the idea of the graphic designer as sole author and toward the notion of the designer as an auteur akin to a film director, whose particular form of agency lies in directing the collaboration of multiple people working together.[11]

In a roughly parallel development, the late 1980s and early '90s saw the establishment of the first master's programs for curating within the European and American contexts, including the École du Magasin in Grenoble, the Royal College of Art in London, and Bard College's Center for Curatorial Studies. These institutions functioned as preprofessional programs meant to prepare their participants for career paths as arts professionals within a newly opening cultural field, yet they also had the effect of solidifying and canonizing a set of approaches to the curatorial field. Significantly, they provided an academic context for moving away from older, more traditional ideas of the curator as "caring" for museum collections toward the role of the independent curator whose authority blurs with that of the artist.[12] This trend followed upon modes of curatorial authorship as practiced by Szeemann and his ilk in the decades prior. Establishing "the curatorial" as a field of study and a *discourse*, as opposed to a *practice*, the introduction of curating into the academy supported the field's perceived cultural value.

11 Michael Rock, "The Designer as Author," Eye 20, no. 5 (1996). Ellen Lupton's essay "The Designer as Producer," from the same period, is helpful in contextualizing those 1990s debates within a larger avant-garde discourse questioning models of authorship. Lupton traces these back to Walter Benjamin's "The Author as Producer." Of another era, but equally relevant, is Roland Barthes's canonical "The Death of the Author," which was first published in Brian O'Doherty's *Aspen* 5+6.

12 Paul O'Neill, *The Culture of Curating and the Curating of Culture(s)* (Cambridge, MA: MIT Press, 2016).

Viewed within the broader context of expanding neoliberalism (capped by the "failure" of state socialism in 1989), the buttressing of ideas of sole authorship, agency, and value undertaken within both the graphic design and curatorial programs of the 1980s and '90s takes on greater significance. Both types of programs sought to elevate what was once considered either a practical trade or an institutionally embedded profession into academic and creative disciplines with greater cultural capital. Graphic design and curating, both of which also require managerial, coordinative, and cooperative skills, sought to balance this understanding of the field's contingency with a more expansive and autonomous self-view. These transformations within the fields and an increasingly individualistic emphasis mirror larger cultural transformations since that period that have helped to destabilize and threaten environmental, social, and political systems.

By seeking to emphasize the individual and insular discourses of the field at the expense of their interpersonal aspects, such programs of the 1980s and '90s (from which I also emerged) may have unwittingly reinforced certain categorical and professional disciplines, despite their claims to the contrary. Sandberg, for example, managed to direct a major museum, shape its exhibitions program, and create highly individual works of design while also inviting broader audiences into the institution to understand and experience art. Operating across the perceived spectrum of individual practice "versus" collective activity, Sandberg demonstrated that one can occupy multiple positions at once. Such resolute straddling of established institutional curatorial roles and personal design or artistic practice appears as an exception from the perspective of today's arts discourse, in which individual genius is the most commonly understood unit of creative valuation, a position that discounts the underlying support systems and collaborations that make any production in the world possible.[13]

Yet as the past twenty-five years have witnessed the spread of personal computing, accessible networked communications, and the progressive deskilling of knowledge-based professions, a space may also be opening up within which to reexamine models of creative practice and consider their renewed social relevance. Starting in the 1990s, one can trace a second arc of practitioners who incorporated the skills of designing, publishing, and exhibition-making in order to simultaneously create space for others,

13 Céline Condorelli, James Langdon, and Gavin Wade's *Support Structures* (2009) is an indispensable compendium of support structures within art, design, and architectural fields. It makes the clear argument that, far from being the exception within the arts, collaboration and mutual interdependency are the (often unacknowledged or willfully elided) rule.

structure narratives in nonnormative ways, and communicate ideas to broader publics while still participating in a rigorous disciplinary discourse.[14] In the educational field, experimental institutions such as the Werkplaats Typografie in Arnhem, the Netherlands, and conferences such as 2012's "Graphic Design, Exhibiting, Curating" in Bolzano, Italy, have provided forums for relevant discussions.[15] The decade just past has also seen the emergence of a new generation of hybrid practitioners, who work fluidly between design, curating, research, publishing, and pedagogy in order to connect timely aesthetic ideas with pressing cultural concerns in unexpected and engaging formats.[16]

As a conclusion to this exploratory sketch: The uncertainties, inequalities, and imminent crises of our current times afford a rare moment to rethink how, why, with, and for whom designers and curators make what they make, and how these skills can be more effectively integrated into broader creative practice. Both fields possess specific tools for both individual creation as well as collaboration; even if the skills belonging to the former category (e.g., typography, layout, image-making, exhibition design, checklist development, etc.) are more typically taught in school,

14 A partial list of such figures might include Åbäke, Andrew Blauvelt, Design/Writing/Research, Dexter Sinister, Jon Sueda, Louise Sandhaus, Mark Owens, Michael Worthington, Na Kim, Silas Munro, Sulki and Min Choi, Tetsuya Goto, and many others.

15 *Graphic Design, Exhibiting, Curating*, Giorgio Camuffo and Maddalena Dalla Mura, eds. (Bolzano: Bozen-Bolzano University Press, 2013).

16 An inexhaustive sampling of more recent figures and their initiatives might include Lauren Mackler of Public Fiction, Hala Al-Ani and Riem Hassan of Möbius Design Studio/Design House, Tereza and Vit Ruller of The Rodina, Corinne Gisel and Nina Paim of common interest, and Anja Lutz of A-Z Presents, each of whom brings a different perspective into the space between curating and graphic design.

it is those of the latter category (e.g., active listening, empathic feedback, group facilitation, research and discovery, organizing and project management, etc.), typically learned "on the side" over years of professional practice, that must begin to occupy equal footing within the pedagogy and mentorship of coming generations.

By expanding the curriculum of both fields to include not only "hard skills" but also these "soft" ones, can design, curating, and art help to support broader social transformations? The intersubjective tools embedded within both design and curating, if used well, could serve to emphasize the importance of understanding bias and positionality through a participant-observer mode; they can allow for opportunities to reconsider given briefs and institutional formats in order to open space for others. Through public presentations and communications, design and curating can help provide resources to those most in need and reimagine platforms for virtual interchange beyond the normative, centralized, and corporatized forms at hand. Learning from historical lessons and examples, these fields may continue to reshape each other—as well as other, adjacent areas of creative practice—in generative and generous ways.

What is Design? Manifesto for the Gwangju Design Biennale Academy series

By Project Projects (Adam Michaels, Prem Krishnamurthy, and Rob Giampietro)

(2011)

Originally presented at Storefront for Art and Architecture, May 17, 2011.

1

Autonomous design is at best a myth; at worst, a backwards, solipsistic slide away from responsibility and broader societal engagement. Instead of pursuing separation from external ideas and impetuses, designers ought to embrace the discipline's communal and contingent nature. Design is embedded in culture and always in dialogue with specific conditions and contexts.

2

History is often mistakenly presented as testament or truth. Today, we have unprecedented access to historical materials and a commensurate ability to archive the present ever more thoroughly. As such, a nuanced perspective acknowledges that history itself is never fixed; it is in continuous flux based on timing and viewpoint. In contemporary design work, it is not enough to simply cite the past. History must be actively and reflexively engaged in order to craft new meanings and synthesize existing knowledge with speculative possibilities.

3

The “ideal” user, reader, visitor, or participant is a simplistic invention of another age. Design should neither seek to impress through pretension nor condescend to a perceived baseline; rather it should use its powers of persuasion to reach new audiences. We advocate for design that translates specialized and complex knowledge into a form that is comprehensible to anyone who might be interested. Rather than vagueness, obfuscation, and visual rhetoric, this requires clarity and precision.

4

There are too many shoddy, unconsidered things in the world already. Given the widespread distribution of today's digital production tools, it's remarkably simple to make nearly anything, especially things claiming to critique design through the rejection of formal rigor. Making things well, making them beautifully, making them with craft, making them with an excess of effort, demonstrates a respect for one's own labor and an expression of love for the world that dissolves perceived categories of work and pleasure.

5

Typically, design helps to further entrench the interests of the powerful. Design work always embodies and advances a political ethos, though all too often a regressive one. A more critical and ethical design must not only acknowledge its relationship to power, but also wield its own strategies of cultural influence—including proximity to networks of production and distribution—to offer alternative glimpses into the near future. Ruptures and rejection of normative ideas are the basis of progressive design practice.

6

In past eras when “the public” seemed homogenous, design accordingly claimed reduction, uniformity, and purity as its mode. Now, as heterogenous, dispersed, and radically different publics come to the fore, contemporary design work is by necessity a combination of hybrid forms. These new approaches demonstrate that easy consensus is less successful than a hard-won balance of often conflictual desires. Instead of sameness and inbreeding, we propose dispersed ingenuity through dissimilarity and cross-pollination.

7

At its best, design's cultural value—as opposed to its commercial value—functions as an abundance, a resource to be shared. As design work makes its way through more hands, its overflow leaves something behind to inspire and instigate change. Seen with this focus, design's basis shifts from the production of forms by its practitioners to the production of actions by its recipients.

Close Encounters

By Project Projects (Adam Michaels, Prem Krishnamurthy, and Rob Giampietro)

Originally published in *The Way Beyond Art: Wide White Space*, Jon Sueda, ed. (San Francisco: CCA Wattis, 2013).

(2013)

PRESENTATION

SPACE, THE FINAL FRONTIER. An advanced visitor to this planet circa 2012 might marvel at our wealth of digital devices designed to convey virtual experiences. What relevance do real, physical exhibition spaces have to offer at this late date? Images and objects can be designed and modeled, examined in microscopic detail, even rotated and manipulated in multiple dimensions, all without the user needing to leave the comfort of his or her home or office. So why do people still insist on considering, admiring, and enjoying actual objects on display? With information increasingly networked and readily available from devices that are "always on," what's the use of specific institutions dedicated to the presentation of only a selected group of works, from 10 A.M. to 6 P.M., Tuesday through Saturday? Isn't the present world one of everything, anytime, anywhere?

Despite the virtual options that we enjoy, people still flock to exhibitions in ever-increasing numbers. The recent Alexander McQueen show at the Metropolitan Museum of Art in New York drew 661,509 visitors and increased the membership of the institution by 23,000 (joining was the only way to dodge the three-hour queue). The first New York exhibition of Christian Marclay's *The Clock* (2010), a 24-hour film composed of clips from other films that show the time of day—and which itself is always synchronized to local time—had lines snaking around the block even in the bitter winter cold. The visitors' experience became an extended meditation on temporality, beginning while in line outside and extending to the motionless hours spent hushed in a dark space, watching a film full of watches and timepieces. Like a public clock in a town square, Marclay's film gathered groups of strangers together to participate in a collective yet authored experience. What is the appeal of these physical encounters that are so limited in their availability, that require arduous preparation and waiting? Why not just watch films at home? (Marclay has announced no plans to exhibit *The Clock* online.)

As popular as traditional physical exhibitions are, institutions manifest an increasing enthusiasm for annotating them through virtual means. Pushing older models of technologically mediated exhibition interpretation (cheap Xeroxes and laser printouts, audio guides, cell phone call-in systems) even further, the physical space is now connected to virtual information outside the gallery in ways that are ambitious, and sometimes distracting. The 2011 exhibition of design and interactivity *Talk to Me: Design and the Communication Between People and Objects* at the Museum of Modern Art in New York featured wall labels with QR codes that visitors could scan with a smartphone to access additional content and social networking features, as well as Twitter hashtags to be used in online commentary. This type of exhibition seems to both revel in and undermine its own physicality; a visitor is constantly pulled toward retreat into virtual realms accessed through a tiny mobile screen. In addition to the exhibition and the objects themselves, the visitor experiences, in real time, their virtual mediation.

The responsibility to sensitively frame and translate content is a daily task for designers. Given their role as professional mediators, it should come as no surprise that graphic designers routinely turn their own methods to bear upon themselves in the public presentation of their work, documenting their designs in highly staged photographs that reinforce the sense of a highly authored, directed message. As certain forms of presentation come to prominence—the poster held up in front of its author's obscured body, the 3/4-angled book cover that floats on a neutral ground—they become generic, overwhelming the specificity of their contents. This approach to portfolio image making emphasizes a graphic design object's most attention-getting visual characteristics while flattening out many of the particularities and peculiarities that are essential to the actual craft of design: its heft, its subtle hues, its tactile qualities. At the same time, such presentation elides deeper underlying specificities essential to understanding design: why a particular piece was made, for whom, under what circumstances, at what cost.

A number of recent design exhibitions have encouraged a high level of mediation as a means to address questions of representation. *Graphic Design Worlds* at the 2011 Triennale Design Museum in Milan and the Gwangju Design Biennial 2011 both commissioned installations from participating designers instead of displaying existing works. This reversal of traditional graphic design exhibitions—instead of presenting a mediated display of designed works, each installation itself became a work on view—posited the works as something closer to understood definitions of "art," since they existed less to solve a communication problem than to communicate the self-expressions of the designers and design groups. Other exhibitions of the past several years, such as *Graphic Design in the White Cube* (part of the 22nd International Biennale of Graphic Design in Brno, the Czech Republic, in 2006) or the traveling show *Forms of Inquiry: The Architecture of Critical Graphic Design* (2007-9), hewed closer to a traditional design "brief" in the commissioning of work, although these briefs were intended to reflexively both manifest and produce the conditions of the exhibitions themselves. In *Graphic Design in the White Cube*, the participating designers created posters that were shown in the gallery and also used as publicity materials for the show, thereby becoming advertisements for the very idea of a graphic design exhibition. *Forms of Inquiry* included not only commissioned posters, but also the architectural inspirations for each work together with a set of informally arranged books and works (including signage and objects) to invite hands-on investigation.

In the United States, the largest overview of graphic design in the past decade, *Graphic Design: Now in Production*, first presented at the Walker Art Center in Minneapolis in 2011, functioned more as a classical museum exhibition of a broad set of graphic design objects. The display avoided any overt mediation of the exhibition's contents (which included several pieces and design input by the authors of this essay), instead preferring a categorical approach to organizing the materials. Products by graphic designers were for sale in the "Storefront," a fully functional retail area that also served as a thematic section of the show, while most works were presented as aesthetic objects distinct from their usage: Books and magazines were encased in vitrines; identity and branding systems were displayed as pure graphic forms, without documentation of their usage; two-dimensional works were presented in frames on the gallery's white walls. In contrast with the exhibition's major institutional precursors, *Graphic Design in America: A Visual Language History* (at the Walker Art Center in 1989) and *Mixing Messages: Graphic Design in Contemporary Culture* (at the Cooper-Hewitt, National Design Museum in New York in 1996), both of which were activated by public-oriented architectural displays highlighting the prevalence of graphic design in daily life, *Graphic Design: Now in Production* focused its attention on the aesthetics and materiality of current, often designer-"authored," objects as objects. It's almost as if, in the decades of desktop publishing and cloud computing since those earlier shows (when graphic design was barely recognized as a discipline), the field has become so virtual that now the job of graphic design exhibitions is to bring the work itself back down to Earth.

Exhibitions are physical, and logistically complicated to produce. They are intrinsically social and often unruly. The communal nature of any exhibition is brought to the fore whenever we peer around someone blocking our view of a painting. Numerous artists in the past half-century have undertaken as a theme the participatory aspect of exhibitions instead of focusing on the production of objects. Well-known examples range from Rirkrit Tiravanija's communal cooking spectacles to older and more critical works such as Graciela Carnevale's 1968 exhibition in Rosario, Argentina, in which gallery visitors were locked into the exhibition space and forced to break a window to escape the show.

The design of exhibitions is also social in another sense: When an exhibition consists of a collection of works, the works themselves socialize with one another. *Artist's Choice: Vik Muniz: Rebus*, curated by the artist Vik Muniz at the Museum of Modern Art in New York in 2008, combined objects from all of the museum's departments in a chain of leapfrogging association. The exhibition consisted of a single row of objects–from paintings and sculptures to readymades and commercial goods–presented one after another, without captions or explanatory materials. This blunt yet effective structure emphasized the literal and often humorous connections between works, and highlighted the ways in which works from radically different disciplines can function as a coherent whole when meaningfully arranged and juxtaposed. When works are in the company of other works occupying the same space in an exhibition, you as a visitor are in the company of both your fellow exhibitiongoers and the works gathered during your visit to the exhibition space.

On the other hand, exhibitions can also explicitly demonstrate that there are many possible paths through a given set of objects and that the frame through which we encounter them also colors their reception. *The Pilgrim, the Tourist, the Flaneur (and the Worker)*, presented in 2011 at the Van Abbemuseum in Eindhoven, the Netherlands, took the museum's role as mediator to a provocative extreme. Each entering visitor played a different specific part (as listed in the show's title), which then expressed itself through a set of tools (a tourist map, audio guides, identifying stickers) that guided his or her experience of walking through the show. Visitors were encouraged to change characters in order to have multiple experiences of the same artworks. In this manner, the exhibition made clear how its overt presence as a frame conditions a visitor's experience. Its structure was the guide that organized particular narratives, and the show emerged as a site for self-conscious role playing–a mode related to analog gaming structures as well as to the fluidity of online identity and presentation.

This idea of user-driven rearrangement in order to produce an "active viewer" has been explored repeatedly at key moments in exhibition history. Frequently cited examples include El Lissitzky's radical *Abstract Cabinet*, developed in Hanover in 1927 for the display of modernist and Suprematist artworks, in which wall slats painted different colors on their two sides created the effect of a changing background field that shifted with the viewer's position; and Frederick Kiesler's 1942 design of the stands for the paintings in Peggy Guggenheim's Art of This Century gallery, the viewing angles of which could be adjusted by visitors. More contemporary examples include the Pontus Hultén Study Gallery at Stockholm's Moderna Museet, an exhibition system composed of multiple large screens with artworks hung upon them. The screens can be accessed and reordered in the manner of library stacks or deep archival storage. On a practical level, this system allows more artworks to be shown than in a conventional space, and on a conceptual level it creates a uniquely engaged way to experience the art, as the viewer assumes the role of a curator or designer who must root through art storage in order to examine particular works. Nowhere is this self-directed curation more in effect than at the Luce Foundation's study centers, located at the Metropolitan Museum of Art in New York, the Smithsonian American Art Museum in Washington, DC, and other institutions. In the study centers, objects are held in "visible storage," positioned in a moment of semi-exhibition, their significance to be determined not by a curator in an official capacity but by visitors. In these examples, the modernist goal of transforming the exhibitiongoer from passive viewer into active participant in reconfiguring the work begins to be realized through the unique technology of display.

CONFUSION

Technology is only one way in which exhibitions may become reflexive; oftentimes this happens even earlier on a deeper conceptual and structural level through the questioning and reversal of typically assumed functions. Martin Beck's video *About the Relative Size of Things in the Universe* (2007) shows a reconstruction of George Nelson's Struc-Tube exhibition display system being assembled. Nelson developed his simple system in the mid-20th century for traveling displays and trade fairs. In the video, Beck looks at this system to comment on both distribution and global capital; the original Struc-Tube system could be cheaply and easily installed and disassembled by unskilled laborers anywhere in the world. The display unit itself becomes a self-conscious reflection on representation and display. Since the system is both an artwork (his reconstruction has often been exhibited as such) as well as an armature for other works, claims of what is presenting and what is being presented get complicated, to say the least.

In the 1980s, exhibition design became a medium for artists with a critical agenda. The artist Judith Barry, when invited to take part in the exhibition *Damaged Goods: Desire and the Economy of the Object* at the New Museum in New York in 1986, decided that her contribution to the show would be to design the exhibition. Building off her previous works such as *Casual Shopper* (1980-81), which critically examined American consumer culture, Barry undertook the role of exhibition designer and created displays and furniture for other artists' work. The scenography of the show took on the slightly lurid, provocative look of a slick 1980s retail space, in stark contrast with the proverbial white cube. In this and other important exhibitions of art and popular culture designed by Barry (later in collaboration with Ken Saylor), the once-distinct roles of artist and exhibition designer, artwork and commodity, were blurred in uncomfortable but revealing ways, complicating (as in the Struc-Tube example) the usual assumptions about the neutrality of exhibition spaces.

Such confusions can function also to extend the exhibition space recursively through the complex interplay of installation and documentation. Julia Born and Laurenz Brunner's *Title of the Show*, first shown at the Galerie für Zeitgenössische Kunst in Leipzig, Germany, in 2009 (and included in *Wide White Space*), consists of reproductions and re-creations of the designers' work at wall-scale. These huge reproductions then became the catalog documentation through a fluid transformation: The gallery walls were photographed and reproduced, one to a page, without alteration, in the book. The point of overlap between installation and documentation occurred in the inclusion (as wall vinyl in the space) of the typical armature of an exhibition catalog: folios, captions, title page, credits, et cetera. These elements were scaled as super-graphics in the exhibition, and thus showed up as normal-book-size text in the catalog. Through this humorous, yet tightly executed play with medium and scale, Born confounded the typical expectations of both exhibition and catalog.

DISTRIBUTION

Though usually unacknowledged, the interdependence of an exhibition and its external mediation is intrinsic to the exhibition. The artist Joseph Grigely has coined the term "exhibition prosthetics" to refer to the various accoutrements of exhibitions—press releases, brochures, wall labels, website texts, catalogs, and so forth—that are not typically considered part of an exhibition yet nevertheless imprint and influence how the show is received. These prosthetic pieces serve both to mediate the exhibition inside its four walls and to represent it outside of them. Ironically, such designed ephemera become the primary lenses for viewing exhibitions now and in the future, and thus in some sense are the defining features of the show as it manifests in the world for posterity.

Similarly, an artwork's representation or documentation can eclipse the actual object, or at least become its primary manifestation. Frequently cited as the most influential artwork of the 20th century, Marcel Duchamp's *Fountain* (1917) was only ever seen by the board of directors of the Society of Independent Artists before being removed from the Society's exhibition (the premise of which had been to display all work submitted). The piece's subsequent notoriety has come entirely through the famous photograph of the urinal taken by Alfred Stieglitz and published in the second issue of *The Blind Man*. This example makes explicit an essential fact about exhibitions: Given that they are bounded in space and time, every exhibition is *not* seen by more people than the number of people who do see it. This singularity lends the exhibition its aura of exclusivity, even sometimes a peculiar sacral power.

In the early 20th century, the philosopher and economist Otto Neurath attempted to strip this elitist aura from exhibitions and make them more broadly accessible. Founded more than a decade before the publication of Walter Benjamin's influential 1936 essay "The Work of Art in the Age of Mechanical Reproduction," Neurath's Gesellschafts- und Wirtschaftsmuseum (Museum of Society and Economy) in Vienna was open every evening of the week so that working people could visit. The exhibitions consisted of printed plates and a standardized display system that could be distributed to multiple cities simultaneously. This ambitious approach presaged such forms of presentation as the website, which can be viewed simultaneously by anyone who has access to a computer with an Internet connection.

Yet the limited reach and exclusivity of exhibitions can be a peculiar strength of the form. How often do we hear about a great exhibition that, sadly, "just closed today"? These unseen presentations can become perfect screens for each nonvisitor's projections, whether specific to the exhibition or relating to broader cultural desires. The seminal exhibition *This Is Tomorrow*, staged at the Whitechapel Gallery in London in 1956, featured multidisciplinary contributions by 12 different working groups of artists, architects, musicians, and graphic designers. However, as the architectural historian Mark Wigley has pointed out, most reports of the exhibition grossly distort its contents by focusing almost exclusively on the contributions of Group 2, which included Richard Hamilton, John McHale, and John Voelcker. Their work for the show included proto-Pop art pieces such as Hamilton's *Just What Is It That Makes Today's Homes So Different, So Appealing* (1956) as well as found objects and sculptures. The iconic photograph of a crowd packed into Group 2's installation to catch a glimpse of Robby the Robot from the recently released film *Forbidden Planet* has passed down into posterity as the defining view of an exhibition that more people wrote about than ever actually went to see.

This example underscores the reality that most historical exhibitions of the past century, represented after the fact, are shown primarily through photographs of a portion of the installation. Other components that might contribute to a more holistic understanding–plans, elevations, checklists, drawings, and models–are rarely circulated. In the case of a design exhibition, in which the actual conceptualization and installation often self-reflexively impact the contents, these other process-related components become even more important, not only to the scholar but potentially to the exhibition visitor and his or her understanding of the display's function.

The first volume of Bruce Altschuler's invaluable resource *Salon to Biennial: Exhibitions That Made Art History* (2008) demonstrates that carefully researched archival materials about specific exhibitions can begin to suggest the complexities of how shows were conceived and received in their time. These materials show that an exhibition is not a singular snapshot, but rather the sum of a subjective navigation through objects in space—a temporal and spatial experience that, like a film or performance, cannot be described merely through two-dimensional manifestations. For those unable to see an exhibition for themselves, the closest way to understand it might be through a dispersed approach involving not only traditional installation photography but also video walkthroughs, audio clips, visitor interviews, and crowd-sourced photography, reflecting the multitude of perspectives and angles of an exhibition experience. In addition to working within the exhibition as interpretive or informational aids, these technologies could serve as a means for sharing an exhibition after its closing.

CONTEXTUALIZATION

Whereas most contemporary artworks are conceived specifically for the constraints of the white cube—to be viewed semi-autonomously, with a minimum of external interference—graphic design is usually created for a client in response to a brief, and is meant to be viewed in some "real world" context, whether on the street, in a store, in an office, or at home. This means that when graphic design is shown in a gallery, it is most often being thrust into conflict with its intent.

This is a critical point: Design lives first through its usage. A book is most usefully a book when a person is looking at it, turning the pages. If the book is on a pedestal under glass, it has been transformed into a relic. Though it still possesses aesthetic value, it no longer embodies its original meaning, origins, or function. To allow design to perform best in public, then, it is critical not to change its nature. Rather than conflating and confounding the effects of design with other art forms, exhibitions of designs should be structured to emphasize the designs' inherent qualities as social and contingent.

With this restructuring and reprioritization comes possibilities for alternative forms of display. One such might be to re-create the more natural habitat of the "street." Venturi, Scott Brown and Associates' 1976 exhibition *Signs of Life: Symbols in the American City* (presented at the Renwick Gallery in Washington, DC) used large-scale tableaux of the American street to continue the firm's analysis of urbanism begun in Las Vegas. In 1980, Paolo Portoghesi's first Architecture Biennale in Venice featured as its centerpiece the Strada Novissima, a corridor of 20 building facades created by 20 different architects that together functioned as a kind of theatrical set. Both of these exhibitions attempted to transpose something of the street into the museum. Yet while such strategies beyond the modernist white cube were significant historically, their kitsch overtones and reliance on simulation ultimately distracted from the real possibility of creating an effective semiotic and communicative evocation of context.

A complementary approach elides the gallery and simulation altogether, taking design directly to the street: exhibiting design objects not within the walls of a gallery or museum, but rather finding a way to position them almost virally within an everyday space of encounter. The potential problem, however, is how to clearly differentiate such presentations from the normal objects of life. Hence the proliferation and rhetorical claims of several recent in-between modes: the pop-up store (a space for exhibition located outside of the gallery, facilitated more by consumption than aesthetic encounter) and the reading room (a common area for reading books in a natural manner, although still located within the controlled environs of the museum).

Alternatively, the display of design and its context could be approached even more discursively. For example, in a museum, where the handling of the work must necessarily be limited, the gap is often bridged by text-based explanations that attempt to answer the critical questions: Why was this object made? For whom, and under what conditions? How much was paid for the design, and what were the limitations that arose in its development? There are notable examples of this approach in the realm of product design, for instance the modestly named Dokumentationszentrum Alltagskultur der DDR (Documentation Center for Everyday Culture of the GDR) in Eisenhüttenstadt, Germany, which presents consumer objects from the former East German Socialist Republic in order to tell the cultural history of a vanished state. Here, the task is made even more complex and ambitious by its twofold goals: to re-create and represent a context that has disappeared entirely, while explaining how and why particular products and objects existed in the form they did.

Apart from anthropological and didactic approaches, there are also more purely visual means to demonstrate the aesthetic context of a given set of works (which is sometimes just as valuable as understanding their economic context). *Signes quotidiens: Designs, fashion, tattoo etc.*, presented in 2005 at the Centre Culturel Suisse in Paris, juxtaposed historic Swiss packaging for pharmaceutical and food products with contemporary Swiss graphics by NORM, Optimo, Elektrosmog, and others, revealing a legible lineage from the commercial packaging's sans-serif typography and visual abstraction to the more radically systematic approaches of Swiss design today. The works were differentiated through careful presentation—the historical packaging in vitrines between two parallel walls, and the contemporary design hung directly on the exteriors of those walls—which served to demonstrate that the deliberate collocation of works oftentimes allows the multiple contexts and histories of objects to resonate more clearly.

We are left with several reasons for exhibitions of graphic design and, moreover, for the design of exhibitions. On the one hand, design objects themselves possess an enduring materiality and a unique presence, best experienced in close physical proximity. And in addition to the sheer aesthetic appreciation of individual objects, exhibitions offer a rare glimpse into the unique sociability of works and the connections that can be made between them: "...as beautiful as the chance encounter of a sewing machine and an umbrella on an operating table," as phrased by Comte de Lautréamont, whose words were later promulgated by André Breton and the Surrealists. When works of graphic design are deliberately placed in a room together, they gravitate in unexpected ways for each viewer, revealing that a set of seemingly discrete points are in fact nodes of a constellation. In the most memorable examples, a spatial presentation made reflexive—whether through architectural intervention, participatory framing, user-modulated display, interpretive obstruction, or embedded technology for documentation and dissemination—can create a critical rupture, producing awareness of design itself. "Design" is simultaneously a noun and a verb, a subject and a frame, an object and an action. It is a mass-produced medium that can orbit the globe in multiples, reaching other places and people at the same moment but in distinct, surprising, and unfamiliar ways.

Time, After Time

Originally published in *One Here Now: The Brian O'Doherty/Patrick Ireland Project* (Cobh: Sirius Arts Centre and Paper Visual Art, 2019).

(2019)

> *A thing is just a slow event.*
> —Stanley Eveling[1]

I BEGIN THIS ESSAY in a room in Tensta konsthall, Stockholm: day two of a one-week mini-residency. Despite my best attempts to wake up early, it is now past 10 A.M. My overambitious travel schedules and jetlagged body of the past weeks have kept me in bed—as did the slight sense of dread of having to start writing this piece. Where, when, how, and *for how long* to think about a subject

1 I have not yet been able to locate this original quotation. Scholar Barbara Kirschenblatt-Gimblett cites it as "A thing is a slow event" in essays from 2004 on. Katharine Galloway Young mentions the idea that "an event is a quick object and an object is a slow event" in a paper from 1987, with the source as Stanley Eveling's unpublished lectures in philosophy. I first encountered this paraphrase as a standard feature of the email signature of Marvin J. Taylor.

Barbara Kirschenblatt-Gimblett, "World Heritage and Cultural Economics." *Museum Frictions: Public Cultures/Global Transformations*, Ivan Karp, et al., eds. (Durham, NC: Duke, 2006), 180.

K.G. Young, "Multiple Contexting: The Story Context of Stories." *Taleworlds and Storyrealms*, vol 16 (Springer, Dordrecht: Martinus Nijhoff Philosophy Library, 1987). https://doi.org/10.1007/978-94-009-3511-2_3

like Brian O'Doherty's imposing *One Here Now* and its apparently endless future?

§

Let me begin again, with a question: What is the relationship between a thing's time of production and its eventual lifespan?

The most famous medieval churches took over a century to build; while some have fallen prey to war and different factors, others still stand, having outlived their production time by a factor of many. A Galapagos tortoise egg gestates for only four to eight months, but the turtle then lives up to one hundred years. In contrast, a book such as Irish writer Brian Dillon's *I Am Sitting in a Room* (2011)–authored, edited, and designed in only twenty-four hours–might last for a decade or longer, its existence multiplying the production time by thousands.

On this spectrum, Brian O'Doherty's *One Here Now* at Sirius Arts Centre falls into an unusual zone. Intending originally to create a temporary work over the course of a one-week artist residency, O'Doherty found himself inspired by the site and context. He eventually made six trips to Cobh from 1995 to 1996 to paint the murals, which cost him his day job at the National

Endowment for the Arts (NEA) in Washington, DC.[2] So a piece that began as an experimental production—a short respite and interim work by way of an artist residency—led to the end of the artist's more remunerative occupation, while opening up a field for speculation.

Artist residencies themselves are often seen as a hallowed forum for impermanent production, lightweight periods where process is paramount. Instead of emphasizing the necessity to create a "finished" work (the province of the "real" world of professional artistic work), residencies typically offer less-structured time to wander. *Un*productivity, even outright failure, is lionized as a way station towards future developments in the artist's thinking and practice. O'Doherty's own book-length essay *Studio and Cube* (2007) explores the complex and entangled relationship between this unresolved space of making (the studio, the residency) and the finished space of presenting (the gallery).

Yet in his work in Cobh, these two levels are collapsed: the site of the residency also became the later site of exhibition. Created in situ, the finished artwork is the residue of this labor. O'Doherty's stay at Sirius Arts Centre was intended from the start to produce the next in his

2 In conversation with the author, January 6, 2019, New York.

3 In conversation with the author, January 6, 2019, New York.

4 Ibid.

series of "rope drawings," room-sized ephemeral installations dating from the early 1970s through to the present day. The end process and its product, however, far exceeded the artist's initial expectations. In O'Doherty's own estimation: "It was a residency that became way too ambitious."[3] We might also add from the sidelines: It was an artist's residency that became quite *heavy*, with much more at stake than usually is the case.

As the artwork's production time multiplied, so did its lifespan. The initial invitation from Sirius Arts Centre assumed that the final product would exist as an impermanent work. This implicit constraint was clear to O'Doherty from the start.[4] Through his ongoing work as a grants officer at the NEA, he knew the necessity for exhibitions to come to an end in order to make space—literally—for the next generation. Ongoing renewal and "innovation" within the contemporary-art ecosystem are accomplished through the logic and format of the temporary exhibition.

On a deeper level, O'Doherty's rope drawings for museums and independent art spaces represented a disavowal of the fixed nature of artworks as well as their commercial market. In the 1960s, he was embroiled in the Conceptual and Minimal art scenes in New York, exhibiting as an artist while simultaneously editing and designing the groundbreaking magazine issue *Aspen* 5+6. During this first wave, Conceptual art attempted to "dematerialise" the art object through a range of strategies. This position became more nuanced as O'Doherty entered into the next phase of his work and took on the political pseudonym of Patrick Ireland. Characterized by his iconic rope drawings, Ireland's short-term, performative installations tested arguments around the purpose, history, and ideology of the white cube gallery space. These rope drawings—ephemeral by design—were captured for posterity primarily in documentary photographs as well as drawings by his artist alter ego, while displaying a symbiotic relationship with O'Doherty's most widely known critical writing and thinking.[5]

In contrast with other Minimal and Conceptual artists of the period—for example, those most closely associated with Heiner Friedrich's gallery and later with Dia Art Foundation—O'Doherty's rope drawings embraced the limiting constraints of *human* time, space, and experience. When creating and exhibiting his rope drawings, O'Doherty emphasized that they were meant to be encountered from an embodied,

5 Indeed, Patrick Ireland's spatial experiments can be viewed as the applied instantiations of and companions to Brian O'Doherty's now-famous 1976 essay series *Inside the White Cube.*

particular perspective, rather than from an abstracted, objective standpoint. Bound closely to the space of installation and surviving only until the end of an exhibition, his public practice of rope drawings represented a rebuke to the white cube's sacralising, transhistorical pretensions.

Yet over this same period, O'Doherty continued a divergent, private path of in situ painting quietly, in another space: his own. In 1975 he bought a house in Todi, Italy, with his wife and intellectual partner, art historian Barbara Novak. From 1977 O'Doherty began a project there, *Casa Dipinta*, which continues to this day. Set in the abstract ogham script (used throughout O'Doherty's work from the late 1960s), it is a lively, ambitious, house-scale installation of brightly painted large-format murals. Comparable in ambition to Kurt Schwitters's *Merzbau* and other environments-as-artworks, *Casa Dipinta* represents a subtle amendment to O'Doherty's earlier notions of time and the concept of an artwork as a passing event. *Casa Dipinta* is a long-term, dynamic, and organic artwork. Although nearly every surface of the house is already filled with paintings, the project continues to change with each of the artist's visits. Both a registered museum as well as a space for periodic living, the house represents a specific model of an artwork's permanence: rather than being frozen in memory or memorialized as a finished work, it remains in use and always in flux.

As O'Doherty himself writes [in the volume where this essay first appeared], when approaching the commanding site of Sirius Arts Centre to create *One Here Now*, he abandoned the earlier, lightweight approach of his rope drawings and instead learned from his own ongoing project in Todi—covering the walls with layers of paint to unify the space. And so, despite its original aspirations to ephemerality, *One Here Now* became semi-permanent from the start—left on view by commissioner and director Peter Murray for two years. Now, after its meticulous restoration, reinstallation, unveiling, and subsequent enclosure within the architecture of Sirius Arts Centre,[6] it will become a permanent, yet invisible, exhibition—a nearly oxymoronic case. Caught in this double-bind of historic preservation versus programmatic necessity, the artwork's life will continue to unfold behind a wall. What will it be, then? An ongoing masterpiece, a troubled ghost, yet perhaps also a seedbank for unknown futures, all at the same time?

6 EDITOR'S NOTE: Following its unveiling, restoration, and year on view, the mural was subsequently covered again in drywall to protect it while also allowing other works to be exhibited in the space.

§

In traditional folklore, when a ghost appears it is motivated by trauma left over from mortal life—pains inflicted that have not yet been released. This negative energy coalesces into a ghostly form until the charge is dissipated. We might speculate: What pain will howl in the future heart of *One Here Now*? What burning remainders will keep it alive, lurking silently under the surface of every future exhibition at Sirius Arts Centre?

Maybe its metaphorical resistance to move on follows its early traumas: the initial pain of birth, where, instead of emerging easily from its creator, it was forced out through multiple passes and a long period of labor. Following an unexpectedly extended lifespan, the artwork was laid to rest and nearly forgotten, while suffering continued violations quietly. This early damage compounds with its current conundrum: after revival and nursing back to health by caretakers—replete with visits by its artist-parent and celebration by many—it nevertheless finds itself slated for a new banishment.

We might associate the artwork with other literary and historical examples of burial: from Edgar Allan Poe's *The Tell-Tale Heart*, beating within an enclosed wall, to an Iron Age human, preserved perfectly within a peaty bog. Or a more grandiosely intentional example: the Egyptian pyramids, where mummified Pharaohs are readied for an eternal afterlife.

Unlike these worldly examples, the specter in Cobh will not suffer from deterioration or decay. Having been resuscitated fully and then buried again, *One Here Now* will be preserved perfectly in an architectural limbo. Its continued existence will require neither oxygen and water, nor any typical form of nourishment. If climate and other conditions are maintained correctly, the exhibition-as-ghost might remain almost entirely intact, forever.

But what should we call an exhibition that no one sees? Etymologically, exhibitions are *placed on display*. Can an exhibition without *publics* still be an exhibition? Is this incompleteness, this painful lack of viewership and lifeblood, what feeds the ghost in the walls? Will this ghastly momentum maintain its unearthly, undead existence over the next decades, generations, centuries, even millennia?

Perhaps the problem here lies in how we think about an object's lifespan. What if an exhibition's life looks less like a line in a space—with a discrete beginning and end—and more like a spiral over time, which could continue indefinitely, depending on the resolution at which you view it? For before the exhibition formally began, it *came* from somewhere; and after it appears to end, its manifold effects are still felt in one way or another. Rather than representing a wholly atypical case, this "permanent" exhibition might simply visualize a general principle of how matter and spirit move in an ever-changing cycle within the closed system of the world.

After these walls are closed up, I wonder what eyes will see *One Here Now* next. Perhaps by the time of this rediscovery, its new publics will have radically different ideas, expectations, and uses for an artwork. Uncovering a brilliant mural, hidden cleverly beneath a wall, they might see within its colorful, encoded abstractions a nearly religious affect and a mystical method. Puzzling over the purpose of this late 20th-century cave painting, would these future viewers reproduce it perfectly in another site, to protect the painted surfaces? Or, with increasing pressure on space and resources, might they take *One Here Now*'s warm glow as an invitation to gather closely to it? Would they marvel at its surfaces, while also feeling at home to add to them? Like architectural *spolia* from one period that are built upon in the next, or a house of worship that changes faith from generation to generation, these walls might accrue other objects, ideas, significances, from those who come to live here in Cobh. In this projection, *One Here Now* might become more of an expanding, collective idea rather than a fixed artwork—a master plan, a blueprint, a framework that changes with the lives around it.

§

These may appear idle questions, gathered together over the short sojourn of thinking through this text. With time, though, even unfinished words become, like O'Doherty's murals, permanent marks to circulate ideas in the world. Who knows what meaning they will have for the next generation of readers of this book. As in any process of residing, of creating, in the testing out of thoughts that is an "essay," I hope that their publication might suggest other relationships between the temporary and the permanent and even potential next lives for our hidden gem in Cobh. Let's just say, it seemed like a good idea at the time.

板
板
地蓆
lasciate ogne stranezza voi ch'intrate
sociability
P!
p!
KOGA

Endless Exhibition

The Ceiling Should Be Green (天花板應該是綠色的), 2013
P!, New York.
Curators: Ali Wong, Prem Krishnamurthy

Endless Exhibition is a curatorial-manifesto-as-polymorphic-artwork by Prem Krishnamurthy that surveys the overproduction, mass consumption, and fleeting attention span of the contemporary art world. To reframe the stakes of exhibition making, *Endless Exhibition* proposes a temporal play: starting today, every exhibition, biennial, and art fair mounted should be permanent, remaining on view forever. This performative proposal poses timely questions of space, waste, labor, and future histories.

Endless Exhibition also challenges the supposed autonomy of discrete artworks, fulfilling, in Krishnamurthy's own words from a 1999 notebook entry, "[Principle] 5: reappearance of the project—the project should never be 'done'—it should always invite addition, rethinking, recontextualizing..."

In 2019, Kunsthal Gent acquired the piece as part of its inaugural institutional framework, "Kunsthal as City." Here, it accrues layers of architecture and programming to construct an ongoing archaeology. In flux and constantly expanding, *Endless Exhibition* rehearses new approaches to changing the global art ecosystem by rewriting its rules.

A thing is just a slow event.†

—Stanley Eveling

† See page 206

The Winchester Mystery House in San José, California, was built by Sarah Winchester, heiress to the weapon manufacturer's fortune.

1. First team meeting at Kunsthal Gent. June 2018.

Convinced that she was being chased by ghosts—the ghosts of all those killed by her family's rifles during the colonization of the American West—Winchester commenced a 38-year program of non-stop, day-and-night construction on her grand mansion.

2. 15th-century mural in the Old House of Kunsthal Gent. A damaged Calvary group (Christ, Mary, and apostle John), with several other layers on top, was laid bare during renovations in the 1990s. The 15th-century layer has been violently treated with an axe or knife. It is likely that the damage was an intentional and symbolic act and that the painting was a victim of the iconoclasm of 1566. The mural is an emblem of what Kunsthal Gent aims to do. July 2018.

Winchester Mystery House
San Jose, California

She believed that by constantly adding new rooms, secret passages, trapdoors, and more, she could confuse and trick the phantoms.

3. Chris Fitzpatrick talking about "[a]ll the exhibitions that don't immediately seem to be exhibitions" at Kunstverein München. Part of a series of talks in which Kunsthal Gent tested its plans and ambitions by inviting inspiring curators, artists, and directors from other organizations. November 2018.

I can’t help but connect this odd case with the current proliferation of art fairs, exhibitions, and international biennials, which are built up every day,

Installation of Brian O’Doherty, *Walk the Line*, 2017
Simone Subal Gallery, Art Basel Miami Beach 2017
Curators: Prem Krishnamurthy, Simone Subal

4. Construction of *Spatial Intervention KHG#01*, a monumental three-storey wooden structure that creates new working and exhibition spaces and shifts the public entrance. The Spatial Interventions gradually change the building into its new form as a “city of contemporary art,” in which different identities come together and interact with each other. Design by Olivier Goethals. December 2018.

only to be torn down the next, in a continuous cycle, all over the world.

Aaron Gemmill removing the awning of P!, New York, May 30, 2017

5. Outside view of Kunsthal Gent. Chain banner design by Michaël Bussaer. January 2019.

Mounted at great cost for a terribly short time, these shows quickly disappear, leaving so much waste in their wake.

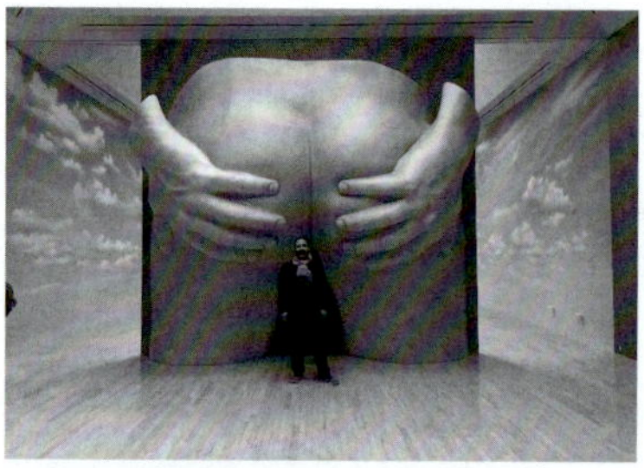

Anthea Hamilton, *Project for Door (After Gaetano Pesce)*, 2015
Tate Britain, London

The question lingers: In our relentless pursuit of the new, which ghosts are we fleeing?

→

Forensic Architecture at Venice Architecture Biennale, 2016
Curator: Alejandro Aravena

6. *Crisis of Masculinity* by Thomas Min and Egon Van Herreweghe. An installation of a replica of the blue steel fence at Muscle Beach Venice in Los Angeles, CA. Muscle Beach is seen as the birthplace of fitness hype and played an important role in popularizing and legitimizing the physical culture as we know it today. January 2019.

7. *Autocorrect (neon)* by Steve Van den Bosch. January 2019.

As curator Vasif Kortun remarked some years ago, “Exhibitions are fugitive, imperfect, fragile machines.”

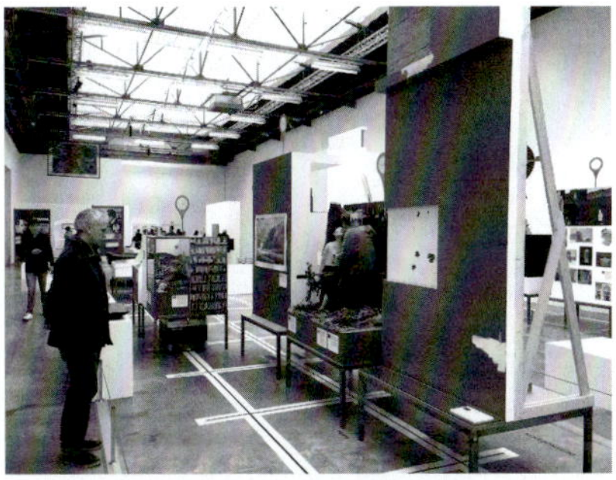

Neïl Beloufa, *L’Ennemidemon ennemi*, 2018
Palais de Tokyo, Paris
Curators: Guillaume Désanges, with Marilou Thiébault and Noam Segal

In their brief physical manifestation, exhibitions have a truncated lifespan and are *not* seen by most people.

Group Material, *AIDS Timeline*, 1991
Whitney Museum of American Art, New York

8. *Spatial Intervention KHG#01* by Olivier Goethals. January 2019.

They may have an afterlife, an existence in rumor and reputation.

Damaged Goods: Desire and the Economy of the Object, 1986
New Museum, New York
Curator: Brian Wallis. Exhibition Designer: Judith Barry

9. Construction of *Spatial Intervention KHG#02*. A cinema and lecture room realized together with Art Cinema OFFoff. Design by Olivier Goethals. April 2019.

But, as a lover of exhibitions, I desire to see them *all*.

So today I'd like to make a speculative, perverse, performative proposition:

Post-Speculation, Act II, 2014
P!, New York
Curators: Carin Kuoni, Prem Krishnamurthy

235

10. *Housebroken* by Nina Beier. Five marble and stone lions, scattered throughout Kunsthal Gent in places like the garden, toilet, and a meeting room, thereby expanding the exhibition space. Curated by Chris Fitzpatrick. May 2019.

From now on, forever, and into the future,

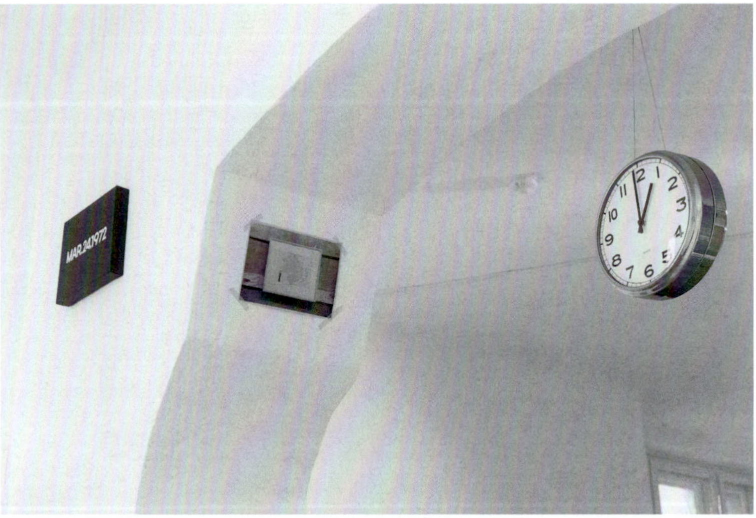

K,, Berlin, January 19, 2019

every museum or gallery show, every art fair booth or site-specific project, every biennial or triennial or quadrennial,

Department of Non-Binaries
Included in Fikra Graphic Design Biennial 01: *Ministry of Graphic Design*, 2018
Former Bank of Sharjah, United Arab Emirates
Artistic directors: Prem Krishnamurthy, Na Kim, Emily Smith
Curators: Nina Paim, Corinne Gisel

11. *Spatial Intervention KHG#02*. A cinema and lecture room realized together with Art Cinema OFFoff. Design by Olivier Goethals. April 2019.

should be treated as a permanent presentation, an immortal installation, an endless exhibition.

12. *Everything in this World Has Two Handles* by Rudy Guedj. Replacing two broken door handles for Kunsthal Gent. May 2019.

13. *Crisis of Masculinity* by Thomas Min & Egon Van Herreweghe. Cut No. 1. The replica of the blue fence of Muscle Beach has been on display in Kunsthal Gent since January 2019. The artists regularly make cut-outs from the work, varying from fifty centimeters to four meters. These cut-outs have been moved to private gardens and interiors at home and abroad. June 2013.

Our new motto trumpets: *Zombie exhibitions, forever!*

ONE HERE NOW: The Brian O'Doherty / Patrick Ireland Project, 1996/2018–19
Sirius Arts Centre, Cobh, Ireland
Curator: Miranda Driscoll

239

14. *Everything is at Play* by Apparatus 22. Confetti fills the air with thought-provoking questions. A celebration and a critical examination of Kunsthal Gent's ambition to radically reimagine what a "kunsthalle" could be. August 2019.

Let’s freeze them in their immediate architectural and spatial context.

Process 01: Joy, 2012
P!, New York

Let’s keep them on continuous view.

Céline Condorelli, *Epilogue,* 2017
P!, New York
Assistant curator: Patricia Margarita Hernández

241

15. *La Fabrique d’un Single screen.* A film performance by THAT’S IT! at Dia:Beacon, realized by Joëlle Tuerlinckx. October 2019.

Or, better yet, seal them up for a period,

Aaron Gemmill, *Provopoli (Wem gehört die Stadt?)*, 2012
P!, New York

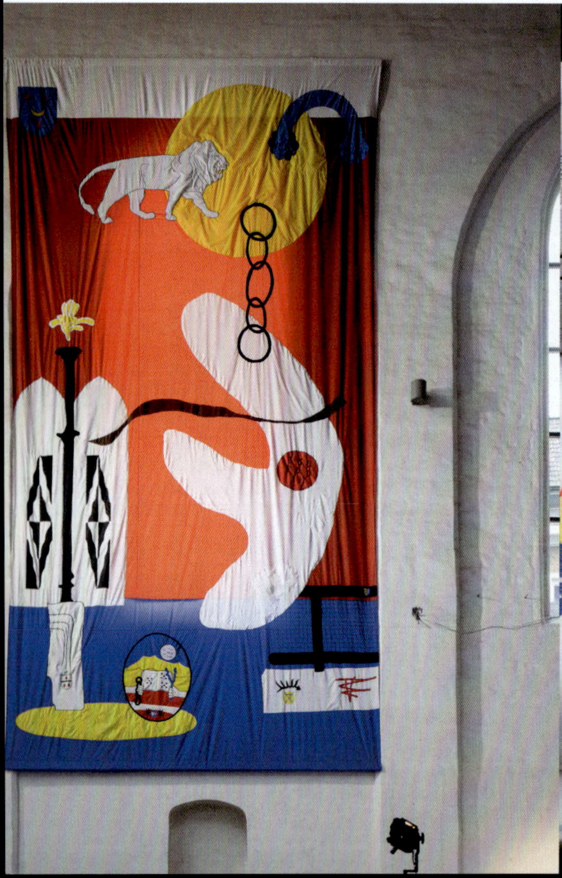

to be reopened one day like fresh sarcophagi or time capsules,

Mathew Hale, *5TH HELENA …*, 2015
K. (a.k.a. P!), New York

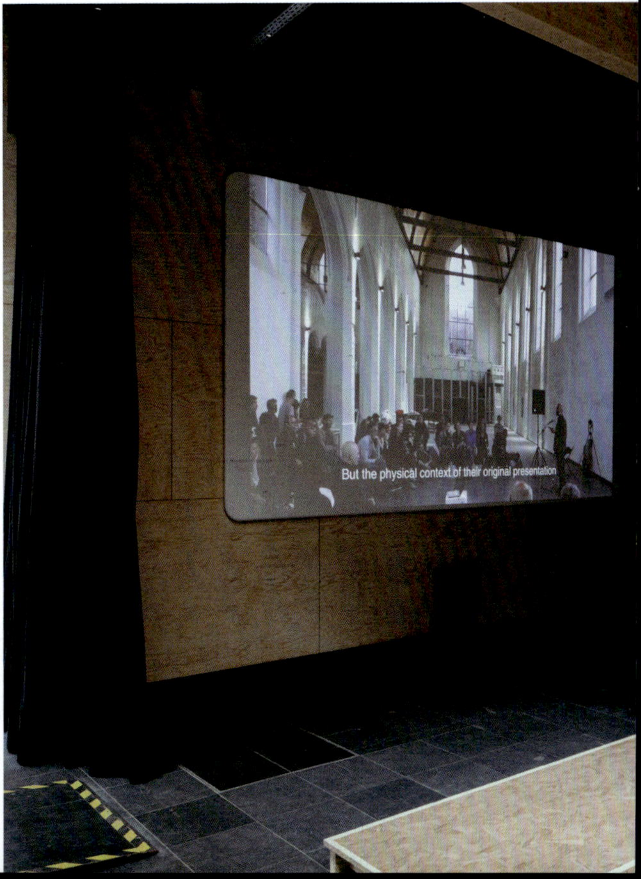

16. *Keepsake* by Charlotte Stuby. A textile piece in which additions to the *Endless Exhibition* are translated and added to this ever-evolving artwork. November 2019.

months or years
or decades or millennia past
their initial moment,

Céline Condorelli, *After*, 2017
P!, New York

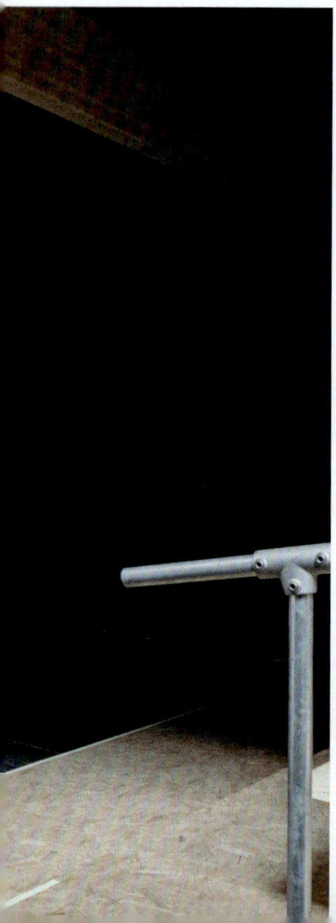

17. *Endless Exhibition* by Prem Krishnamurthy. January 2020.

when they can be experienced anew by some intrepid, seeking soul.

→

Possibility 02: Growth, Part IV, 2012
P!, New York

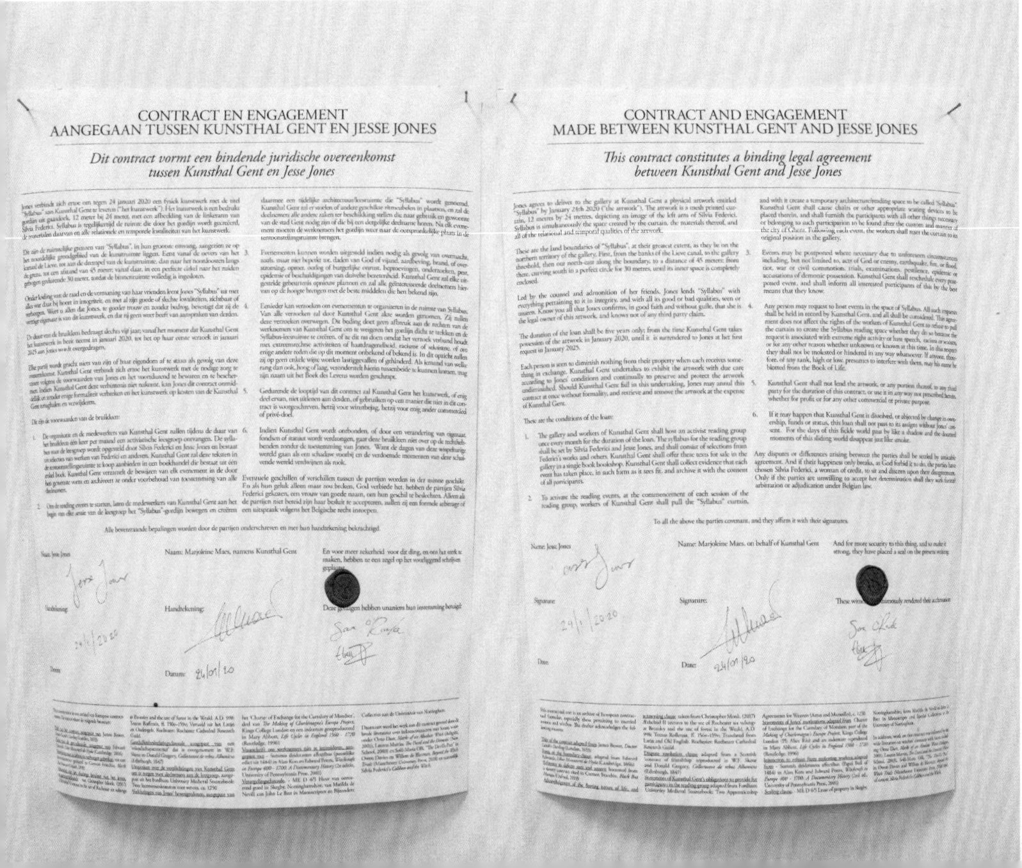

18. Jesse Jones, contract between Kunsthal Gent and Jesse Jones. Drafted by Mairead Enright and Jesse Jones from an archive of European contractual formulae, especially those pertaining to married women and witches. January 2020.

19. *When it Changed*. An exhibition consisting of nine different screensavers installed on the personal computers of the Kunsthal Gent coordination team and interns. Curated by David Reinfurt / O-R-G. January 2020.

Now, individual artworks can enjoy a long lifespan, particularly if their survival is staked to museums or institutions.

Ethnological Museum Dahlem, Berlin, 2014

247

20. Jesse Jones, *Syllabus*. A monumental, twelve-meter-high semi-transparent curtain moves through the gallery, creating a space-filling moving image of a floating, giant arm. It is the left arm of the well-known feminist and activist scholar Silvia Federici, embracing the institution and creating a new protective space in Kunsthal Gent. January 2020.

But, isolated and forcibly restrained, they often lose the physical, social, and spiritual context of their original presentation.

On Kawara, Installation view of
Pure Consciousness, 1998–, Goa, India, 2013

21. Curators Anonymous invited by Nein. A nonprofit, non-affiliated association of curators, offering a platform for exchange on pressing issues affecting curators. February 2020. Courtesy Leontien Allemeersch.

In the case of exhibitions, longevity is an even more complex issue.

The Center for Land Use Interpretation Exhibit Hall
Wendover, Utah

249

22. *Spatial Intervention KHG#03* by Olivier Goethals. June 2020.

As we know from Brian O’Doherty’s *Inside the White Cube,* context is content—all of which disappears the moment a show closes its doors.

Brian O’Doherty, *Connecting the ...*, 2014
P! and Simone Subal Gallery, New York

23. *Remuer Ciel et Terre* by Martin Belou. September 2020.

Even when an exhibition is reconstructed— in part or in whole—

P!CKER, Part I
Elaine Lustig Cohen, *Looking Backward to Look Forward*, 2017
Stanley Picker Gallery, Kingston University London
Curators: Prem Krishnamurthy, Stella Bottai

24. *Keepsake* by Charlotte Stuby (outside version). July 2020.

the recurrence of its original display often signals an absence even more clearly.

→

Klaus Wittkugel, *Plakat, Buch, Ausstellung, Packung, Marke*, 1961
Pavilion der Kunst, Berlin

25. *Spatial Intervention KHG#03* by Olivier Goethals. June 2020.

26. *Memories of things to be done* by Ritsart Gobyn. Temporary exhibition. September 2020.

We trust that exhibition archives can give us a glimpse into their origins, process, and players.

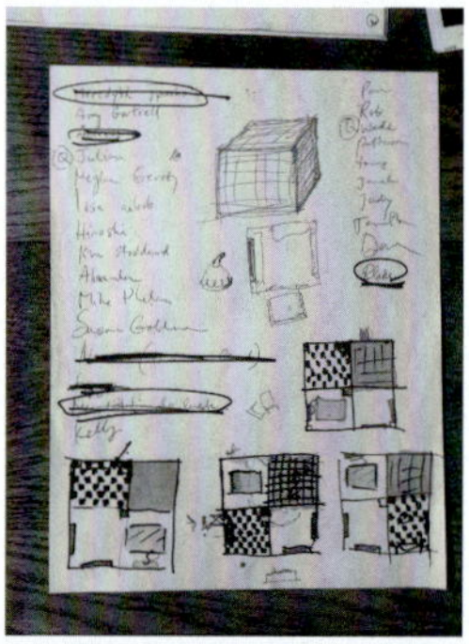

Ricci Albenda, *Answer Yes, No, Don't Know*, 1999
Andrew Kreps Gallery, New York

Still, how could such relics possibly resurrect that complex, contradictory thing called *context* after an exhibition's shelf life has expired?

Downtown Collection at the Fales Library
Elmer Holmes Bobst Library, New York University

27. *Wishbone* by Bram De Jonghe. January 2021.

It seems like any documentation is doomed to fail in preserving an exhibition's power, its timeliness, its urgency–

HOWDOYOUSAYYAMINAFRICAN?,
Thewayblackmachine (24-channel version), 2014
P!, New York

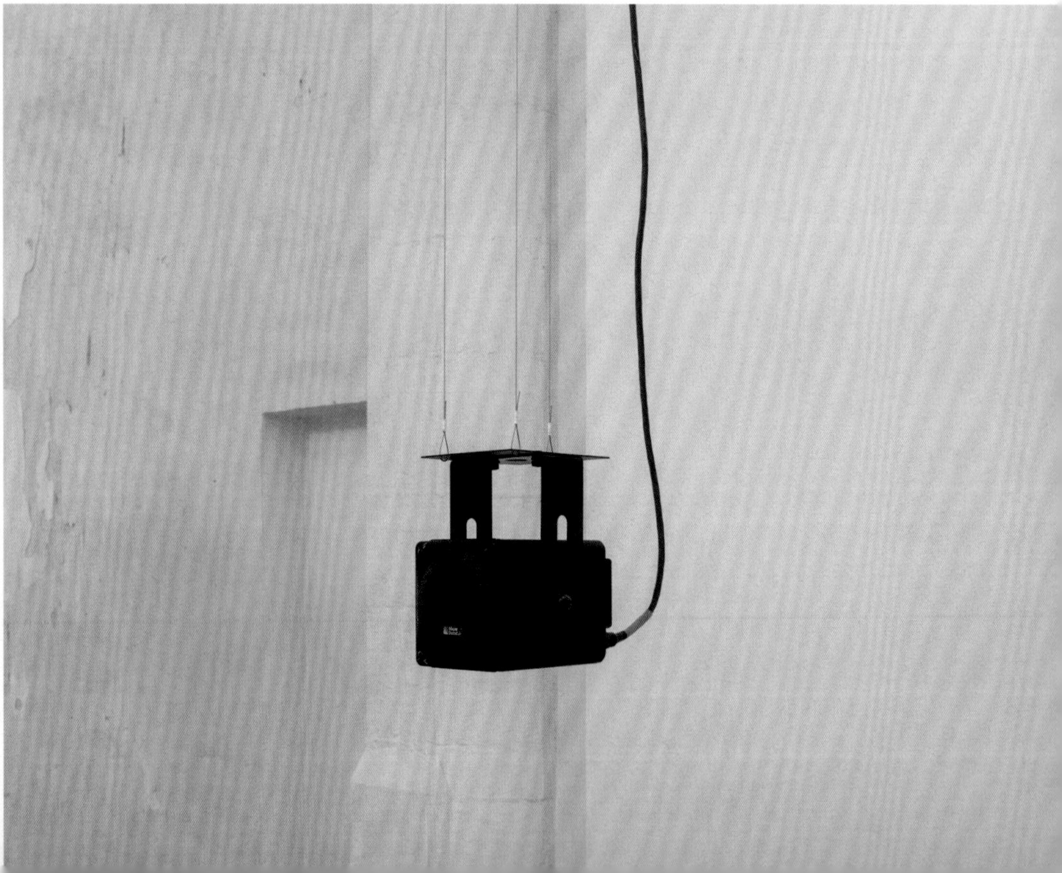

28. *As Sirens Rise and Fall* by Aline Bouvy. Temporary Exhibition. January 2021.

what it felt like
to actually *be* there.

→

Book launch for *Beyond Objecthood: The Exhibition as a Critical Form Since 1968* (MIT Press, 2017), April 30, 2017. P!, New York.

29. *Interplays* by Felix Kindermann. March 2021.

30. *Crisis of Masculinity* by Thomas Min & Egon Van Herreweghe. Cut No. 4. Private collection, Bø, Telemark, Norway. December 2019. Courtesy the artists.

How, then, to capture exhibitionary presence? One approach looks like Walter De Maria's *The New York Earth Room.*

Walter De Maria, *The New York Earth Room*, 1977

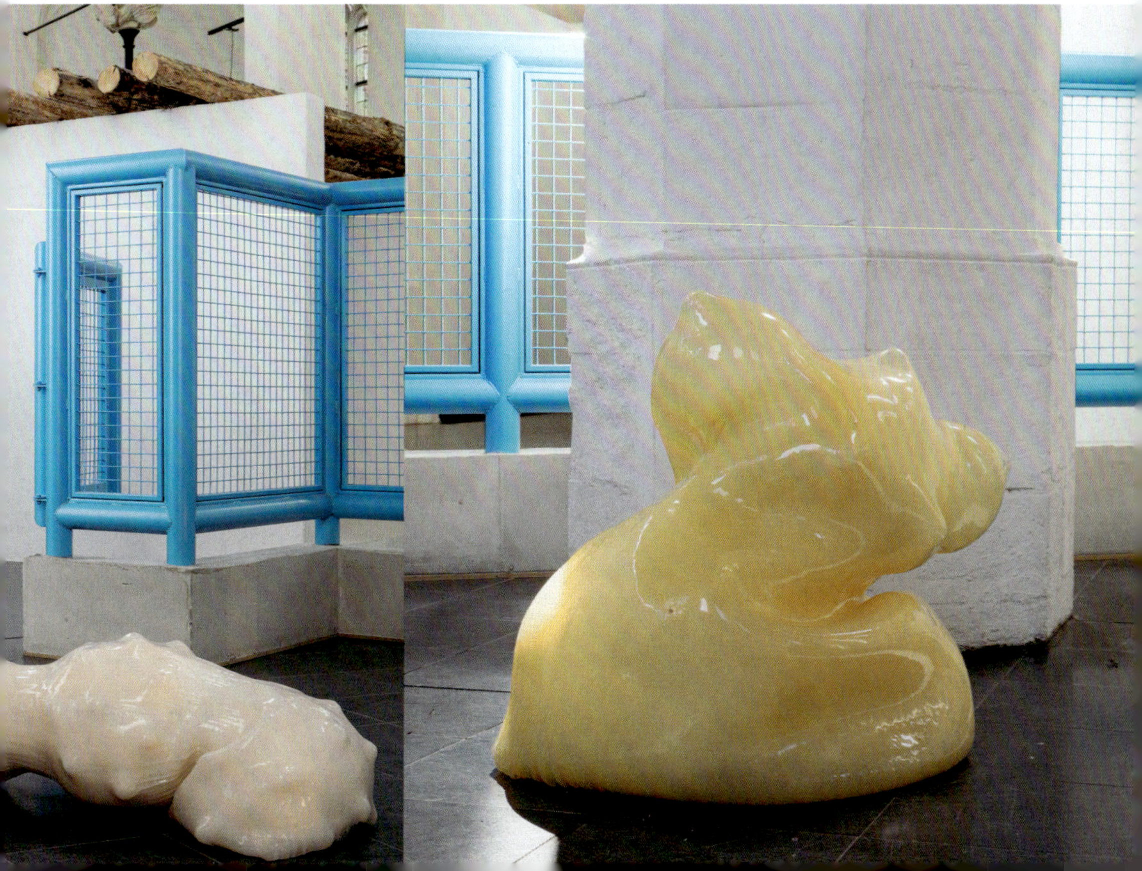

Built in 1977, the installation is to be preserved in perpetuity by the Dia Art Foundation. Yet maintaining this status quo requires regular watering and raking to ward off mushrooms, and other growth.

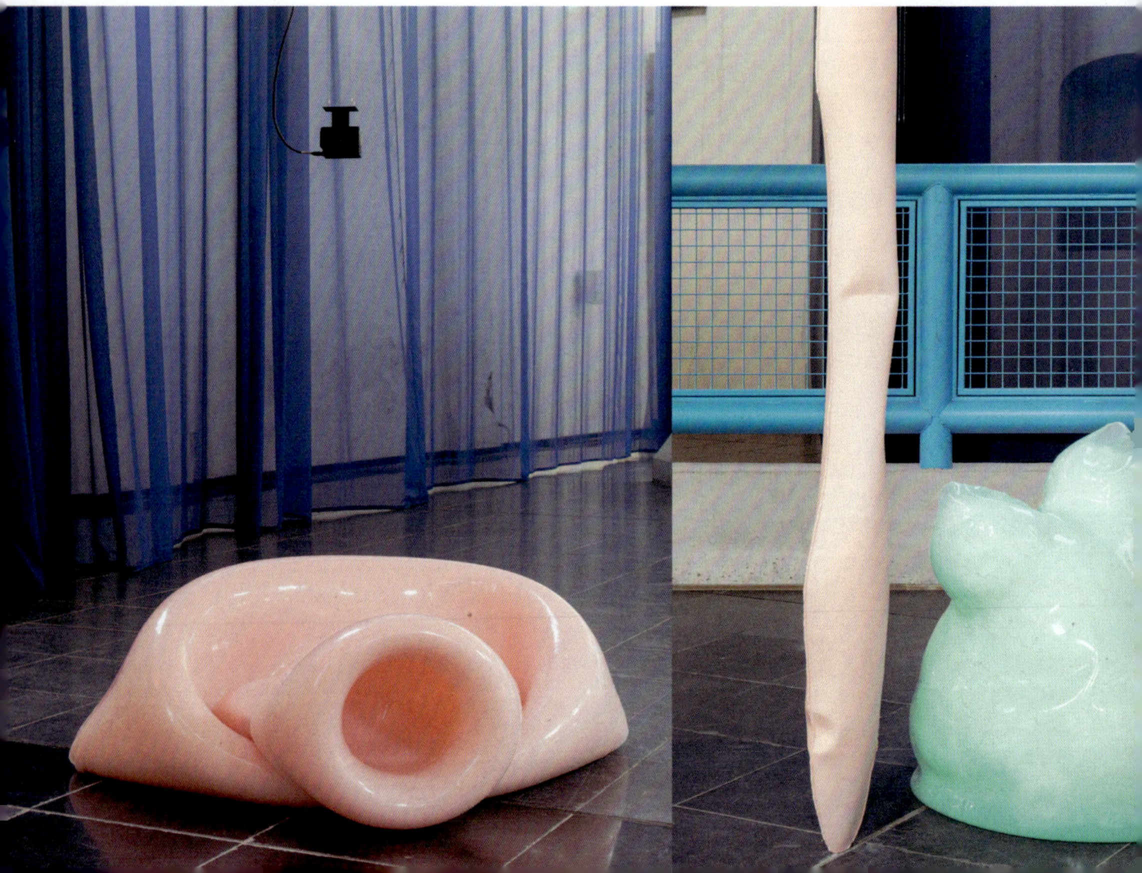

Seen from today, the *Earth Room*'s proud claim to permanence flies in the face of our terrifying political, cultural, and environmental uncertainties.

Doug Ashford, *Bunker (Clippings 1982–2016, Group 1)*, 2016

261

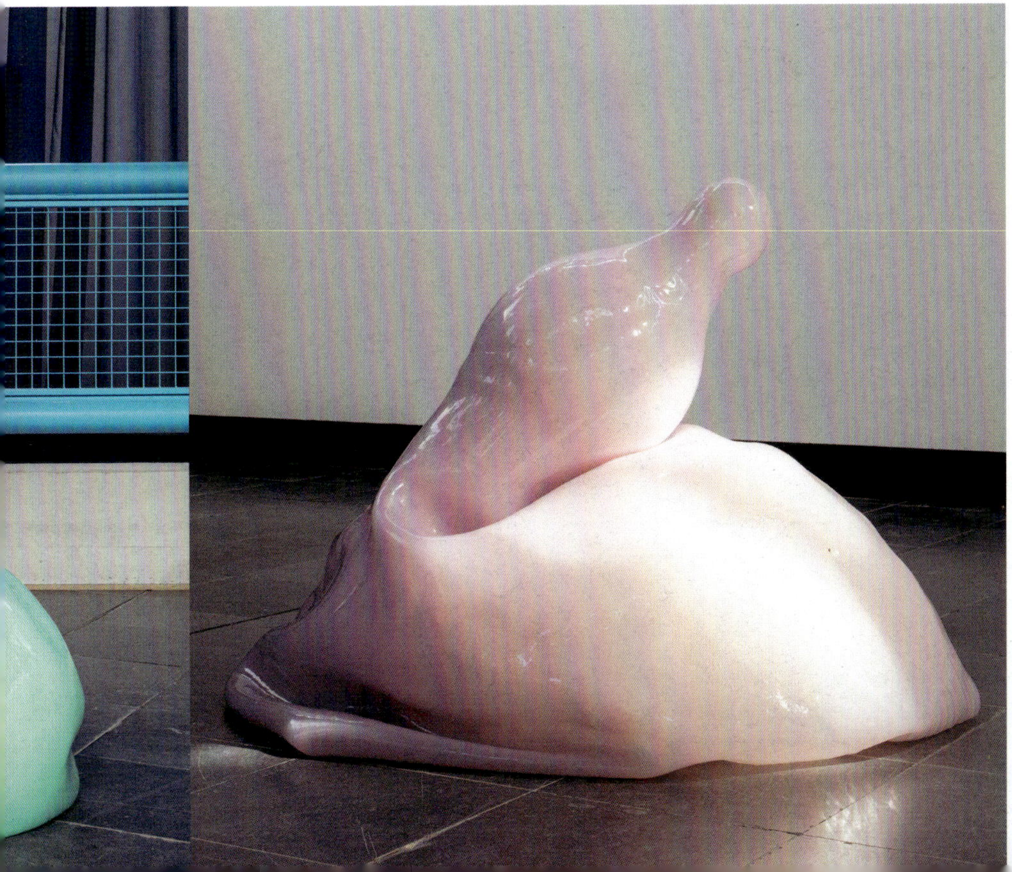

31. *Skin-Like* by Eva Fàbregas. The materiality and the longing for touch that is expressed in Fàbregas's colorful and monumental work form a great contrast with the strictly male and religious origins of the building of Kunsthal Gent. May 2021.

A mere year after the *Earth Room* was installed, Stephen King published his apocalyptic novel *The Stand*,

263

32. *Crisis of Masculinity* by Thomas Min & Egon Van Herreweghe. Cut No. 5. Private collection, Landegem, Belgium. May 2020. Courtesy the artists.

in which a government-
created superflu leaks out
and kills 99.4% of
the human population.

It's an uncanny look at life beyond the end.

The Stand, 2017
P!, New York
Curators: Anthony Marcellini, Prem Krishnamurthy

33. *Sous Les Cieux Et Les Nuages* by Thomas Renwart. September 2021.

In King's fiction, does the *Earth Room* live on in the necropolis of New York?

34. *Bioscopic Books* by Tine Guns, Inge Ketelers, and Isolde Vanhee. Temporary exhibition. April 2022.

Or, as the real-life rising tide engulfs Manhattan, will the artwork stand watch underwater one day?

35. *Sunny 16*, *Looney 11* by Rudy Guedj. February 2022.

36. *Sunny 16*, *Looney 11* by Rudy Guedj, in combination with *Remuer Ciel et Terre* by Martin Belou. February 2022.

Perhaps what we need to counter accelerating art-world (and *world*-world) time is a new necropolis:

Société Réaliste, *A Rough Guide to Hell*, 2013
P!, New York
Curators: Niels van Tomme, Prem Krishnamurthy

37. *Sous Les Cieux Et Les Nuages* by Thomas Renwart, in combination with *Skin-Like* by Eva Fabrégas. March 2022.

A graveyard of exhibitions—

270

James Wines / SITE,
Detail of *Ghost Parking Lot Model*, 1977

38. *Housebroken* by Nina Beier. March 2022.

frozen in form,

Wong Kit Yi, *Futures, Again*, 2017
P!, New York

39. *Crisis of Masculinity* by Thomas Min & Egon Van Herreweghe.
Cut No. 10. De Vooruit, Ghent, Belgium. September 2022. Courtesy the artists.

yet still fecund,

Connie Samaras, *The Past is Another Planet: Huntington Desert Garden, Cacti; OEB 1723, Novel Fragment, Parable of the Sower, 1989*, 2016

40. *We Once Were One* by Femmy Otten, September 2022.

like so many verdant, decaying monuments to change.

Permutation 03.3: Reproduction, 2013
P!, New York

41. *Sheela's Bar*, Theo De Meyer & Olivier Goethals, September 2022.

Just imagine this silent set of sentinels watching over us, an endless archive of shows that lives forever.

274

→

Egress, 2015
K. (a.k.a. P!), New York
Curator: Sarah Hromack

42. *Casting Call* by Eleni Kamma. Temporary exhibition. January 2023.

43. Installing *Cura's Garden* by Ben Thorp Brown with Jan Minne. April 2023.

I proclaim that, starting today, every exhibition we mount will be *permanent*.

Let these exhibitions accumulate. They will colonize the space around them until they are the space. There will be no more forgetting.

44. *Nessy Extreme* by Lochness. A temporary skatepark inside Kunsthal Gent where skaters, artists, and the public can meet. May 2023. © Lukas Neven.

Now, how will we reconsider our production, our consumption, our understanding of these fragile and fugitive creatures?

Maryam Jafri, *Economy Corner*, 2016
P!, New York

In making new exhibitions under this curatorial regime, will we grow conservative, fearful, or nostalgic?

OST UND ~~oder~~ WEST: Klaus Wittkugel and Anton Stankowski, 2016
P! and OSMOS, New York
Curators: Prem Krishnamurthy, Cay Sophie Rabinowitz

45. *Cura's Garden* by Ben Thorp Brown with Jan Minne. Unfolding over time through choreographed and natural processes, this installation creates an idyllic and foreboding landscape that deepens links between our senses, emotions, and earth itself. May 2023.

Or will we instead find ourselves emboldened,

Hitting It Off, 2014
P!, New York
Curators: Sarah Demeuse, Manuela Moscoso

280

46. *Zomersalon: Buy Local 3*. A temporary show with the radical but deliberate decision that any Ghent artist can participate. 650 artworks fill the space to the brim with a cross-section of Ghent's visual arts scene. July 2023. © Lukas Neven.

driven to greater risk-taking and experimentation?

The Ceiling Should Be Green (天花板應該是綠色的), 2013
P!, New York
Curators: Ali Wong, Prem Krishnamurthy

47. *nes•nor•nae* by Apparatus 22 unfolds in its own peculiar space in the penumbra of the main entrance of Kunsthal Gent. An immaterial artwork placed between the wooden construction of the entrance and the original walls of the church. It is a protective shell for commissioning artistic interventions exploring utopian feelings and futures. September 2024.

With this expanding palimpsest of perpetual exhibitions overtaking the world,

Aaron Gemmill, *Camera Drawing*, 2016

48. *dankEconogy1_ALIENVillage*, a visitation at Kunsthal Gent by Sahjan Kooner. January 2024.

will we finally lose the luxury of believing that today is only today?

Karel Martens, *Recent Work*, 2016
P!, New York

49. *Installing Spatial Intervention KHG#04* by Olivier Goethals. March 2024.

The clock counts—our eternal program unmaking every illusion that the future is yet to come,

Wai Kong Lui and team removing the flooring of P!, New York, May 30, 2017

284

50. *The Endless Walkthrough*. A contemporary remake of the movie *Ghent, 10 June 1989*, For Geraldine Nerea by Jan Vromman with Alain Platel. Thirty-five years later, the hall church, renovated in the 1990s, looks completely different. And after five years of Kunsthal Gent, fifteen works of art are now part of the *Endless Exhibition*. Jimena Perez Salerno and Shivadas de Schrijver have developed a participative choreography *parcours* through the Endless Exhibition, which is recorded in a single take with real-time audio. May 2024.

rather than trembling already, transformed to dust beneath our feet.

P!CKER, Part II
Céline Condorelli, *Prologue*, 2017
Stanley Picker Gallery, Kingston University London
Curators: Stella Bottai, Prem Krishnamurthy

51. *An Experiment with Time* by Ailbhe Ni Bhriain, inside *Spatial Intervention KHG#04* by Olivier Goethals. May 2024.

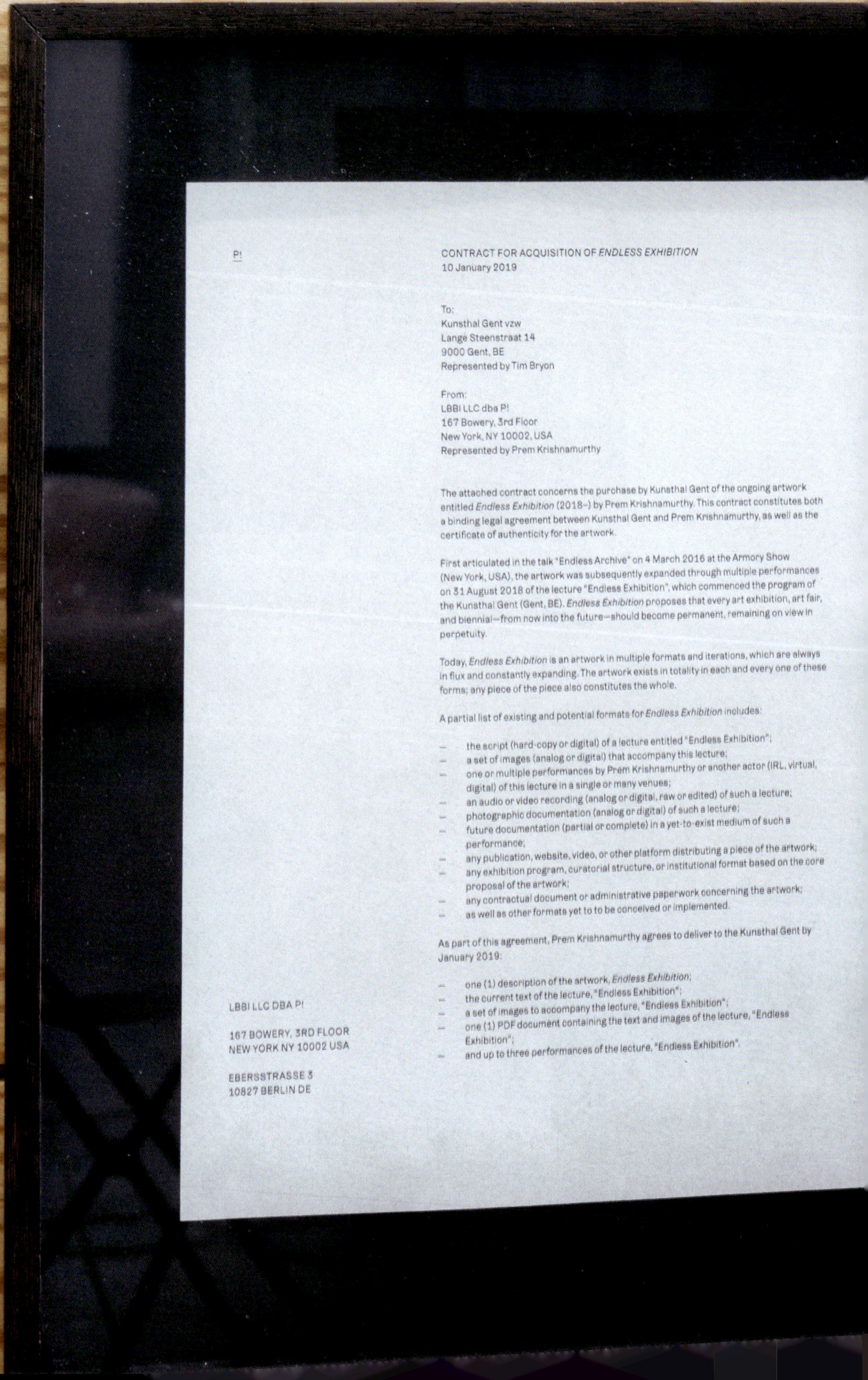

P!

CONTRACT FOR ACQUISITION OF *ENDLESS EXHIBITION*
10 January 2019

To:
Kunsthal Gent vzw
Lange Steenstraat 14
9000 Gent, BE
Represented by Tim Bryon

From:
LBBI LLC dba P!
167 Bowery, 3rd Floor
New York, NY 10002, USA
Represented by Prem Krishnamurthy

The attached contract concerns the purchase by Kunsthal Gent of the ongoing artwork entitled *Endless Exhibition* (2018–) by Prem Krishnamurthy. This contract constitutes both a binding legal agreement between Kunsthal Gent and Prem Krishnamurthy, as well as the certificate of authenticity for the artwork.

First articulated in the talk "Endless Archive" on 4 March 2016 at the Armory Show (New York, USA), the artwork was subsequently expanded through multiple performances on 31 August 2018 of the lecture "Endless Exhibition", which commenced the program of the Kunsthal Gent (Gent, BE). *Endless Exhibition* proposes that every art exhibition, art fair, and biennial—from now into the future—should become permanent, remaining on view in perpetuity.

Today, *Endless Exhibition* is an artwork in multiple formats and iterations, which are always in flux and constantly expanding. The artwork exists in totality in each and every one of these forms; any piece of the piece also constitutes the whole.

A partial list of existing and potential formats for *Endless Exhibition* includes:

– the script (hard-copy or digital) of a lecture entitled "Endless Exhibition";
– a set of images (analog or digital) that accompany this lecture;
– one or multiple performances by Prem Krishnamurthy or another actor (IRL, virtual, digital) of this lecture in a single or many venues;
– an audio or video recording (analog or digital, raw or edited) of such a lecture;
– photographic documentation (analog or digital) of such a lecture;
– future documentation (partial or complete) in a yet-to-exist medium of such a performance;
– any publication, website, video, or other platform distributing a piece of the artwork;
– any exhibition program, curatorial structure, or institutional format based on the core proposal of the artwork;
– any contractual document or administrative paperwork concerning the artwork;
– as well as other formats yet to to be conceived or implemented.

As part of this agreement, Prem Krishnamurthy agrees to deliver to the Kunsthal Gent by January 2019:

– one (1) description of the artwork, *Endless Exhibition*;
– the current text of the lecture, "Endless Exhibition";
– a set of images to accompany the lecture, "Endless Exhibition";
– one (1) PDF document containing the text and images of the lecture, "Endless Exhibition";
– and up to three performances of the lecture, "Endless Exhibition".

LBBI LLC DBA P!

167 BOWERY, 3RD FLOOR
NEW YORK NY 10002 USA

EBERSSTRASSE 3
10827 BERLIN DE

P!

Furthermore, Prem Krishnamurthy agrees to:

- assist Kunsthal Gent by providing oversight of the editing of the video documentation from the lectures, "Endless Exhibition", to be completed by March 2019;
- include *Endless Exhibition*, with reference to Kunsthal Gent, within the next version of his book, *P!DF* (preliminary release date: April 2019);
- and deliver at least three (3) additional lectures entitled "Endless Exhibition" at other locations throughout the world over the course of 2019. These performances, which may take place as part of another lecture or event, will be credited appropriately with reference to Kunsthal Gent.

Artwork purchase price: 5000 EUR
Payment Terms: 50% of the purchase price is due upon signing of this contract; 50% is due upon completion of agreed upon deliverables in January 2019.

LBBI LLC DBA P!

167 BOWERY, 3RD FLOOR
NEW YORK NY 10002 USA

EBERSSTRASSE 3
10827 BERLIN DE

P!

ADDITION

Ownership
Upon execu
LBBI LLC sh
reproduce
presentatio
are allowed
license may

Please note
list of delive
associated
the sole res
the rights t
belong to th
and usage r

Publicity an
Kunsthal Ge
in any publi
Prem Krishn
may be cha
has been ag
artwork, Ku
Krishnamu

Samples ar
Kunsthal Ge
manufactu
represent t
Endless Exh
documenta
recordings

Project ma
Kunsthal G
Kunsthal G
dba P! abo

Miscellane
Kunsthal Ge
into this ag
in accordar
a breach by
not cured w
party may,
breaching
become im
available by
cumulative
existing at l
parties. It m
by the party
to be bound

This agreem
and the inte
of Arrondis
upon and in

LBBI LLC DBA P!

167 BOWERY, 3RD FLOOR
NEW YORK NY 10002 USA

EBERSSTRASSE 3
10827 BERLIN DE

On the Art of Adaptation

Originally published in Deem Journal, *Pedagogy for a New World* (Issue Two, W/S21).

(2021)

DEEM JOURNAL How do friendship and love fit into your models of education and work?

PREM KRISHNAMURTHY Prem means "love" in Sanskrit. I have an older sister whose name means "affection," so I like to say that I won (not that I'm competitive!).

Here's a childhood scene to answer your question: When I was eight years old, my parents sent me to a "Hindu Heritage" summer camp in the Poconos, which was quite an unusual situation. Imagine a sea of South Asian children led by a bunch of white folks in orange robes who called themselves Swami Krishna, Swami Parvati, and Swami Lakshmi. To be honest, we found out later it was something of a cult—but the image I hold onto is that at the end of every night, we were supposed to hug three people. I took it upon myself as a young child to hug every single person in the camp.

Nowadays, that would make me a super spreader! But I think it shows how love and friendship are intrinsic to what I do. I couldn't do any of this without the friendship, support, and love of a lot of other people.

DJ In our participation in, and observation of, your digital work and gatherings, you have been leveraging the lecture performance format, which we really enjoy because it feels like a virtual collage. It's an expansive approach to pedagogy, opening up, in real time, a beautiful synthesis of information. What role does sharing play in your work?

PK Sharing is crucial. More and more, I'm trying to make my process and the tools that I'm developing for projects available to people along the way. For example, when I'm asked to give a talk—whether it's at a conference, in a class, or otherwise—if at all possible, I share all of my notes and slides with everyone in real time, so that they have access to those materials during my talk and afterwards.

Everybody learns and experiences in different ways. Rather than taking a more "proprietary" approach, where I'm only going to give you the final version of my thinking, I'm much more interested in the porosity of things. I call almost everything I make these days a rehearsal. It's definitely a personal strategy to avoid the inevitable anxiety that comes with performing or making sure something is "final." But it's also more than just rhetoric. In any given configuration of people in a room, there's so much to be learned, mutually. If I present my contribution as a draft or a prototype or a rehearsal, it leaves more space for other people to give something, too, to provide feedback, and to feel some agency in shaping what's happening. In other words, I'm offering something that still has room to grow.

DJ In March, around the beginning of lockdown, you started *Present!* which you refer to as a combination of a virtual lecture, a talk show, and a Sunday sermon, with a dose of karaoke. We'd love to hear more about how this came to be and how it has evolved.

PK *Present!* started as a direct response to the isolation of the first lockdown in March 2020, but it also represented a synthesis of a lot of thinking and organizing that had come before. I had already been working for years on an ongoing electronic publication called *P!DF*. The book's newest edition, in development well before the pandemic, included a chapter on what I call "bumpiness": the idea that productive friction can help to slow things down and offer a moment of reflection amidst the increasingly smooth, fast consumption of contemporary life. It was planned as a publication, an exhibition, a set of performance lectures, and a set of workshops and teaching engagements. The project involved artists, designers, curators, writers, musicians, and others from all over the world.

In mid-March, when so many things came to a standstill, I found out that the exhibition would be postponed indefinitely. My practice is formed in constant dialogue with other people—present, past, and future. I was really feeling the isolation and anxiety of the first lockdown, as if part of myself had been cut off. Thankfully, I had the presence and privilege to pivot: I took what was meant to be an exhibition and instead invited nearly all of the contributors to participate in a live Sunday event, which was meant to be a one-off, performative mix of many different modes. As you said, I called it a "sermon," but it was also a talk show with conversations and a presentation, and it included group karaoke and dancing. It's related to my past work, but it definitely represented a new format for me.

At the end of that first episode, several people who attended, some of whom I didn't even know, said, "Please, you need to keep doing this. This kind of a gathering is really important right now." So I kept doing it, first as a loose "season" of six Sundays in a row that all built on *P!DF*, then with a couple of additional episodes featuring a slightly different format. Now we're in the "third season." It was originally designed as a communal gathering that would make people feel welcome and allow them to be themselves, yet also with a clear artistic structure. Now, it's transitioned into being much less about "presentation" and much more about "being present."

One recent episode featured a social dreaming matrix with LA-based psychoanalyst George Bermudez. It was free and open to the public, but it wasn't recorded. It consisted of a group of 50 or 60 people from all over the world, sharing their dreams as a way to make sense of this contemporary moment. Our last episode of 2020 will be called "A Conflict Party"; it's a workshop teaching tools for using conflict productively towards building community, organized by the artist-facilitator duo Adult Kindergarten, plus a dance party. Our next event will be even more open in structure. So it looks like *Present!* will continue for the time being, while also shifting responsively. I'm thinking of it less as a time-based "event" and more like a virtual gathering place—or maybe a combination of the two.

DJ What types of infrastructures do you think we need to design to continue to hold support for learning at the moment?

PK I often consider two separate approaches that might seem at different ends of a spectrum. On the one hand, we have platforms and technologies which have certain affordances; for example, each new Zoom update includes different features, whether it's featuring open-access breakout rooms or chatting in different ways. These can be useful, for sure. Yet I'm pretty platform agnostic: I've been trying out every single platform for group communication, assuming that each one is designed differently and can teach me something. These platforms are made with specific intentions and ideologies, but they also allow certain opportunities for misuse. None of these platforms were really optimized for group karaoke, but that won't keep me from trying!

I also maintain that what's even more important for designers, curators, artists, and others are so-called "soft skills": the relational skills needed to create a generous, productive space for other people. These are facilitation skills, how you listen actively to people, and how you give and take feedback. It's about holding space and creating spaciousness. It's about timing. It's about breathing. It's about engaging with different bodies in different ways, not forgetting these virtual encounters are also embodied. It's about shifting scales to consider more intimate encounters within a larger group dynamic. It's about mixing things up and responding to people's capacities. It's exhausting to look at 20 or 40 or 100 people's faces all at once. That's a huge cognitive load to take in. So I often think about ways to switch modes. I recently participated in a live-action role-playing game by artist Susan Ploetz that was audio only; it freed you to feel your body and senses in different ways. I thought it was remarkable and have since started to use switching video on and off in a strategic, designed way.

Moving forward, we need to think about platforms but also about behaviors. It's not one or the other, it's both. Many people have already hit fatigue around digital interactions; designers and others need to work on how to treat our bodies well and in ways that offer more agency in relation to these gatherings. It's as important of a design question as "What's the interface?" and "What does the interface let you do?"

DJ As we come up on a year of COVID-affected life, how have some of these virtual gatherings developed and shaped pedagogical thinking?

PK It's a feedback loop—a lot of the ways that I've been thinking about virtual gatherings have come out of teaching and pedagogy, and then curating and organizing the gatherings informs the teaching in turn. Of the many people I've been in dialogue with during this time—new friends and old—those who are thinking about the complexities of interacting with people online in the most interesting ways are often educators. They're imagining how to engage with different kinds of people, different tech setups, different home situations, different capacities, capabilities, and attention spans. The first time I ever used Zoom was with a bunch of students in Beijing in mid-March of 2020. I tried to get them to karaoke with me! It only partially worked because of the network latency and lag, but it already got me thinking: "If the audio and video are out of sync, what possibilities might that 'failure' open up?" Or in May, when I was speaking with art students at Goldsmiths on Jitsi, and the bandwidth was so low that none of them could turn on video, I ended up improvising and asking a lot of questions for the students to engage with in the chat! It was a lot of fun.

In teaching over the past sixteen years, I've been interested in creating situations that are less about the hierarchy of teacher and student and more about acknowledging how much everybody in the room can learn from each other. It requires tools, practice, and presence to keep things open–improvisation needs foundations. But with that foundation, you can also embrace the unexpected, the unplanned, and bumpy experiences as potential opportunities to grow.

A Tribute to Brian O'Doherty, 1928–2022

Originally published online in
The Brooklyn Rail

(2023)

In Spring 2014 at Simone Subal Gallery in New York, I helped install a rope drawing by Brian O'Doherty for the first time. Trying to make the piece's symmetries of twine and tone rhyme in the room, I pulled out a measuring tape and spirit level to make sure things were exact. A learned habit, a desire for clinical precision that years of graphic design had taught me.

With a semi-stern look, Brian waved away these tools: "You need to use your eyes to look at how an artwork is hung, not a ruler."

This came as a surprise, given how accustomed I was as a curator to making sure artworks are installed perfectly. Yet Brian continued to insist that his rope drawings were meant to be measured only by the eye. They needed to respond to the room and to the viewer. If they looked straight, then they *were* straight. An empirical, human way of taking stock of the world. I put my measuring tools away.

This moment stuck with me over the next nearly decade of our close exchange, in which I played different roles with him: curator, dealer, writer, designer, installer, and even once as his performer. For all of the tools that he had at his disposal–from his razor-sharp mind to his far-seeing eyes to his unwavering hand to his inimitable, booming, boisterous voice–Brian O'Doherty was always eminently *human*. His talents seemed to require little outside of the basic organism with which most people arrive equipped.

Annie Murphy Paul's 2021 book, *The Extended Mind: The Power of Thinking Outside the Brain*, articulates how the human mind encompasses much more than just the physical brain. Combining neuroscientific research with memorable stories, she demonstrates that cognition happens in the body and gestures, in spaces and objects, and, most significantly, through relationships with others. It's a compelling framework for rethinking thinking itself that perfectly captures Brian's expansive genius.

Although he may have rejected yardsticks and levels, Brian instinctually embraced outward-facing modes of thinking in the world: for example, his performances from the 1960s and '70s tied movement to language. His paintings, sculptures, and installations encoded words and letters into physical materials and spaces using the ancient Irish alphabet of Ogham. And Brian's "extended mind" included his rich relationships with the people around him: whether as an editor and curator, encouraging writers such as Roland Barthes to publish unreleased works, or in the implicit and explicit ways that he collaborated with others—in particular with the brilliant Barbara Novak, who accompanied him throughout life and work as a second mind and pair of eyes to help him evaluate his art, writing, and rope drawings alike (of course, Brian's rope drawings were most often installed to line up correctly from her eye level).

Once upon a time, Brian said to me, "Every person is actually many people." He meant this with regards to his many personae, but it suggests not only that he contained multitudes, but also that many others also carry parts of him with them. There are traces of Brian everywhere. It's in these different extensions of his mind that he lives on with us now—in the installations that persist from Italy to Ireland into infinity; the words that wind through museums and galleries the world around; in the ideas that have shifted the very language of art; and in the ephemeral ways that his love touched countless people and changed their lives—including my own.

When I hang an exhibition these days, I usually squint first at the artworks for a long while before reaching for a bubble level. Who knows: maybe I *do* know better than a five dollar plastic tool.

Thanks, Brian, for all the large and small things you've taught me about being human. The truest measure of a person's path is how they point others toward their own futures.

Dearest O________,

Originally published in *Oh, Gods of Dust and Rainbows*, Brian Sholis and Prem Krishnamurthy, eds. (Cleveland: Cleveland Museum of Art and FRONT International, 2022).

(2022)

Dearest O________,

Oh wow, what a slog it's been! Sorry that I never got back to you—everything else came in between. Let me tell you: directing a contemporary art triennial is no joke, on top of this never-ending pandemic, war across the world, political regression—and who knows what else is on the horizon! Phew. I don't mean to overwhelm you, just making sure you know how I'm showing up today. Deep breaths.

By the time this message reaches you, the show will already have opened, maybe even closed. It's tough to tell with the speed of global postage at the moment, paper and supply chain issues, all that fun stuff. But our conversation continues.

Do you remember when I first came to visit and told you about the triennial? It was a different world. I was still playing the role of graphic designer; the idea of directing a thing at the scale of FRONT was well out of sight. But by the second visit, it was clear: I was checking out FRONT 2018 with an eye toward the future. Driving between Akron and Oberlin, I rocked out to The National and recorded wild voice memos to keep myself awake at the wheel. I never was much of a driver—when my knee isn't acting up, I'm a committed perambulator, or at least a public transportation person, gladly sharing space with other folks. That fact alone could have, should have, probably kinda sorta given me a clue about how *hard* a triennial like this might be for me, in particular.

It can be difficult to go against your instincts, your strengths, your personal proclivities—for intimate dialogue, for vulnerability, for tight-knit community, for connection—and instead strive for

1 Adapted from Case Western Reserve University Social Justice Initiative's Land Acknowledgement: https://case.edu/socialjustice/sites/case.edu.socialjusticefiles/2019-03/Land%2 Acknowledgement.pdf

something large scale, spread out, institutional, and maybe even alien. Plus, I was unfamiliar with the cultural landscape of the central United States. Even if it's true that this area was once known as the Western Reserve—after it was wrested from the Lenape (Delaware), Shawnee, Wyandot Miami, Ottawa, Potawatomi, and other Great Lakes tribes who lived here for eons before[1]—and that it was ruled from afar in Connecticut (where I grew up), I knew next to nothing about this place, O____, beyond my wife's murky family history. Creating something meaningful here might seem like a fool's errand, perhaps, an Icarian flight. But I guess getting too close to the sun is what it's all about, right?

I want to be the first to break it to you, dear O____: this show, this whole multiyear project, might very well be a big failure. A tragic, expensive, destructive one.

It sounds harsh, but I mean it as fact, not as opinion.

For if the stated goal of our not-so-little art exhibition is to change the world, to transform and heal our sick selves, our sick communities, our sick structures, isn't it obvious that the only thing we could do is fail? Isn't every utopia a failure—quite literally, a no-place?

"Try again. Fail again. Fail better." Samuel Beckett's mantra is something to hold on to in the pale of night. Or, as The National's Matt Berninger ambiguously croons, "The system only dreams in total darkness." Despite the gloom of these times, we tried our best to dream: about what art might do, for ourselves and for others. How art might be an agent of transformation, a mode of healing, and a therapeutic process amid a world that seems to be spiraling out of control.

What an impossible task. What a challenging project. If you had asked me six months ago, I might have begun my statement about the show with the preamble, "If I make it through this show alive..."

But here I am, today: alive, writing to you.

So instead of trying to craft a single, neatly buttoned-down narrative, O________, I will just start from the beginning and share some fragments with you. Pieces of a bumpy tale that never ended up settling into a singular story, but that still reveal the process, the experience, some of the pleasures and the pains. Would you bear with me a bit?

§

Zoom back to January 2019: the first trip to Cleveland for the curatorial process of the second edition of FRONT International. Tina Kukielski and I, proud co-artistic directors, have gathered many of the triennial's partner institutions for a workshop. It's part of our approach. Rather than showing up and telling people what we intend to do, it seems necessary to start with listening: asking what worked in the first FRONT, what was challenging, what everyone hopes the next exhibition will look like. It's a useful though sometimes fractious conversation: there are mixed feelings about the first edition and a lot of cruft under the surface we're not yet reaching. Afterward, though, over glasses of wine and crunchy snacks, people seem more relieved—and even excited to start working on the next iteration. Tina and I have pages and pages of notes. A good start.

We worked in earnest from there, visiting Cleveland, Akron, and Oberlin multiple times; meeting up at international art exhibitions and biennials; conducting studio visits and conversations with artists in Cleveland, Oberlin, Akron, New York, Berlin, London, Sharjah, and online; beginning to jot down thoughts in Google Docs and discussing our ideas on long calls. We shared the artists on each of our minds and drew maps outlining what connected them. We made plans for a road trip across the Midwest. We were excited about finally working together after having been friends for years. Collaboration emerged as a key method. We wanted others' voices in the mix. Could we convene an artistic team of curators, artists, designers, editors, community organizers, and more—based both in Cleveland and abroad—to accompany and help guide us in this process? It seemed like a novel idea, and the triennial approved our budget for it.

The idea of healing first came up in early conversations in Ohio. After one visit that included stops at the National Museum of Psychology and Dr. Bob's House, the birthplace of Alcoholics Anonymous, in Akron, as well as the Cleveland Clinic, we talked about therapy at length. It's a topic that Tina and I are interested in and it seemed embedded in the social fabric of this particular place. At first, we were a little skittish: healing might seem too hippy-dippy, not intellectual enough for the oh-so-serious Art World. But the more we considered northeast Ohio and its many historical scars, the more we talked with artists from around the world, the more the big idea of healing seemed to resonate.

Specific subthemes emerged. There was the notion of human capital: how the city's great prosperity and civic institutions were built upon the remnants of the forced labor of enslaved people in the United States followed by the exploited labor of industrial Cleveland (which has since been supplanted by the service-based biotech and health care industries). Or the recognition that those same extractive industries had degraded Cleveland's more-than-human landscape, its great lake and river. This culminated in 1969, when the mighty Cuyahoga burned (again). Although the heavily polluted river had caught fire at least a dozen times before, this particular incident caught the attention of national magazines such as *Time* and *National Geographic*. It marked a major turning point in the environmental movement's efforts and led to the eventual formation of the Environmental Protection Agency.[2] While the backdrop of ecological catastrophe bolstered Cleveland's unfortunate moniker, the Mistake on the Lake, that pejorative also came to encompass the ongoing racial segregation and discrimination in the city. These were exemplified by the Hough Uprisings of July 1966, when Black residents of Cleveland rose up to protest discrimination and were put down by the armed National Guard.[3] In recent years, the ongoing

2
Lorraine Boissoneault, "The Cuyahoga River Caught Fire at Least a Dozen Times, but No One Cared Until 1969." Smithsonianmag.com, June 19, 2019. Accessed July 3, 2022 at https://www.smithsonianmag.com/history/cuyahoga-river-caughtfire-least-dozen-timesno-one-cared-until-1969-180972444/

3 "The Hough Uprisings of 1966." Accessed July 3, 2022 at https://clevelandhistorical.org/items/show/7

4 Langston Hughes, "Two Somewhat Different Epigrams." *New Poems by American Poets #2* (New York: Ballantine, 1957), 81.

killings of unarmed Black citizens by police, most notably the murder of twelve-year-old Tamir Rice in 2014—and, all too recently, the bone-chilling death in June 2022 of Jayland Walker at the hands of Akron police, who shot down his fleeing body with forty-six bullets—serve as the brutal face of decades of racially motivated disinvestment, redlining, and police violence across the region.

Yet amid such great past and present wounds, we also witnessed shimmerings of hope and renewal. Today, new urban farms such as Rid-All or Château Hough sprout up in former dumping grounds and empty lots. On one five-block drive through Cleveland's Glenville neighborhood, Tina and I counted eighteen churches of different denominations. Clearly, community is deeply rooted here. We imagined that such places—along with the dance clubs, music halls, and choir rooms of Cleveland's heyday, as well as unmarked AA gathering spaces everywhere—might offer security, safety, and a sense of support that help people make their way through difficult times. Could an exhibition enable a similar sense of belonging? Could our collaborative approach help provide this nudge?

Alongside this optimistic viewpoint, institutional pressures began to build. Three months into the process, we were asked for a working list of artists, a concept, and our approach. So we drafted a presentation to collect our thoughts, which was well received. Next on the to-do list: an exhibition title.

Thankfully, I forget many of our faltering initial attempts. I think they tried to evoke eco-futures and sci-fi dreams. What I do recall is stumbling upon our eventual title in summer 2019 while reading through a PDF of Langston Hughes's collected poetry. Tina and I were already curious about that prolific, polymathic writer's influential teenage years in Cleveland, as well as his later return to the city to produce plays at the present-day Black-focused theater Karamu House. I started a Google Sheets file to collect resonant phrases from the poems. Tina picked out "Dust and Rainbows" from the long list and asked after its original context—what do dust and rainbows have to do with each other?

TWO SOMEWHAT DIFFERENT EPIGRAMS

I
Oh God of dust and rainbows, help us see
That without dust the rainbow would not be.

II
I look with awe upon the human race
And God, Who sometimes spits right in its face.[4]

After reading the poem on the page, Tina proposed using its entire first phrase, "Oh, God of dust and rainbows," as our exhibition title. An epic invocation, a piece of language resonant with the immediacy of speech, of dialogue, of calling to some other outside of yourself. Its length was odd, unexpected, even ungainly. Coming from a polytheistic background, I proposed tweaking the phrase to the plural: "Gods." At first some people were uncomfortable about this change; others stumbled over the title's length. But most eventually accepted it. Dust and rainbows brought to mind powerful images and associations. The whole poem captured the complexity of human experience in its exultation and its woes. The name gained traction.

Things developed. Things changed. Tina had a beautiful baby in late July 2019 and took a short leave before jumping back into work. We began to gather curatorial staff. We established our artistic team, whose members were enthusiastic about the show's name and the approach. Inspired by other biennials that had invited cohorts of commissioned artists to visit a place at the same time—a way to spark conversations, even micro-communities, from the start—we convened our first set of artists and the artistic team in Cleveland that October. It was powerful to finally have such incredible individuals interact with the city and with each other. Things were moving along well.

In January 2020, amid faint news reports from China of a novel coronavirus, we announced this title, and the theme of art and healing, at Karamu House in Cleveland and at a private event in New York. The announcement was accompanied by a quirky visual identity by our graphic designers, The Rodina, in a typeface originally designed in Cleveland in the 1880s. Ready to rock!

And then, within eight weeks, the world as we knew it shut down. Countries went into lockdown, innumerable people became ill and died, communities broke down, anxiety and uncertainty became the norm. Infrastructures groaned under the weight of collective care. A social movement for racial justice became even more widespread. Everything transformed.

We pivoted the show, pivoted the team, pivoted the structure: postponing the exhibition by a year to 2022; canceling artist trips and projects amid budgetary uncertainty; struggling to research a locally rooted show amid lockdown; and, eventually, losing Tina's full involvement as co-artistic director due to lack of childcare and the working pressures of the moment.

Yet the title stuck. I began to feel like it was the one solid thing I had to hold on to. Not just on an aesthetic or poetic level, but on a deeply personal one. "Oh, Gods of Dust and Rainbows"—its acceptance and acknowledgment of the inevitability of both joy and suffering, its nearly Buddhist equanimity, felt aspirational amid the tumult. What an apt name for this odd, unexpected, and often punishing more-than-just-an-exhibition project.

§

How can art heal? Ask twenty people and you'll get twenty different answers.

We spent our first year of curating the show thinking about artworks that touched on healing, both in their subject matter and in how they were made. Art and healing are deeply intertwined in many cultures, through the figure of the magician or shaman who so often aligns with the otherworldly channeling of the artist.

5
adrienne maree brown, *Emergent Strategy: Shaping Change, Changing Worlds* (Chico, CA: AK Press, 2017), 13.

6
Bessel van der Kolk, *The Body Keeps the Score: Mind, Brain and Body in the Transformation of Trauma* (London: Penguin Books, 2015), 358.

During the fall of that first, eventful pandemic year, I began trying to distill the exhibition's thematics and many artistic approaches into a single framework. It had been such a trying time, with Tina leaving FRONT, health issues, relationship strife, creative exhaustion, global tumult, and more. Artmaking had definitely proved healing for me on a personal level, yet I also had faith that art could, in some cases, also work to heal societal structures. Were these one operation or multiple?

I found a starting point in the now-classic 1969 diagram that legendary designers Charles and Ray Eames made for the exhibition *What Is Design?* The original drawing articulates how the work of the design office is neither the act of a pure service producer nor that of an autonomous genius. The best work emerges at the intersection of multiple interests: those of the designer, client, and society as a whole. Over the past few years, I've taken the liberty of redrawing this diagram and substituting what I find to be more broadly applicable terms: artist, commissioner or community, and planet as a whole

Around the time I was working to comprehend this diagram by tracing and retracing it by hand, I happened to reread organizer and writer adrienne maree brown's landmark book *Emergent Strategy.* As she says:

> In the framework of emergence, the whole is a mirror of the parts. Existence is fractal—the health of the cell is the health of the species and the planet.[5]

This fractal, multiscalar way of thinking sparked a hunch: if healing is necessary at all of these levels, then we might begin to think about how art—a uniquely human modality, in both its making and its reception, yet also a primal one that every culture has discovered in its own way—might contribute to healing in different forms.

Bessel van der Kolk's *The Body Keeps the Score*, a work that articulates an embodied and holistic perspective on individual trauma, offered further suggestions. Have you read it already, O________? During the first COVID-19 lockdown, I bought nearly 150 copies of the book (many with FRONT's backing) and sent them to friends and colleagues—that's how essential I found it. In the last paragraph of the book, after writing for hundreds of pages about modalities for treating different forms of trauma, van der Kolk makes an unexpected leap of scale:

> The same is true of societies. Many of our most profound advances grew out of experiencing trauma... Trauma is now our most urgent public health issue, and we have the knowledge necessary to respond effectively. The choice is ours to act on what we know.[6]

It sparked the thought: could the modalities of artmaking that work on a personal level also function for groups or for society as a whole? Even to my elastic mind, it seemed like a bit of a stretch,

7 Eugen Herrigel, *Zen in the Art of Archery* (New York: Pantheon Books, 1953), 40.

but rather than interrogate, I rolled with it. In my typical way, enhanced by being stuck in lockdown, I pulled out piles of books and started looking for examples and references across disciplines. All to answer a basic question: how can art function as a healing force at multiple scales?

1. DAILY PRACTICE...

Let's start at the individual level. How can art heal an individual?

It's something about daily writing. I should have woken up early this morning to write: at 5:33, when I first looked at the clock; at 7:00, when the alarm first went off; or at 7:09, when I first hit snooze. By 7:33, I got out of bed for sleepy morning yoga and meditation, but at 9:00, when my assistant texted me that her kids are sick today, I replied that we should both just work from home and went back to bed. Now it's shortly after 11:00 and I'm lying on the couch, head propped up by a pillow, hands outstretched toward the keyboard, banging out words.

Some days things work; some days they don't. That's the nature of daily practice, and perhaps artmaking in general. If my whole career as a creative person was judged on this single morning, then you might not think much of it. But it's the persistence of doing this, day in and day out, that leads to its meaning and, ultimately, to its healing potential.

The artist who best exemplifies this for me is the late, great On Kawara. His *Today* series, started in 1966 and ended in 2013 before his passing the next year, codified the idea of daily practice into rules. He set himself the lifelong task of making paintings that were started and finished on a single day. They were to include no information apart from the date on which they were painted and to be rendered in a cool, sans serif-style white lettering.

Kawara didn't actually paint every day of his life, but he did set a high bar for what a rigorous practice of daily artmaking can accomplish. It seems to have transformed his individual consciousness. After all, Kawara's later projects, such as *One Million Years*, move from meditating on a single day to encompassing the entire span of historical time.

Kawara's practice resonates with what philosopher Eugen Herrigel, in his classic *Zen in the Art of Archery*, tells us about the mastery of a craft.

> As though he had no higher aspirations he bows under his burden with a kind of obtuse devotion, only to discover in the course of years that forms which he perfectly masters no longer oppress but liberate.[7]

Herrigel highlights the seeming contradiction that the rigor of a daily practice—whether archery, meditation, or artmaking—is eventually freeing.[8] Although he doesn't use the term, one could see here psychologist Mihaly Csikszentmihalyi's idea of "flow"—how you can lose yourself in the making of work. I only read Herrigel recently and wish I had encountered it twenty years ago, although I might not have understood it then. His invocation of Zen practice also connects, in my mind, with the Korean-German philosopher Byung Chul Han, whose timely book *On the Disappearance of Rituals* highlights how rituals become incorporated into our bodies.[9]

A more easily accessible version of daily practice is captured in Julia Cameron's wildly influential *The Artist's Way*, a best-selling self-help manual for frustrated artists. Some people find its language and approach tough to swallow, not least because of her penchant for religious phraseology (such as her frequent invocations of a "Creative God") and potential indebtedness to the Alcoholics Anonymous twelve-step program. For me—mostly bedridden during month two of the pandemic with three slipped discs from working myself to the point of collapse—her book was a godsend.

Cameron's self-guided twelve-week program for finding your individual creativity starts with a basic tool: Morning Pages, the practice of starting each day by writing three pages longhand in a notebook before you do anything else. (It's how I began this entry, though I'm fudging the rules by typing.) It sounds simple, and, actually, I think it is; if you can muster the dedication and time to write every day, it helps to shake out many anxieties, uncertainties, and loose thoughts. I came to recognize it as a kind of "mind scan" or mindful meditation, though in my experience, it's equally significant that it involves actual, physical mark making, the creation of something that you can later refer back to. I often feel that if only every human had the privilege of fifteen to thirty minutes a day to make something uninterrupted, sustained, and purely for themselves—whether writing, drawing, weaving, printing, making ceramics, or whatever captures their fancy—the world would already be a slightly better place.

This approach to artmaking as daily practice is widespread across FRONT 2022 and this catalog: in the work of Julie Mehretu, whose painterly practice at all scales, from epic to intimate, comes from a meditative and mindful approach to the medium; or Karel Martens, who follows in Kawara's footsteps in a lightweight way. He has made for the show a set of 365 individual monoprinted numbers, one for each day of 2022, which are posted daily online and in specific FRONT locations.

Other artists in our show who use art specifically to address their traumas also come to mind. Dexter Davis, an artist whose work spans several FRONT locations, uses the iterative visual vocabulary of block printing, painting, and collage to work through violent episodes of his life. In my encounters with both Davis and his pieces, I've been struck by the juxtaposition of the frenetic, layered quality of the final works with the calm that making them seems to create for him. Paul O'Keeffe's iconic, abstract sculptures, spread across multiple venues, work through the suicide of his son Christian a decade ago. Incorporating Christian's poetry and texts into his artworks, O'Keeffe uses his craft to integrate the

8
There is a challenging historical complexity at work here, too: Herrigel was a member of the Nazi Party and used his ideas of Zen to justify its politics. This was elided from his biography for years and only recently acknowledged. It may seem problematic to use the words of a former Nazi to argue for individual liberation, and yet it also must be accepted that high-ranking Nazi officials believed strongly in the practice of yoga. Neither of these facts, I believe, disqualifies the use of Zen or yoga as transformative, healing tools on an individual level, although they lend strong credence to the fact that these methods in isolation are not a sufficient cause for ethical behavior in the world—instead, they are tools that are best taken in context with other, interpersonal ones.

9
Byung-Chul Han, *Vom Verschwinden der Rituale: Eine Topologie der Gegenwart* (Berlin: Ullstein, 2018), 20.

painful memories of this event into his life. I've learned a lot from our conversations in recent years about how formal methods can produce a therapeutic effect.

The link of art to individual therapeutic practice is even more direct in certain artists' biographies. Although they're not included in the show, a handful of names come to mind: Charlotte Posenenske, who left the art world to become a social worker; or Lygia Clark, who moved to France and developed experimental, material modalities for psychotherapy. But for me, the figure who most stands out is Chauncey Hare, who transitioned from engineering to social photography and finally into a career as an occupational therapist. He was a mysterious, elusive figure whom I've spent the past twenty-five years listening to from afar. Before disavowing his career as an artist and nearly destroying his archive, he dedicated the photographic images he had produced to all the working people who labor under the domination of corporate overlords. This kind of everyday labor—which is coerced, recorded by a clock but stripped of its essential individuality, agency, and joy—is the opposite of daily practice. Perhaps it's why, in our evermore consumptive and alienating world, we each need something as simple as fifteen minutes of artmaking a day to help us slow down and heal.

2. SHARING JOY!

March 19, 2020: the first lockdown has gone into effect. Alongside about half of the world, I am in disbelief. How can everything suddenly be closed? How can we be locked into our homes to avoid contact with others? For humans, an inherently social animal, this seems unfathomable. For me, a person who loves other people more than even myself, it is a dire sentence.

I turn to one of the best forms that I know for bringing people together: karaoke. It's a great way to generate mild to serious discomfort in many people while also creating community through that shared vulnerability. "Spontaneous Zoom Karaoke," a WhatsApp group including more than thirty artists, designers, curators, and others from a dozen time zones, was born. It dovetailed well with *Present!*, an experimental, weekly Zoom extravaganza I organized throughout the early pandemic months, where out-of-sync online karaoke became a staple.

Of course, if I hadn't been so desperate for connection, I might have realized there are other modes of human expression that create a shared sense of space even more effectively and with greater lasting power. One good example: art!

A major purpose of art, since humans drew the first cave paintings, has been to commune with other forces and beings—whether human, animal, spiritual, material, or elemental. This is still the basic goal of art as I see it: a way to convene communities, particularly unruly ones, composed of unlike participants.

Art does this through aesthetic pleasure itself. Pleasure is embedded within so many visual decisions—color, composition, materials, craft, or touch—as well as within the even more fundamental human modalities of dance and song.

Here, Audre Lorde offers an exceptionally useful frame:

> The sharing of joy, whether physical, emotional, psychic, or intellectual, forms a bridge between the sharers which [sic] can be the basis for understanding much of what is not shared between them, and lessens the threat of their difference.[10]

Put even more simply: sharing joy allows for those who are different to come together.

Music, movement, and aesthetic pleasure are core human forms as well as beautiful, useful tools. Barbara Ehrenreich's essential *Dancing in the Streets: A History of Collective Joy* offers ample arguments for the ways ecstatic dancing has been an effective tool for group formation—one that is sorely lacking in contemporary society, with the exceptions of sports rallies and rock concerts.[11] Why, she asks, has Western society lost its capacity for ecstatic dancing? How does this relate to the loss of community that we have encountered increasingly in recent decades?[12]

Ted Gioia's crucial volume *Healing Music*, a good companion, also offers nuanced arguments for the inseparability of music and healing across human cultures and eras. Many medical and healing forms began with rhythm, as he notes.

> Rituals that involve only a single individual ... do not contribute to social cohesion, do not inspire or inflame the emotions of onlookers, do not normally lead to emulation and the preservation of the techniques used. Music, in contrast, is not only able to do these things but may even be the single most powerful tool we possess in achieving them. What force better contributes to group integration, ritualistic power, visionary inspiration, or emotional intensity than music?[13]

Music is one of the best ways to gather people. It has the power to travel over distance, over time, to link people together. Take, for example, Cory Arcangel's *Hail Mary*, which is an algorithmically composed automated score for carillon, played daily at the McGaffin Carillon at the Church of the Covenant as part of FRONT 2022. The resonance of Cory's artwork is amplified by a network of carillonists across Ohio and the world who will perform this synchronously. As you may know, O________, the McGaffin Carillon also figures in my family history: it's named after my wife's great-grandfather Alexander McGaffin (1870-1929), a beloved pastor of the church. He represents my only direct personal link with Cleveland. McGaffin's letters to his wife, carefully chronicled by my wife's aunt Susan Moore, hint at ongoing struggles with mental health, breakdown, and possibly addiction.[14] And yet despite this, he was a well-respected pastor at multiple churches, including the one whose bell tower bears his name.

10 Audre Lorde, "Uses of the Erotic: The Erotic as Power." In *Pleasure Activism: The Politics of Feeling Good*, adrienne maree brown, ed. (Chico, CA: AK Press, 2019), Kindle, 29-30.

11 Although one wonders what Ehrenreich would have added to her book to account for events such as the 2021 insurrection at the Capitol building or other nationalist protests that seem to nudge a kind of ecstatic joy and chaos into something destructive.

12 Barbara Ehrenreich, *Dancing in the Streets: A History of Collective Joy* (London: Granta Books, 2008), 19.

13 Ted Gioia, *Healing Songs* (Durham, NC: Duke University Press, 2006), 32.

14 Susan Ferries Moore, *The Tip Top Letters* (Wicomico Church, VA: Tip Top Publications, 2020).

Martin Beck, one of the triennial's artists and a dear friend, has created a musical memorial to a community he never experienced firsthand in the form of an immersive thirteen-and-a-half-hour film installation of records playing. This musical work, an echo of a past gathering, nods toward the richness of community embodied within the long-running series of Loft parties organized by David Mancuso in the 1970s and '80s. Music and the joy of dancing is such a vector for gathering diverse people. Well before FRONT 2022 began, my friendship with Tina was cemented by going to *Joy*, a Loft-inspired party with Martin in Brooklyn and learning something new: that even the often unloved form of prog rock, and in particular the Steely Dan song "Aja," can be highly danceable under the right circumstances and with a great sound system. Try it! Move your body to that sax solo!

Of course, dear O________, this is the key: music is not just meant to be received from afar but is also a participatory experience that many kinds of people can engage in. FRONT 2022 includes several examples of this. Lenka Clayton and Phillip Andrew Lewis's *Five Hundred Twenty-Four* is partly inspired by the statistic that one in five US families has a member in a choir. The pair engaged with over twenty choirs in the Cleveland area to create a video work featuring only large groups of people singing numbers together—and yet this simple act of gathering in song made me, and others on the FRONT team, weep the first time we watched it. Jace Clayton's *40 Part Part* takes sonic interactivity a step further, constructing an audio artwork featuring forty speakers that visitors can connect to via an audio cable or Bluetooth. My dream is to see groups of Cleveland youths gleefully geeking out to loud music in the main hall of Cleveland Public Library's former reading room. Bluetooth is also the protocol underlying Dansbana!'s new public dance floor in Akron, which they developed together with youth in the city and which anyone can now connect to in order to play music and shake their booty. I first encountered the all-female collective's work in Stockholm just before the curatorial work of the triennial began and was moved by their generous gesture to create open spaces for dancing together in the city. Joy is even embedded in life's most painful moments: grieving and loss are the focus of Every Ocean Hughes's *Help the Dead*, planned for the closing weekend of FRONT at CWRU's medical education center. Colin Self and Geo Wyeth, the two musicians who perform the piece, have developed a suite of catchy vocal hooks to accompany this profound meditation on death. After I first experienced it in 2019 at KW Institute for Contemporary Art in Berlin, I couldn't help but hum the main tune to myself on the way home. And Wong Kit Yi's new video work, on view both at CWRU and in Akron at the Emily Davis Gallery, uses a format that the artist has employed to great effect for the last five years: the karaoke essay-film. Creating webs of association connected to the first voice box transplant, which was performed at the Cleveland Clinic in 1998, she has commissioned new music with running karaoke subtitles that takes her complex ideas and makes them highly engaging. I curated several exhibitions with her before the pandemic; by now, I can also now sing along to much of the work.

It's easier than ever to listen to music, but most of us, I fear, do it alone: while wearing headphones, isolated from the communal experience of sound. Many of the artists I admire most challenge this atomizing, isolated approach. They use singing, movement, aesthetic beauty, and even karaoke as ways to bring people out of their bubbles and into something that is shared, something that is potentially messier, vulnerable, and more awkward, but hopefully also more rewarding and connective.

CURATING AS A CONTAINER

IN WHAT WAYS ARE curating and therapy connected?

Perhaps, first of all, by the simple fact that I just drew the link. But beyond my gut association and the fact that any two things can be brought into relation by evoking them through language, let's dig a little deeper—"peel back the onion," as one of my therapists used to say.

One of the core practices of contemporary curating is the studio visit: a ritual in which one arts professional, whether an artist, curator, or collector, visits another arts professional, usually an artist, in their studio (whether physically or virtually) to look at their art and exchange ideas. In my experience of being on both sides of this encounter, these visits are typically forty-five to ninety minutes. The visited artist explains their work, either in an comprehensive or more focused fashion. The visitor then says what they think, oftentimes freely associating, interpreting, and perhaps offering some degree of critical judgment of the work. After years of being both subject and object of studio visits, I have developed my own approach to this form.

As an artist, this usually involves making sure that the visitor feels at ease, allowing myself to be vulnerable, and yet maintaining my boundaries. As a curator, I feel a responsibility to be caring: I ask open-ended questions and avoid making statements or giving feedback, at least until I feel like I've first listened closely.

Since I started to experience frequent studio visits in this form about fifteen or so years ago, I've been struck by their unexpectedly rhyming relationship with the rituals of individual psychotherapy. There are some easy parallels: the often one-to-one modality, the time frame, the sense of sharing and feedback, the real risks of projection, transference, and harm. Also, divergences: except for when they're in art school, artists don't typically pay others to do a studio visit; typically, studio visits are one-offs or at least directed at a specific end, rather than open-ended, repeat engagements. At the same time, I have the sense that both these formats support transformation, insight, understanding, and, ultimately, liberation from constraining patterns of behavior and reaction.

Maybe this perception is colored by my own relationship with therapy; I first took psychology classes at the local community college while

15 My visual essay "Workshop of Workshops," first released in 2019 and subsequently revised in March 2020, offers a more comprehensive account of my experience with and relationship to individual psychotherapy: https://bit.ly/Workshop_of_Workshops

still in high school and studied Freud as literature as an undergraduate. I turned theory into practice in early 2008, beginning in individual psychotherapy around the same time of my first professional identity crisis, when I started to fancy myself a curator and visit professional artists (many of whom were close friends) in their studios. During the same period, I delved into the work of artist Amie Siegel, whose feature-length films *Empathy* and *DDR/DDR* examine psychoanalysis through the rigorously self-reflexive lens of an artist. My first psychotherapist was a trainee at a prestigious New York psychoanalytic institute who offered me sessions for a modest fee, just within range of what I could afford. He became my therapist for over four years, until he left New York City for a job at an institution upstate. I then worked with another therapist from 2012-21 with only one pause due to her having a child. Our richly generative dialogue weathered a move to Berlin and more. In summer 2021, we ended our formal work and transitioned into being friends and colleagues. To be honest, though, the circumstances of this triennial and its related stresses have pushed me to resume my weekly sessions with her, at least until the project is complete.[15]

OK, let me admit: this aside feels a bit patchy and probably deserving of a larger, more expansive container. It would take much more space and time to articulate the methodological overlaps between curating and therapy, the many conversations and connections I've made with artists around ideas of therapy, and the ways in which a studio visit and subsequent exhibition might help an artist to unpack their own personal history. There are specific examples I might cite, long-term conversations, studio visit after studio visit that were part of curating FRONT and which, I believe, might have helped certain individuals to unlock certain traumas. But it's a big, big claim for the work of curating to say that it can be actually curative on the level of healing trauma. That it can be not only about art and exhibitions but also about understanding substantial individual truths. Instead of overreaching, I'll leave this stub as it is for now, here, and perhaps pick it up in a context still to come. Let's call it a future-note, an encapsulated counterpoint to a footnote. But sidebars are often best when they also have practical tips. With that in mind, here are humble suggestions for those who would give or receive studio visits:

FOR ARTISTS

DO offer the visitor a beverage and snack of some sort—blood sugar usually helps in taking in and processing unfamiliar information.

DO be as transparent as you're able—although inviting someone into your studio is itself a risky move, sometimes leading with vulnerability can inspire others to also let down their guard.

DO articulate your own boundaries by expressing what kind of feedback you're seeking or in what form you would like to receive it.

DO acknowledge that studio visits (like therapy) are work—hard work—and often exhausting; give yourself enough time to process them.

DON'T assume that the curator or interlocutor is an objective or impartial authority.

DON'T offer unsolicited feedback or critique without first asking many questions, especially open-ended ones.

DON'T rely only on memory to hold the conversation—a notebook is a great expansion of your mind's capacities.

DON'T make assumptions about the artist's work, compare them to other artists with whom you're familiar, or try to fit them into a favorite theoretical or discursive framework—it's better to let them lead and try to listen on their terms.

DO be empathic, respectful, and aware of your own power: the safer the container, the more honest and generative the conversation.

DO ask questions about the artist's childhood, parents, geographic origins, how they came to artmaking. One of my standard first questions, "What is your

16 For more information, you can also refer to the Paper Monument book *I Like Your Work: Art & Etiquette* (New York: 2009), which contains useful entries on studio visits.

family's relationship to art?" often yields useful context and insights.

DO accept that your role and unique privilege is to potentially support an individual on their own path toward discovering and inhabiting their own best selves. Take this responsibility seriously; never abuse the space of the studio visit.[16]

3. SPEAKING WITH POWER?

In winter 2021, I found myself on Zoom well past midnight in Berlin, facilitating a community meeting between residents of the Fairfax neighborhood of Cleveland (including their councilman Blaine Griffin), representatives of the Cleveland Clinic (including Dr. Charles Modlin, founder of Cleveland Clinic Minority Men's Health Fair), and FRONT 2022 artist Jacolby Satterwhite. I was nervous: what if this didn't go well? The conversation was an important first encounter between an artist, a community, and a commissioning entity. The Cleveland Clinic, one of the world's largest and most respected institutions of healing, has a historically charged relationship with its mostly Black neighbors. It had decided to hire an artist to create a public artwork for a new medical facility in the neighborhood; FRONT had introduced the Clinic to Jacolby's boundary-crossing work and helped shepherd along the project. The whole situation was fraught with potential pitfalls.

I remember my anxiety at a critical moment: Jacolby was talking about his past efforts as an artist, including his now-canonical 2012 work *The Matriarch's Rhapsody*, for which he digitized an archive of his late, schizophrenic mother Patricia

Satterwhite's inventive drawings and used them to populate a virtual gaming world. He used this wildly creative—and also visually advanced—3D environment to introduce his intention to conduct a similar process of digitization with drawings and "assets" from the Fairfax Community. His descriptive language was nuanced, a mix of personal, pop, and art historical references with a smattering of high-theory vocabulary. The prompt to which he wanted participants' responses: "What does utopia look like to you?" My response: trepidation. Shallow breathing. Most probably perspiration on my fingertips.

Forty minutes of the allotted hour had already passed. I asked everybody in the room to use the chat to share how they felt about Jacolby's project. I did this according to a protocol inspired by something artistic team member and FRONT 2022 artist Kameelah Janan Rasheed once demonstrated in an online *Present!* session: I asked everyone to take a deep breath, type their response but not hit "send" until the count of three. A way to give everyone space for their own thoughts and reflections before they became collective knowledge.

I counted off: *1-2-3, send!* Texts, most positive and excited about the possibilities, trickled in. My body relaxed. Phew. One thing, done.

Don't get the wrong impression: the rest of the project wasn't an entirely smooth road. Any collaboration between a powerful institution, an artist, and a particular community is bound to be bumpy. One time I got a late-night call and had to jump in, on short notice, to play the role of conflict mediator or relationship counselor between two parties, trying to help them to listen better to each other, to find a shared vocabulary for agreement and conflict, harmony and friction. There were sometimes unspoken, sometimes articulated tensions around race and representation, power and language, budgets and value. I was only part of a very small portion of these conversations; there were many many more hours of discussion and negotiation for everyone involved.

So you might ask, O________: Why add complexity to an already complex project? Why make this damn triennial any damn harder? Unfolding over several years, it had already proven to be the most challenging professional project of my brief life. Due to the pandemic and the inability to travel, I had to direct the whole thing from afar with a six-hour time difference. The project's shifting conditions had caused me back problems, knee issues, insomnia, marital conflicts, depression, breakdowns, and raging anger. And that does not even take into account multiple global-scale crises. What a fucking mess! Why even try, amid this chaos, to create a new configuration for collaborating with people on Zoom, of all possible means for group communication?

I suppose it's because the stakes are so high—personally and politically—that it seems necessary to insist upon meaningful collaboration between unlikely actors. In the contemporary art world, established artists are often treated as geniuses—or as powerfully privileged small children. They're given a budget and

17 Caroline Levine, *Forms: Whole, Rhythm, Hierarchy, Network* (Princeton, NJ, and Cambridge, UK: Princeton University Press, 2016), 23.

space within which to play, then set loose. I've witnessed how this can lead to frustrated expectations on each side. And, even more significantly, this may or may not serve the larger concerns and needs of society. On pessimistic days, I fear that much of the expensive, high-profile art produced and exhibited around the world today is completely irrelevant to the biggest problems we face as a society—problems that cannot be solved by any individual.

A book that has influenced me greatly in recent years is Caroline Levine's *Forms*. In it, she identifies how the formal structure of a thing itself contains a political meaning.

> I seek to show that there is a great deal to be learned about power by observing different forms of order as they operate in the world. And I want to persuade those who are interested in politics to become formalists, so that we can begin to intervene in the conflicting formal logics that turn out to organize and disorganize our lives, constantly producing not only painful dispossessions but also surprising opportunities.[17]

That she manages to connect social and formal structures without being entirely reductive is testament to her impressive intellectual prowess. Also, the fact that *The Wire* is her crowning example of an artwork in which formal structures resonate with political meanings also seems pretty great!

Perhaps I'm attracted to Levine's argument because it gives me an easy way to reconcile my deep-seated belief that art should engage in the world with my truest, and most fundamental, pleasure: the act of reading fiction.

Science fiction was my go-to genre until I got to high school and felt pressure to read "serious" literature. My recent reacquaintance with the genre came with a book that I actually could have read as a teenager upon its initial publication in 1993, if only I had looked in the right places: Octavia E. Butler's *Parable of the Sower*, a powerfully prescient near-future dystopia that opens in July 2024. It describes a potential United States in which the environment and society are beginning to collapse. Its protagonist, Lauren Oya Olamina, must find new ways of bringing people together, collectively, in order to survive in this harsh, brutal, and all-too-near world.

Another act of (potentially dystopian) worldbuilding manifests in the work of Isabelle Andriessen, a wildly talented Amsterdam-based sculptor whose art I first encountered in a studio visit in early 2019. Her metabolic sculptures accomplish their work by animating inanimate materials; this allows her pieces to inhabit the liminal space between sculpture and performance. Their uncanny anatomies suggest dormant agents acting out dark agendas, envisioning grim speculations about our (near) future. In one of our conversations she told me about *Eldorica*, a utopia published in 1986 by her father Jurriaan Andriessen, who was a visionary artist, composer, and futurist. Affected by *The Limits to Growth*, the landmark 1972 study by the Club of Rome that articulated the fatal dangers to humankind of unchecked economic and population growth, the elder Andriessen spent over fifteen years imagining and illustrating The Eldorian Empire, a world with a fictional narrative based on scientific research into statistics, architecture, and technological systems that reject the logic of capitalism. Exhibiting both artists' works in the same venue reveals an intergenerational paradox—of how utopian speculations from the 1970s can become ever more dire amid the horrific crises that have unfolded since.

Kameelah Janaan Rasheed, whose influence is embedded across the triennial, often cites Butler's groundbreaking work in her practice. In a 1998 interview that she turned me on to, Butler discusses her method as a kind of "primitive hypertext"—a way of reading across many different books and reference points at once.[18] This approach is surely in dialogue with the way that I'm connecting disparate ideas here.

> All that you touch
> You Change.
> All that you Change
> Changes you.
> The only lasting truth
> Is Change.
> God is Change.
>
> EARTHSEED: THE BOOKS OF THE LIVING
> Saturday, July 20, 2024[19]

Another dystopic reading experience—though its author Elvia Wilk might reject the surety of the term—is *Oval*. This novel, set in a near-future Berlin, highlights the role of artists in prototyping new forms of society. In this fictional world—one that real artists participating in FRONT 2022, such as Christopher Kulendran Thomas, might thrive within—artists no longer work in a gallery system. Instead they are embedded within startups and companies on multi-year retainers with the express mandate to "disrupt" society. One artist, the boyfriend of the book's protagonist, develops a club drug that makes people more generous. It's a magic pill that's meant to save the world, the ultimate work of socially engaged art.[20] I don't want to spoil the book, but let's just say it doesn't end quite that rosily.

But art, I believe, can be a force for change in society, if only we can understand and accept more thoroughly the mechanisms by which it accomplishes its work. As a prime example, I would cite Kim Stanley Robinson's novel *The Ministry for the Future*. In my mind, this is one of the best artworks that I encountered during the lockdown, during which most museums and exhibitions venues were closed. This brick of a book, written in a highly engaging style from many vantage points, is a literary masterpiece in its construction. Yet it is also a complex, multiscalar thought experiment about how

18 "Octavia Butler, Samuel Delany." Accessed July 3, 2022 at https://web.mit.edu/m-i-t/science_fiction/transcripts/butler_delany_index.html

19 Octavia E. Butler, *Parable of the Sower* (New York: Four Walls Eight Windows, 1993), 3.

20 Elvia Wilk, *Oval* (New York: Soft Skull, 2019).

21
Kim Stanley Robinson, *The Ministry for the Future* (New York: Orbit, 2020).

22
Amitav Ghosh, *The Great Derangement: Climate Change and the Unthinkable* (Chicago: University of Chicago Press, 2016), 80.

to address the looming climate catastrophe.[21] It's commendable how readable Robinson makes that message, which has enabled it to inspire people to take the climate crisis more seriously, even catalyzing new companies that are turning some of its technological thought experiments into reality. This is a true Trojan horse: a gripping, complexly structured artwork that can deliver a bitter but desperately needed pill.

The writer Amitav Ghosh highlights this role of art today—to influence the structures that govern our contemporary world—in his essential *The Great Derangement: Climate Change and the Unthinkable*. As he articulates:

> Similarly, at exactly the time when it has become clear that global warming is in every sense a collective predicament, humanity finds itself in the thrall of a dominant culture in which the idea of the collective has been exiled from politics, economics, and literature alike.[22]

Ghosh's argument, elucidated throughout the book, is that a core problem of our time, underlying all of the other crises we face, is how contemporary society has banished the idea of collective action. Instead, an undue focus is placed on individual agency. He argues that the largest, most "wicked" challenges can only be solved by *collective* means.

This brings me back to collaboration and to why it makes sense to encourage a world-famous artist to work with an exclusive hospital in an underprivileged neighborhood. Over the past five hundred years, artists have become ever cozier with those who possess power, whether economic, political, social, or spiritual. Yet one thing that art has always been good at is creating visions of how society might function differently. As Martin Heidegger outlines in *Der Ursprung des Kunstwerks* (The Origin of the Work of Art), the artwork opens a new world and way of being.[23] And so, through the artist's unique skills, when she is sitting at the table with those in control, I believe she has the ability to speak *with power*—to use her ability to present ideas in enticing, engaging ways to challenge, influence, and transform the structures that govern our contemporary life.

Jacolby's project does that, giving people in a neighborhood that is rarely asked the chance to share their visions of utopia, and then translating them—through his laborious handwork of digitization and animation—into a permanent, striking, and *totally gonzo* public sculpture. It's something that looks like it could have been dropped by futuristic aliens into Fairfax, yet it also becomes a kind of time capsule, rooted within the community. It's a thing that changes the artist, the institution, and the neighborhood in unexpected ways.

Maybe I had already been primed for conflictual group processes by the artworks in the show. The challenging social hierarchies embedded in every gathering is at the core of Leigh Ledare's 2017 film *The Task*, which proved essential to how Tina and I approached making the show. Although the film primarily explores the dialogue

23
The fact that I am citing Martin Heidegger, another former Nazi, in making my arguments about art may seem suspicious to you; in fact, it starts to appear questionable even to me at this point. Is this the result of my formative intellectual education and most profound recognitions around the role of art having taken place in Germany, while studying aesthetic philosophy and beginning my career as an artist/designer? Or out of some deeper connection between destructive, authoritarian, and centralized political systems with the framework I'm espousing? I dearly hope it's not the latter. Perhaps with more time after this project is done, I can reflect further upon this.

and uncomfortable dynamics of a diverse group of people, the key moment is the artist's unexpected decision to step out from behind the camera and seat himself within the crowd. The move elicits upset reactions within the participants of the Tavistock group-therapy conference where the work was filmed. At first, I felt similarly, given that the perpetrator of this intervention, the artist, presents as a white, straight, cis-gendered male. Yet this troubling moment, which Tina and I argued about at length, highlights how an artist can generate useful friction, question implicit boundaries, and create greater awareness within a particular community or context.

This attitude toward unexpected intersections is also at play in our efforts at curatorial matchmaking. Artists Sarah Oppenheimer and Tony Cokes did not know each other until we introduced them on Zoom in 2020. I had a hunch that, although their work demonstrates no outward formal or thematic overlaps, they might get along. Having known Sarah for over twenty-five years and worked on smaller projects with her, I thought something could gel. My gut was confirmed when they decided to make a new work in dialogue with each other, resulting in an immersive, interactive installation in Transformer Station's Crane Gallery that invites visitors to take real agency in configuring and reconfiguring the work. Here collaboration exists both on the level of artmaking and for those who encounter the work.

Such collaboration is also essential when artworks leave the gallery and inhabit wider social realms. Cooking Sections, who joined us for the first artist trip to Cleveland in October 2019, has developed a long-term project around regenerative farming practices in Ohio that takes the form of an installation on Lake Erie that celebrates farming practices engaged in saving the lake ecology as well as a three-year commitment to working with farmers in the region. Having witnessed their works in the flesh, over long spans of time, I'm excited to see how the project unfolds in ways we can't even imagine right now. This planned yet emergent approach also resonates with the work of Asad Raza, a friend and dear collaborator—some people even take us for doppelgängers!—whose practice defies the fixed definition of artist. He has made feature-length films, organized a graduate-student strike, written about tennis for the *New Yorker*, produced live art works in major museums, and convened people in any number of configurations. One of his works in Cleveland is a physical structure for observing the heavens that is scaled for children, while another involves bringing a group of musicians on a boat trip across Lake Erie and co-composing music informed by Indigenous oral traditions and the Seneca language. Asad is interested not only in *what* is produced, but also in *how*.

Other participants in FRONT work with the structures of the museum itself, such as artists like Ahmet Öğüt, who intervenes within a collection to unpack questions of art and revolution—and also implements this on the level of conceptual contracts—or Julie Mehretu, whose exhibition at the Cleveland Museum of Art is the first time this august bastion of culture has allowed an artist to curate using its collection. Julie's approach cuts across all of the museum's departments, implicitly calling into question the accepted hierarchies and categories of an encyclopedic collection. I learned immensely from the grace with which she navigated institutional norms. Even more deeply embedded in issues of institutional practice is an artist like Renée Green, whose work over several decades has self-reflexively probed the boundaries of the institution. Here, her work—as both artist as well as curator of others' artworks—inhabits every aspect of moCa, from its display and acoustic spaces to its public programming to the manner in which it produces and distributes didactic materials. Born in Cleveland, she was one of the first artists Tina and I invited to be part of FRONT. We had the hunch that, with her dual experience of both the city's many histories and the challenges of museum practice, she could reimagine what a group exhibition might be. Through this expansive exploration of what "contact" means today, Renée proposes different ways for institutions to act and be present in the world.

As is probably obvious from this partial account, O________, many of the artists whom I've had the privilege of working with on this show are people I now count as co-conspirators, sometimes even close friends. It's what happens during the process of making a long-term project together. But this is also an important methodological and psychological point: doing something that tries to change the reigning structures of the world, even just a tiny bit, is really, really hard. How many times during this process did I dream of ending it, one way or another?

Working with others is not easy: it involves friction, conflict, betrayal, and heartbreak. And yet going at it alone is even harder. I'm convinced that the only sensible way to approach this process—this never-ending attempt to make the world seem a little more habitable every day, to paraphrase Bertolt Brecht—is together, with others.

Not every intervention or structural move has to be large-scale or all-encompassing. Sometimes it's just about shifting how we relate to each other on a personal level. Here, Cassie Thornton's *The Hologram* comes to mind. On view as an intervention at the National Museum of Psychology—an institution located in Akron that tells the history of psychology through works from its extensive archive and includes surprising objects such as the control consoles from the infamous Milgram experiment—Thornton's project is a decentralized, feminist, peer-to-peer network for mutual support and care. Begun as a speculative fiction—and expanded with writings including a Wikipedia article ostensibly authored in 2038—it has now become a format for community care that is practiced by over a thousand people across the world. In summer 2021, I had a transformative experience in *The Hologram*'s seven-week online course for male-identifying folks called "Why be vulnerable?" Among other things, it taught me how to ask for help from others. As Thornton has written, "Needing support does not make you weak."[24] It's a lesson I wish I had learned earlier and still sometimes forget—but better late than never!

24
Cassie Thornton, *The Hologram: Feminist, Peer-to-Peer Health for a Post-Pandemic Future* (London: Pluto Press, 2020), 55.

Funded and supported in its early phases within the context of art, today *The Hologram* has begun to outgrow that limiting framework to become, perhaps, something even more consequential: life.

§

Oh, O________, dear O________, it's hard to know where to end this letter. Reckoning with failure is what motivated me to write to you in the first place. Now, it seems, failure to tell the whole story might be how I must wrap it up. Anyway, things—such as the work of healing, on an individual or more-than-individual scale—can never properly be completed. "It's a process," as they say. It's been a crazy time. I know I'm not through it quite yet. And you, you grand, majestic, contradictory state of mind, O________: you keep changing, too.

Even if we limit ourselves only to "art": an exhibition, as neatly delimited as it might seem, is never clear cut. Every exhibition is latent within the world well before it opens and leaves traces for generations after its close. This is the deep time of exhibition-making and of everything else in this world. So many of our projects continue. Renée Green's *Contact* stays on view—and keeps growing—for months to come. Cooking Sections will be working with Ohio farmers for the next three years. Julie Mehretu is already planning her ten-year-long public mural in downtown Cleveland. And these are only the more visible manifestations. What about the effects upon the bodies, minds, and spirits of those who participated in the show, upon the institutions that partnered in it, and the many people who came to visit it? How can these be summed up in a mere piece of writing, locked into squiggly black marks on paper?

I guess I can accept this as a small comfort: to know that whatever work we do is a momentary flash, like a thunderstorm that brews up, and yet it waters the soil for whatever is next to grow.

For now, I feel both happy and tired. There's still so much to do. But if there's one thing I've learned through this long, twisting path, through our meandering conversation across time and space, it's that a hard journey is much more manageable with others. In writing to you, I'm already a bit lighter. Thanks for taking the time to exchange with me. I look forward to seeing you again before too long.

With love,
Prem

To Zia

Originally published in *Best! Letters from Asian Americans in the Arts*, Christopher K. Ho and Daisy Nam, eds. (New York: Paper Monument, 2021).

(2021)

Dear dear Zia,

How lovely to hear that you're moving to Ireland! Bet you'll find it a welcome change from London. I've only been twice, but I feel an odd sense of kinship with the Irish. Perhaps it's a sense of shared or at least sympathetic colonial history, the idea that "we" were all against the same enemy. I remember what my dad used to say: "The British: they'll shake your hand with one hand and stab you in the back with the other!" Delivered in a comedic mode, but it definitely left an impression on me.

I can't believe it's been only (already?) six years since we first met. Or rather, I should say since I "met" your novel—because we actually met IRL later on.

On August 9, 2014, as I was reading *In the Light of What We Know*, Michael Brown was being murdered by police in Ferguson, Missouri. What a brutal and senseless juxtaposition of verbs. His murder sparked a collective uprising against racism and police violence, which I followed from afar. In New York, I happened to be hosting Mitch McEwen, a member of the Black art collective HOWDOYOUSAYYAMINAFRICAN?, for a residency at my gallery P!. It's now a bit of a blur, but within days the entire residency pivoted, and the group responded in their own, all-in kind of way. Over the remaining weeks of August, they created a total installation at P! that featured a 24-channel video piece, *theway-blackmachine*, put together by Richie Adomako. It collected and presented social media from the BLM protests, transformed visually by algorithmic scripts. It also transformed the entire gallery space, and my life.

Since no one will read this letter but you, I can safely admit a sorry truth: I never really began to think consciously about race, especially my own, until I was a lot older than most folks. In high school, my own upper-middle-class upbringing and assimilation into mainstream American culture meant I took it for granted that I belonged to the same category as the other folks in my small, WASP-y Connecticut town. Were there ever moments of discomfort? Sure. Did I feel like I fit in completely? Never. But I didn't make too much of it, and anyway, I had enough support on other fronts to make it work.

That feeling of slumbering safety and oblivious ease continued through my college years. Wasn't I just so *lucky* that I never had to think about race? As a high-achieving Indian American, I felt impervious to most of the discourse around postcolonialism and stuck to the things I loved most: my postmodern American novels and continental philosophy. By the time I was in university, there were enough Black and Brown folks around me to make me feel even more like a good model minority. Maybe it was moving to Germany that triggered something; I remember the moment on a train platform in Berlin when I realized that someone might actually flirt with me *because* of my skin color. The first time, it was thrilling. After a couple more references to *Siddhartha* and Germans looking for Kama Sutra enlightenment, I had a less rosy picture.

But I really don't need to tell you my entire life story, Zia! I've been tending too much to shaggy dog tales these days. Maybe I just need to sit down and finally pen some sort of sprawling memoir or fiction (or combination of both) that can capture these ideas adequately. I suppose that's what you did–though much better than I'll ever be able to do–with *In the Light of What We Know*!

When I first read your novel that summer and fall of 2014, one particular passage struck me: your itinerant and mysterious protagonist, Zafar, is queried about his penchant for wearing dark suits at all times while navigating in Afghanistan, Bangladesh, and Pakistan. His response is telling, though now flipping through the book I realize that I can't find the exact words I remember. Did I make it up or extrapolate from the text? You once told me that there are lots of things that people recall from your books that you never explicitly wrote, but that you actually did intend to imply.

In any case, Zafar tells his friend that his generic but formal clothing choice helps him to avoid certain kinds of attention, to unmark himself. That fall, in the wake of Michael Brown's murder, in the wake of Ferguson, in the wake of *thewayblackmachine*, in the wake of *In the Light of What We Know*, I traveled around the US, moving through the international art world like a fish out of water. Wherever I landed, I would insist, even more forcefully than in the past, on wearing a dark suit or at least a blazer at all times, regardless of temperature or context. From steamy gallery openings to museum dinners to art fair previews to friends' birthday parties, I would answer queries about taking off my jacket with a paean to your book and a line that I guess I invented: "I always wear a dark suit when traveling in a war-torn country."

Until reading your book, I had never thought too carefully about how I dressed, but that passage (even if I invented part of it!), made me realize how my particular garb has served as a shield. In the several years leading up to 2014, as I had started to spend more and more time embedded within the art world, chatting with folks whose skin color was a lot lighter and whose net worth might be a hundredfold or a thousandfold my own, I felt an even greater need for protection: a distinctive layer of clothing that would mark me as belonging to the class of people allowed to frequent these hallowed white cubes of White culture.

Clothing has always been a strong signifier of identity and aspiration. My dear friend Roger, a founder of the art journal and publisher I was telling you about, wrote a trenchant yet humorous essay about clothing and etiquette in the art world for our first book. But beyond signifying belonging to a particular creative class or profession (for example, that of the artist), having uniforms for certain roles and classes also represents an attempt on the part of the wearer to conform, to fit in, to stand out less—and thus to make the experience of social interaction between folks from different contexts smoother.

I'm sure that Erving Goffman must have said something about this, but it's been a couple decades since I read him. The jacket and boat shoes required at a country club (a type of place I've been exactly once, with the upstate New York grandparents of my stepdaughter's close friend, where I suspected, correctly, that I might be the only person with tawny skin not working the service); the basic shirt and shoes required for more modest spaces. I often think of the historical anecdote, hopefully not apocryphal, that a friend once told me about the characteristic garb of the Hasidim. Apparently, they originally donned black suits and hats in order to imitate the Polish or Russian nobility, and therefore blend in better. Except that, in continuing the style for centuries after, their attempt at assimilation, ironically enough, became a highly visible marker of otherness and not belonging.

Eventually, my own habit of wearing a blazer to every art world event or meeting started to seem more like a forced gesture, one I imposed on myself in order to feel a sense of fitting in.

Although, come to think of it, sometimes I also took the opposite tack: one day many years ago, I was meant to gather my then-girlfriend from Tempelhof Airport in Berlin. Her flight had been scheduled for September 12, 2001, and so it was delayed for a week or so by the World Trade Center attacks. I was nervous about being picked up as a suspicious individual in the airport, so I decided to make myself *really* conspicuous: I headed to the airport wearing safety orange pants, a safety orange jacket, and a safety orange hat. Plus, I whistled the whole way into the airport, just to make it clear that I was no threat. The security personnel probably thought I was insane rather than scared.

Although America and Germany are the only countries I've known as a resident, I can feel with clarity the powerful connections between class, race, and clothing in the home country of my parents, India. As Tamil-speaking, highly educated Brahmins, my parents belong to the elite of their own context. Even though they left that context for the USA and arrived as dark-skinned, ill-fitted immigrants with funny accents who lived off of food stamps for the first few years, what they left behind was privilege: as Brahmins, belonging to the highest caste, they could make good use of education, capital, advancement, and social networks, resources withheld from others around them. And this shows in their garb, in the veshtis and dhothis my father might wear to the temple, lined with gold filigree; in my mother and grandmother's nine-yard saris, equally resplendent with precious metals. Those clothes allowed them to lord it over those of lower castes. How was it read by their colonial masters?

It's hard for me to say, since my father was born only four years before Indian independence and my mother three years after—and I, born and raised only on the East Coast, in the US, have little access to the sartorial codes of their native country. Yet within the context of our transplanted Hindu community, I started wearing my black and gray blazers as a badge of pride on the rare occasions that I went to the temple after college. There, it was a nearly aggressive sign of deliberate Otherness, an attempt to represent power from another context in one that was foreign even to me.

Of course, I owe my mother even this badge of honor, this suit of armor (is it a coincidence or a fact of etymological clarity that we call it a "suit"?). For it was my mother, who, if I remember correctly, first took me when I was 14 or 15 to a Macy's department store in our local shopping mall to buy me my first blazer: a navy blue Brooks Brothers jacket with fake gold buttons sewn on the outside of the sleeves, which marked me as a Connecticut man. This blazer, which was probably acquired in preparation for my first serious debate meet, would be the one I carried through college and into my first years afterward in Germany. In my twenties, after having sneered at the extreme privilege and opportunity that allowed me to study, debt-free, at an Ivy League college, receiving an undergraduate degree in fine art (of all possible subjects! For an Asian child to pursue art at an expensive college instead of something more practical! It is a testament to the love and care my parents have for me, something it took me decades to realize, that they even allowed this. A whole other letter to send one day!), that I realized the truth: I owed my parents the fact that they first tried to armor me. They gave me a garment to protect me from the hostile White world that had made a smaller man of my father and worse of too many others.

So today, despite the baggage of a blazer, I can wear it more lightly, thanks to your fantastic book and the journey it began in me. I can wear a blazer to openings, even in the Miami heat (the worst kind of openings, let me tell you! And the place from which I first called you after a raging all-nighter to talk about doing a show together); sometimes, rarely, I even trust myself enough to wear shorts to openings, the way other folks around me seem to do with relative ease.

On that note: a couple of months ago, my dear stepdaughter, who had helped assist a major German artist install a museum show, took her mother and me as *her* guests to the private opening. It was an unusually hot day, and my wife suggested that it was just fine for me to wear shorts. As I walked out towards the door, I asked my very stylish stepdaughter if it was an appropriate choice. She looked me up and down, and told me that it would probably be better if I at least went in pants. I ended up throwing on a blazer—not the worst decision I've ever made.

Big hugs, Prem

August 9, 2020
Berlin

On Letters—
Letter One

Originally published in
Prem Krishnamurthy, *On Letters*
(New York: Domain, 2022).

(2022)

Dear On,

Today, I got up at 5:55 A.M. I had been dreaming about letters.

Letters! What beautiful things. What would we humans have done without letters? If there had never been an ancient Phoenician who drew an ox-head and called it an *aleph*, if there had never been a first translation from the invisible realm of ideas and the ephemeral medium of sound into a visual mark on a substrate, where would we be now? I know that letters are the way I make sense of life, but I can't help thinking that something is lost, something sci-fi genius Ted Chiang or Indigenous scholar Tyson Yunkaporta might describe as a fluid relationship to memories, to rules, to order, to structure, to standards. Yes, letters are a kind of ancient magic; think of the doubled meanings of "to spell" and "a spell." Yet once they're committed to paper—or screen or canvas—ideas become fixed, they become material, they appear permanent. If things are never written down, they also remain open, changing, although they can prove harder to post across distances of space and time.[1]

And so I write to you, On, to get at the heart of the tension between letters as stable things and the myriad changes they cloak. In spite of all appearances, when we look at your Date Paintings, with their white letterforms painted on a flat, monochromatic ground, fixity is clearly not the case. Your project was simple, but vast: on a large number of your 29,771 days, you woke up, wherever in the world you were, and completed a painting containing only a date in the geographic location's primary language, perhaps *OCT. 9, 1966* or 29 *MAJ. 1983* or *4 AOÛT 2006*. Partaking of such an enormous conceptual project, each of your quiet artworks outlasts mortal time as one of the great human creations, its physical presence alluding to something eternally unfinished and resolving at multiple scales. I've often projected my desire for coherent conceptual systems and perfectly rationalized projects onto you. Yet the more time I spend with your work, the more it unsettles the answers I used

1 I might also mention Walter Ong's essential *Orality and Literacy*, the seed for Chiang's short story, "The Truth of Fact, the Truth of Feeling," or Jacques Derrida's *Of Grammatology*, one of my early lessons in unlocking the lore of letters, or even David Abram's *The Spell of the Sensuous*, a more recent revelation for me in terms of rethinking the relationship of speaking and writing—though, damn!, that would be a hell of a lot of dudes for only the second full paragraph of this letter!

to seek from art—your approach to creating the paintings, those coolly curved letters themselves coming to resemble a literary conceit, even an artistic metafiction. Or, perhaps, a lifelong game, one that one of us might just win. For although your paintings might appear consistent, I am beginning to realize that they are anything but. Your letters, like my letters, are also mutable, transforming and transformative over time.

You must have a unique relationship to language and writing. Was the Roman script your second, your third one? By knowing Japanese first, did you enjoy a more complex and multitiered relation to linguistic representation? I've read that Japanese contains both ideographic characters (*kanji*) as well as syllabic ones (*kana*). Using it must require a subtle shifting of the brain's function from the realm of the symbolic to that of the real. Not the real, mind you, in some psychoanalytic sense, but rather the clear materiality and craftiness of a syllabic letter, which exists not only as a self-contained idea, but also as an open-ended building block. I hope you don't take me for an essentialist, On, but is it possible that the mythical sharpness of your mind can be traced to this constant switching of modes while reading, the necessity for the brain to fluidly shift gears, a perpetual motion that keeps the mental transmission well-oiled?

But I never have been much of a car person, so let me abandon unsure roads and stick to what I know I know pretty well: letters, especially of the Latinate persuasion. Let me linger on notions of translation that lie close at hand, theories that land on the tip of my tongue. Like Nabokov's introduction to *Lolita*, where he transports us through his own linguistic tragedy, of never writing in his mother tongue, Russian, but rather always arriving to writing as a tourist. Of course, I've heard that there's a disingenuity in this claim, since as a wealthy White Russian, he learned French and German and perhaps even English from his governesses alongside his native Russian, with its Cyrillic script—yet still, what is it to have to translate at the very moment of laying forth your innermost thoughts? What is it to never feel the "natural" flow of a language, what comes to you in your dreams, when putting pen and brush to paper—but, rather, to constantly be compelled to negotiate signs and their performance for others?

We will never know what that act of waking up, morning after morning, sitting at a notebook or typewriter, might have felt like to Nabokov, but we can evaluate the results. Regardless of his subject, V.N. constructed sentences and crafted metaphors that, I humbly maintain, no native speaker could have deigned to produce. Perhaps it was this embedded foreignness, the discomfort of writing in English for the polyglot Nabokov, which produced such strands of liquid poetry and bumptious pleasure. The tragedy of original loss, the fact that the most profound creators might be alienated from the very letters that they pen, is a starting point for us today.

Yet letters are more than an individual's story: what is a letter, but a dense encapsulation of a tribe, an entire culture, its history? Think of the smoothed-out diamond at the end of a long process of compression, discovery, cutting, and polishing. Unlike a diamond, extracted by forced labor under the worst of conditions, a letter is rarely to be bought or sold; if anything, commerce and trade are what it enables. But when a diamond, like a letter, is framed—set, for example, into a smart metal housing and flashed at a party—it reads not only as a thing but also as a symbol: one discrete component within a communicative system. Sometimes, within an ensemble of jewelry, its unique history and transformation may be nearly forgotten, subsumed within the whole getup. This is when a diamond is at its most powerful—not on display in a vitrine for the scheming of some silent circle of thieves, but rather, as a hidden player within a many-act historical drama. It's also the power of a letter, penned even in a cipher or invisible ink, shaping history behind the scenes.

Neither diamonds nor letters are an end-game of a geologic and cultural journey. Though it may seem static, every diamond will continue its path of becoming something else, long after the humans who polished it for presentation have returned to dust. Much like the alien black monolith in Stanley Kubrick's *2001*, lording over the development of the first human tools, diamonds seem forever. But what if, like glass, they are forever changing, albeit at speeds we cannot easily register? "A thing is just a slow event," wrote Stanley Eveling somewhere, somewhen, and I fervently believe him. Our own, naturally human, alphabetical diamonds, this finite set of letters: they accompany us throughout generations, from place to place, marking out the daily transformations of time and society and ourselves.

So let's make a pact now: never to let these letters that we treasure so dearly appear to us as static things, as points of arrival rather than what they are: endless, perpetual departures. If we can agree to this, On–and I feel confident that, on this, you and I will be one–then I think it might be a marvelous journey together.

Au revoir, bis nächste Mal, sayōnara, dear On.

With warmest regards,
Prem

Afterword for *Notes on Book Design*

Originally published as an afterword in Formal Settings (Siri Lee Lindskrog and Amanda-Li Kollberg), *Notes on Book Design* (Eindhoven: Onomatopee, 2023).

(2023)

MY DEAR FRIEND DAVID GILES is an amateur author of the short form book review. Although David is definitely not a millennial, his book reviews are written in a way that younger generations might appreciate: he types them entirely on his Android phone, two thumbs tapping in alternating staccatos. This might make you think that his texts are short, something like Twitter's famed constraint of 280 characters. No, quite the opposite. They are extended, enthusiastic, even breathless investigations of a book's character, meant to express his great love of books alongside manifold philosophical musings.

Here's the review that first introduced me to his idiosyncratic form. It was sent to me as a text message—the longest and possibly best text message I've ever received. I hope you'll forgive the potentially self-aggrandizing fact that this book review was written about my first book, which no doubt endeared me even more towards David's self-assigned format:

> I finished your book this morning. I loved it. It was very readable for someone who has spent very little time thinking about On Kawara which is seriously nothing to sneeze at. You achieved something in your tone and style that I think about often or used to anyway (I haven't for a while). Is it irony? The Spanish author Enrique Vila Matas writes a lot about this. "Irony is the highest form of sincerity," he wrote in There is Never Any End to Paris. And "I don't like ferocious irony but rather the kind that vacillates between disappointment and hope." Kafka, Walzer, Vila Matas, Marias (maybe) all employ a kind of comedic irony that creates space between the subjective space of the narrator and their story or subject matter. It gives the reader space to move around in and reflect on their own experiences and their own always evolving relationship to the author, narrator, and story. I
> re-read the famous Paul De Mann essay on irony years ago when thinking about this and was struck again with how brilliant it was (despite the personal failings of the author of course). Is it a form of narrative self-consciousness? I wrote a bunch of stuff about this that i can no longer access mentally, at least not right now. The epistolary conceit of your essay, as a fiction in particular (since On Kawara cannot receive them much less answer them) gives you a lot of room to do this, to play around with the greetings and salutations, the indexicality of the writing, etc. It was a brilliant move. But many of your arguments and insights were brilliant as well, particularly when you zero in on the idea that his paintings were a form of lettering rather than typography, and how this assumption could go unanalyzed for so long by so many smart people, an assumption that was difficult for
> people to distance themselves from in part, I imagine, because they couldn't imagine why it was important. It looks like typography, it seems to mimic typography (however

imperfectly as your younger self thought) so it must be typography. And anyway even if it□s not typography what difference does it make? Your essay is an extended rumination on how this seemingly subtle shift in perception creates a whole new vista of interpretative possibility, something that good philosophers do when they pick a part the arguments of their predecessors, pointing out that this seemingly insignificant logical move is not only question-begging but obscures everything interesting about the matter at hand. Wittgenstein's critique of Augustine's theory of language at the beginning of the Philosophical Investigations, for instance, and his discovery that the so-called unity of the proposition is an enormous philosophical problem that no one has every really identified much less theorized about. How do the words in a sentence hold together as a thought when each individual word has no meaning outside the proposition/thought? I loved your playful obsessions in the book, and how you bring in analysis from self-help literature. I have heard you talking about many of the books in there for years (Perec, Foucault's Pendulum) so it was personally delightful to see how they have informed your thinking over many years. It's clear that there was much more at stake in this essay than just properly understanding On Kawara's Date Paintings, which ultimately makes it much more valuable as writing. I hope it finds a broader audience.

[original formatting retained]

David's 577 word paean does not attempt to synopsize its subject. Instead, it expresses the peculiar, personal experience of joy in reading; it follows its own preoccupations without reservation. I wonder whether the review would have received a good mark in a high school class.

Many academic institutions prize so-called objectivity over excitement. Yet the fact that the writing's careening trajectory defies the calculable logic of, say, the recently released ChatGPT AI software, is what makes it valuable. This book note is willful, particular, biased, and, to my eye, beautifully bumpy. I find David's texts brilliant encapsulations of how bibliophilic ekphrasis can, under the right circumstances, become a peculiar art form unto itself.

§

Amid the family photos, nonchalantly sexy selfies, exhibition views, dance videos, yoga ads, and artworld memes that Instagram's algorithms serve me up every day, Amanda-Li Kollberg and Siri Lee Lindskrog's "Notes on Book Design" for Berlin's Hopscotch Reading Room pop up periodically. I usually click on them to read their 2,200-character captions. Although my interests run wide, I started my more mature intellectual life as a graphic designer—so things in this vein win my attention the most.

I don't think one can get away from where you come from. At least, I know that *I* can't. Over the past 20 years, I've called myself a curator, a writer, an exhibition-maker; an artist, an organizer, a facilitator; a teacher, a learner, a performer; a tour guide, a talk show host, a karaoke MC; and more. All of these monikers might be more or less true, but recently I've come to accept that I am, at the core, a designer. It underlies how I experience and process the world.

Embracing the identity of a designer seems to come more naturally to Amanda and Siri. They are unabashed about their love of the medium. The "Notes on Book Design" may summarize the literary aspect of the books they've chosen, but their real interest is honing in on materials, format, typography, tactility, and so on.

In this, their notes appear quite different from those of my friend David, who as a former philosopher and future novelist is obsessed with literary construction and language's nuances. Yet their project is also a kind of generative obsession, just with another focus: the syntax and structure of book design and typography. Although they may or may not type the notes on their phones (you'd have to ask them), they do go deep on the specificities of visual choices, how a certain font or particular binding or paper finish creates complex, embodied meanings. Here, these two very distinct approaches find a common ground: the quest to unravel the myriad ways in which a book means something in the world—what its printed words spark in the reader's brains and how its physical presence transmits information into the reader's hands.

Rather than trying to inhabit someone else's voice or a normative approach, Amanda and Siri burrow down deeper into their own designerly subjectivity. The serial quality of the reviews also suggests a process of learning over time. I wonder if the act of writing these book reviews one-after-another and later reviewing them as a corpus (as they have also done in order to prepare this publication) helps them to understand their own work as designers, their perspective, and their critical lens differently, sharpening the perspective that is their unique contribution.

Critics have honed their craft (and themselves) for decades by pounding the pavement, looking for shows or books to review, digesting those experiences in words, and then, thereafter, more or less consciously learning from them by writing and tweaking how they write. And then they pound the proverbial pavement again, yet with new eyes to bring to bear upon each successive exhibition or volume. It's a transformative process—a successive feedback loop that both creates observations about the world while also reflecting upon the very subjectivity that is doing the looking.

It's a little like the process of writing this text. A slightly rambling postscript for a book of book reviews that has reminded me of a simple fact: I love design, I love books, I love writing, I love the act of thinking through and with books and trying to capture their mysterious ways in a linguistic form, while also acknowledging that these beautiful books—or any given subject, to be honest—will always exceed its description by leaps and bounds.

To paraphrase Kae Tempest's song "Grace," replacing only the word "love" with "books":

> Make books, let me be books
> Let me be booking
> Let me give books, receive books, and be nothing but books
> In books and for books and with books
> In books and for books and with books

So thank you, Amanda and Siri, for inviting me to write this bookish, loving afterword. And I hope that you, dear reader, have lingered over these notes on book design as much as I have: finding love, of all kinds, within them. I hope they find a broader audience.

Prem Krishnamurthy
Berlin, January 12, 2023

A is for Acknowledgments

(and Annotations)

(2024)

It seems nearly impossible to compile acknowledgements for a book of work that spans over fifteen years. I barely remember much of that time, given how insanely busy and sleep-deprived it was. So, if you don't find your name here, know that it probably should be!

As my erstwhile design partner Rob Giampietro[1]—a brilliant writer in his own right—taught me many years ago, a great way to organize a chaotic series of thoughts is through

SUBHEADERS

He learned this, I believe, from Rem Koolhaas's *Delirious New York,* in my humble estimation still one of the best nonfiction novels about Gotham City. Although reducing things to categories may seem unnecessarily atomizing ("Every person is actually many people," the multifarious Brian O'Doherty[2] used to tell me), at least subheaders give us a simple structure to start with.

So, without further ado, let's go!

THE BOOK

Kicking things off are the immediate thank yous: first, to Krist Gruijthuijsen for his initial invitation to start *K,*,[3] his trust in my sometimes-bumpy process, and his proposal (and support) to bring together my writing into this book.[4] Without his insistent urging, *Past Words* would not exist. I know that it became far more complex than he ever imagined, but I guess that's par for the course. Secondly, to Valentijn Goethals[5] for the initial commission to develop *Endless Exhibition*[6] as Kunsthal Gent's first artwork, and then to make this conceptual obstacle the founding curatorial premise of an entire institution. It takes real resolve and courage to tackle something like this, knowing well that it can only fail.[7] Valentijn is someone who, like me, comes to exhibition-making and institution-building from graphic design. This makes me appreciate even more his quiet but steady bedside manner in accompanying challenging projects. I am grateful not only to him but also to Danielle van Zuijlen, Tim Bryon, and the entire team of Kunsthal Gent who have led this inspiring institution so far—and hopefully for many years ahead!

My boundless thanks goes to Steve Pulimood, a colleague, collaborator, and supporter of P! from its start. His downtown gallery, Room East, served as encouragement for my own foray into gallery-ing. His continued friendship and generosity—as well as his discerning sense of design!—has allowed this book to come into being in this form. Thea Westreich Wagner & Ethan Wagner have also been tireless cheerleaders of P! and my work. They seeded *K,* long ago by gifting me a recording of On Kawara's *One Million Years.*[8] With Thea's signature enthusiasm, she has now enlisted the welcome support of Jane Hait, Fred Bidwell, Carin Kuoni[9] & John Oakes, and others[$] to help make this book's wild design and printing possible. Anna Rubin has been Thea's tireless assistant in this initiative.

1 See pages 188–195, 196–205

2 See pages 6, 41, 46, 161, 183, 206–216, 226, 239, 250, 297–300, 358

3 See pages 4–8, 10, 67, 72–74, 81–152, 236

4 See pages 1–360!

5 See pages 10–11, 12, 57–74, 217–288

6 See pages 217–288

7 See pages 27–29, 301–325

8 See pages 81, 99, 107, 114, 118

9 See page 235

$ Thanks also to Gita and Subramaniam Janakiraman and Prakash Janakiraman, as well as Asha Murthy, Dr Radha and Dr Giridharan, Howard Freedman, Kanchana and Venkat R. Ishwar, S. Srinivasan, and Sharda Srinivasan.

Brian Sholis[10] is an exceptionally multifaceted and well-structured human, one whom I've had the privilege of working with on multiple endeavors in different capacities over the past twenty years. One of our first projects at my first studio Project Projects was the design of a website for his writing. So I'm even more grateful that he reciprocated by serving as an editor-midwife to help me to select, sequence, and think through the writing in this book. I'm hopeful that we'll have a chance to work on other projects over the next 20 years!

An incommensurate note of gratitude goes to Judith Gärtner,[11] assistant and extended mind[12] of this book (and to me in general). She helped me establish P!, and later was my partner in everything *K*,. That particularly kooky juggling game would not have existed without her wholehearted support and engagement in the process. It even included translating my alphabetically absurdist texts into equally if not more gonzo German! For the entire two-plus years of creating this book, she has supported editorially, graphically, and emotionally to make sure it gets done. Thanks for having follow-through, focus, *and* excitement, a rare combination indeed.

Charity Coleman's attention to this unwieldy set of words allowed its language to be as clear and error-free (and free-wheeling) as anything in the world might hope to be. She has touched (figuratively, I mean) every word in this book (including this one!). Plus, given her part-time preoccupation as a poet, perhaps, she permitted a more prolific preponderance of non-standard punctuation and anarchically alliterative, poor-man's Perecian play to pass than any other professional proofreader would typically find pardonable.

THE DESIGN

This book's format feels like a beautiful moment of designerly reprise, when people I have known in other graphic performances come back to play leading roles. The four designers of this book[13] have been thinking partners and more for a combined total of over 40 years; I've had the pleasure to be party to their many engagements with my work and their individual pursuits. I am so proud of what they've each accomplished.

David Knowles[14] was my right-hand human at P! for nearly its whole run (until Patricia Margarita Hernández[15] stepped in to steer us to the close). He provided well-needed poise and counterbalance to my frenetic action. I am so happy that he went on to embrace the media of the book fully. Thank you, David, for always being you.

Ann Richter[16] is the designer of this international cohort whom I've known the longest, since her time working with me in New York City during the 21st-century tweens. Even back then, she brought quiet intensity and typographic precision coupled with a wild ambition to make things outside of the norm. She has proved a trusted collaborator since, often sharing design commissions, as well as being a friend and respected pedagogical colleague. Furthermore, she came to nearly every *K*, program, evidenced in the excessive photographic record. I'm honored to have watched her grow to create

10 See page 301 in particular

11 See pages 92, 104, 112, 142–143

12 See page 298

13 See page 3

14 See pages 1–80, 153–216, 289–360

15 See pages 227, 241

16 See pages 81–152

17 See page 57

18 See page 163

19 See pages 96, 163

20 See page 326

21 See page 336

22 See page 19

23 See pages 23, 25, 27, 51

24 See page 188

25 See page 343

26 See page 75

27 See page 174

28 See page 196

29 See pages 66, 153

30 See page 206

31
See page 297

32
See page 47

33
See page 57

34
See page 153

35
See page 323

36
See page 206

37
See page 63

space for other talented designers through Studio Pandan, her practice with Pia Christmann. Thank you for taking the time out of your busy studio life (and life-life) for this.

Mark Foss & Valentijn Goethals represent the design team who were most intrinsically embedded within the holistic ecosystem in their specific section—as I mentioned before, Valentijn actually commissioned *Endless Exhibition*. To be both commissioner *and* designer is a wild and rare double role, one that I understand only too well. And thank you, Mark, for accompanying us in this time traveling, after having made an appearance in some of P!'s programs (look *very closely* at the hands in the bottom left corner of page 258)! I am excited to experience your further adventures in shaping graphics and communities alike.

As you might have gleaned by now, I have a thing for letters and typography. As a recently recovering graphic designer, having hot sexy cool fucking awesome new typefaces is one of the best hits you can take. Believe me! Phew. So thank you to the generous type designers who let Ann use your typefaces in the *K*, section: Fabian Harb & Johannes Breyer (Dinamo), Elias Hanzer & Lucas Liccini (HAL Typefaces), Andrea Tinnes (typecuts), Commercial Type, Florian Karsten, Lisa Drechsel (Apparat Type), Nolan Paparelli, and Siri Lee Lindskrog (Formal Settings).

Another crucial design companion to *Past Words*, embedded invisibly within its pages (appropriate given his inscrutable way), is Benjamin Reichen of Åbäke. We have been circling around each other for a while. His unique "Deep Publishing" process helped me to distill many ideas about this book's direction and *K*, in particular in 2022. He is a beautiful teacher and I am grateful to count him among my closest.

THE WRITING

All of the pieces of writing reprinted in this book owe a debt of gratitude to their original commissioners and editors. To accept my writing at a time when I could not clearly see it myself represents a true leap of faith.[17] These trusting souls include Angela Lammert[18] and Anna Schultz,[19] Christopher K. Ho & Daisy Nam,[20] David Knowles[21] (and yes, he not only worked for me and designed part of my book, but also commissioned, published, *and* designed my last book! I owe this dynamic dude a lot), Dushko Petrovich & Roger White,[22] David Reinfurt,[23] Eva Franch i Gilabert,[24] Formal Settings (Siri Lee Lindskrog and Amanda-Li Kollberg),[25] Geir Haraldseth,[26] Geoff Kaplan,[27] Jon Sueda,[28] Julian Myers-Szupinska,[29] Miranda Driscoll,[30] Phong Bui,[31] Stella Bottai,[32] and Valentijn Goethals[33] (there he is again!). Each of these individuals recognized something writerly in me and invited it to grow.

Several individuals and organizations gave me invaluable space and time for writing. These include Denniston Hill,[34] helmed by Julie Mehretu,[35] Paul Pfeiffer, and Lawrence Chua; Maria Lind during her inspiring tenure at Tensta konsthall;[36] and Asad Raza[37] in his former role as artistic director of the Villa Empain in Brussels. Asad in particular has graced me with his friendship and collaboration through many projects since then, and even participated in one of my most quixotically ambitious outings to date.[38] Love ya, brother.

One of the most multifaceted humans I've met (and, believe me, I've met a couple!) is Cem Eskinazi. His keen insights, alongside those of numerous students and faculty, proved invaluable in helping me live-workshop *P!DF* in public from 2016-18.[39] Zia Haider Rahman, another swarthy polymath (and man of maths),[40] has been a model for errant forms of writing. Elvia Wilk[41] and Liz Jensen are two other speculative novelists whom I've had the good fortune of futuring with. I'm lucky to also have been in dialogue with adrienne maree brown,[42] world- and word-builder without peer.

My intellectual life as a writer was formed by two canny Connecticut coaches, Bob Cox and Professor Howard Stern at Yale. Howard in particular introduced me to George Perec and helped nudge me towards studying in Germany, two God-given gifts for which I can never repay him. Other friends and colleagues helped my writing in more mature years. Tim Aubry was co-author of my first published, performative piece, "The Genealogy of Discussion Club," and helped steer the regular gathering of the same name with me for several years—an informal graduate seminar for those of us who never went to grad school. Sarah Demeuse stands out as a constant source of encouragement, critique, and direct feedback, as well as a close friend. Our curatorial[43] and literary dialogue has been essential to my intellectual process over the entire period of this book's writing. Manuel Cirauqui has been an interlocutor for over a decade, matching my intensity of ideas at every turn with his brilliant meditations. Without him, my last book, *On Letters*, would not exist. Rob Wiesenberger was an ardent observer to P! and has been a design-writing-living friend since. Niels van Tomme is an ongoing curatorial comrade[44] in considering institutional forms and their relationship to politics. Sofía Hernández Chong Cuy has been an essential commissioner and discussant around design, curating, and more. She has witnessed, more than nearly anyone, the multiple forms that my designing can take. Javier Anguera and I have talked about classification systems for over fifteen years now, and there's thankfully no end in sight. Carin Kuoni has been a commissioner, a co-curator, a supporter, and a dear friend alike. John Oakes is an editor, publisher, and writer who is steadfast in his support. Nick Irvin read and commented on many of my texts (including that on Maryam Jafri[45]) during his generative time working with me in the studio. Jessica Loudis, editor-atrix extraordinaire, has exceeded any common expectations of friendship through her reading of the entirety of *On Letters*.[46] She also has the best book tips!

David Giles,[47] a dear friend in all things philosophical since 1999 and a great reader for much much longer, scrolled through versions of this. He may even be, as I type this, compiling proposed corrections for a book that has already gone to print. I love and admire your mind, David.

38
See page 323

39
See page 70

40
See page 326

41
See page 321

42
See page 310

43
See page 280

44
See page 269

45
See page 30

46
See page 336

47
See pages 343–346

48
See page 301

49
See pages 23–25, 200–201, and 233

50
See pages 57–58, 70, 200, 311

51
See pages 99–100

52
See pages 47, 52, 85

53
See page 27

54
See pages 120–121

55
See pages 96, 103

56
See page 103

57
See pages 120–121

58
See page 98

59
See pages 40, 144–145, 240

60
See pages 132–133

61
See pages 34, 39, 179–180, 186

62
See pages 39, 198

63
See page 186

64
See pages 126–127, 237

65
See pages 108–111, 126–127, 237

66
See pages 127, 237

67
See pages 126–127

68
See page 301

69
See page 126–127

70
See pages 67, 72–72, 81–152, 236

71
See pages 142–143

72
See pages 92–93, 98–99, 1001–101, 148–149

73
See pages 127–131

K,, EXHIBITION MAKING, AND DESIGN MORE GENERALLY

From about 2007-17, far too many of my conversations circled around exhibitions. You might say I was a little obsessed. Ken Saylor,[48] Judith Barry,[49] and Martin Beck[50] stand out as the folks I'd most often quaff a beer (or stronger) with in New York City while going deep on display. Paul O'Neill enabled this exhibitionary thinking (and drinking) during his influential time running Bard College's Center for Curatorial Studies, and Ann Butler at CCS remains the stalwart steward of this era of my creative production.

My discussions with a group of Londoners clarified sometimes scattered thinking about exhibitions, curating, design, and art. Emily King[51] has been a sharp conversational partner for nearly the whole period represented in this book. I never would have arrived at the (admittedly unhinged) idea to start a gallery without her. Catherine Ince is always down for some exhibitionary exchanges. Stella Bottai (represented through our collaboration on *P!CKER*,[52] and who gave me empathic feedback on one particularly personal section of *P!DF*[53]) has been a brilliant friend throughout. Sam Thorne, though not so prevalent in these pages (just wait until the next book!), is someone I always go to when I'm needing books, ideas, exhibitions, radical pedagogical models, and dance parties.

The community of designers in Berlin who came together around *K,* are an inspiring cohort. Practitioners like Andre Fuchs, Anja Lutz, Christoph Knoth,[54] Hendrik Schwantes, Imme Leonardi,[55] Jona Piehl,[56] Konrad Renner,[57] Oliver Klimpel, Serge Rompza,[58] and others—many of whom I've known for 25 years or longer—offered support as well as constructive critique. Most importantly, they simply *showed up*. I count among this group of wonderful folks my close friend Christine Hill, a superb designer of art and life alike.[59] Other farther-flung design minds who have proved crucial colleagues include Alexandra Cunningham Cameron,[60] Andrew Blauvelt,[61] Asli Altay, Ellen Lupton,[62] James Goggin, Lauren Mackler, Liz DeLuna, Mark Owens,[63] Mark Zurolo, Maryam Al Qassimi & Salem Al-Qassimi,[64] Michael Christian McCaddon, Michael Ellsworth, Na Kim,[65] Nina Paim,[66] Sulki and Min Choi, Tetsuya Goto,[67] Tereza & Vit Ruller,[68] Uzma Rizvi,[69] Vera Sacchetti, and Zoë Ryan.

Cathrin Mayer[70] helped shepherd *K,* during her fruitful time at KW. Sina Najafi of *Cabinet Magazine*[71] was a co-conspirator in creating Ebersstrasse 3—the hub that hosted *K,* for a year and afterwards. The space itself was constructed through the skilled craftsmanship and care of Dirk Dähmlow (who also took some of the best photographs[72] of it, which were sadly lost on a stolen hard drive) as well as Ole Schmidt and Daniel Rödiger.

Esen Karol is a genius designer and compassionate human whom I'm most fortunate to know. I am exceptionally proud of the afterlife of our projects together[73]; to help her work enter the collection of one of the most esteemed art institutions in the US, the Art Institute of Chicago—where it is collection-fellows to my work with Project Projects—means that this important *oeuvre* will be preserved for many others who need to know it.

My three business partners in graphic design since 2004—at different times, Adam Michaels, Chris Wu, and Rob Giampietro—have each contributed greatly to the arguments within this book. Writing—like graphic designing!—is a craft as much as a set of abstract ideas. Thank you for your creative companionship, friendship, and the challenges that you brought—all opportunities for growth. Chris[74] in particular deserves a note of high-level appreciation for how his precision design sensibility has led the direction of Wkshps since 2018. His friendship continues to support my greater-than-design mission.

THE RESEARCH

Specific pieces have their own thanks to give. My more than decade-long research, publishing, and curating on Klaus Wittkugel[75] has been helped by grants from the Graham Foundation for Advanced Studies in the Fine Arts (not once but twice!) and the New York State Council on the Arts. Steffen Tschesno's friendship and commitment to supporting new scholarship around his grandfather's legacy helped Wittkugel's singular work find contemporary audiences. Peter Zimmerman, Silvia Diekmann, and Anna Schulz at the Akademie der Künste, Berlin, were instrumental to this project at multiple phases. I am grateful to the designers who studied with Wittkugel and his other colleagues and family who gave me their time for interviews from 2008-10.

Endless Exhibition lives on because of formative conversations with Jeffrey Weiss, Martin Beck, Marvin Taylor, Matthew Israel, Michael Findlay, and Paul Elliman[76] (and yes, sorry, that was a list of all White dudes). Jessica Morgan and her excellent leadership of Dia Art Foundation helped lay the groundwork for much of my thinking around exhibitions and time. Michelle Elligott[77] at MoMA went above and beyond in both sharing her voluminous knowledge of René D'Harnoncourt[78] both during her visit to *K,* and in the preparation of this book.

Sebastian Bach[79] doesn't really fit into this section, but he's all over this book. A fantastic photographer and human who took many of the best images of P!, he also helped remind me that before I was a designer, I was a photographer. This was a primary lesson of *K,*. What a gift. Thank you, Seb.

LIFE AND THE REST

Designer, professor, and mover Emily Smith was a creative and emotional companion for over two decades. Her active collaboration on many projects during *K,*[80] and Fikra Graphic Design Biennial[81]—alongside her generous reading and re-reading (and re-reading and re-reading) of most of my texts written from 2015-2022—made

74
See page 112

75
See pages 7, 39–40, 63, 66, 73, 86, 88–89, 92–93, 96–97, 153–173

76
See page 99

77
See pages 188–189

78
Ibid.

79
See pages 235, 241, 243–244, 258, 265, 270–272, 275, 278–279, 282–283

80
See pages 108–109, 115–117, 129–130, 138–141, 148–149 in particular

81
See pages 126–127, 163

82
See pages 82, 109, 152

83
See pages 226, 250, 297

84
See pages 27, 227, 242, 282

85
See page 323

86
See page 265

87
See page 324

88
See pages 47, 185, 241, 244, 285, as well as the back cover

89
See pages 102–103, 321

90
See page 272

91
See page 310

92
See page 323

much of my creative work possible during that period. Her practice connecting embodiment, design, and dance informs many of the ideas that I hope to build upon in the future. Her children Anton and Eloise Hammermeister-Smith[82] have been a source of inspiration in how to live life joyously.

Simone Subal[83] was my dearest dearest gallerist friend throughout the period when I wore that dealer drag. We worked together closely as ambassadors of Brian O'Doherty's seminal work and legacy. Apropos nothing: She's also an incredible dancer. Apropos this volume: Simone once asked me if I would ever make a book of *K*,. I responded: *Why would I do that? It's written in the bodies of me and those who participated in it.* I guess I was wrong about the book, but all of us are marked by the time we've spent with each other.

Thomas Fischer first introduced me to Brian. This connection with a legendary figure and deeply kind man (as well as Barbara Novak, his partner of over sixty years and a brilliant, beautiful person in her own right) altered my life path.

Essential artist friends and collaborators whom I had the great fortune to exhibit and/or collaborate with include Aaron Gemmill,[84] Ahmet Öğüt,[85] American Artist, Anthony Marcellini,[86] Can Altay, Cassie Thornton,[87] Céline Condorelli,[88] Christopher Kulendran Thomas,[89] Connie Samaras,[90] Cory Arcangel,[91] Cooking Sections,[92] Elaine Lustig Cohen,[93] Every Ocean Hughes,[94] Femke Herregraven, Grace Ndiritu, Isabelle Andriessen,[95] James Wines,[96] Leslie Hewitt, Lenka Clayton & Phillip Andrew Lewis,[97] Jace Clayton,[98] Jonathan Bruce Williams,[99] Julie Mehretu,[100] Kameelah Janan Rasheed,[101] Maryam Jafri,[102] Mathew Hale,[103] Nora Turato, Paul O'Keeffe,[104] R.A. Washington, Renée Green,[105] Sarah Oppenheimer,[106] Tacita Dean, Tony Cokes,[107] and Wong Kit Yi a.k.a. Ali Wong.[108] Their work resonates throughout all of my words. Thank you for sharing your ideas and practices with me so entirely, even letting me sometimes swallow them into my own.

Of these generously creative human beings, Karel Martens[109] deserves exceptional praise and gratitude. I never studied with him in a formal way, but working with him was part of my cobbled-together graduate school of life. Without him, I would not have started a gallery or known what I know now about designing and teaching with clarity and conviction. I am so very proud of the work we pulled off together, Karel. Dank u wel!

Friederike Meyer has proved one of my most trusted friends since my early years in Berlin. I am thrilled to watch her son Ede—my godson—mature in the world. My old-school curatorial crew of Andria Hickey, Dan Byers, David Norr, and Tina Kukielski are still much much more than the world can handle (particularly at karaoke!). Alla Rachkov, Elizabeth Moller, and Stephen Hanmer D'Elía have been beloved companions since our crucial time in Berlin in the 1990s. Murtaza Vali and Annie Wischmeyer were both dear collaborators in Cleveland[110] as well as literal life-savers. Lisa Koby and Meghan DellaCrosse proved a true friend in those times of existential curiosity. Tamar Cohen[111] and Tamara Sussman are

93
See pages 47–50, 180, 251

94
See page 311

95
See page 320

96
See page 270

97
See page 311

98
Ibid.

99
See page 265

100
See page 323

101
See page 321

102
See pages 30, 39, 278

103
See page 243

104
See page 308

105
See page 324

106
See page 323

107
Ibid.

108
See pages 68, 218, 271, 281, 311

109
See pages 34–43, 134–135, 138–141, 283, 308

110
See pages 301–325

111
See pages 47, 251

112
See page 289

113
See page 113

absolutely the best friends one could wish for–always present, always checking in. What a blessing! I'll add to this motley roster Andrew Berry and Cara Maniaci, who helped me in the path of understanding myself–and also helped me to realize when the path is best undertaken in other formats.

Additional friends have been a great support in both work and life for several decades. A wholly incomplete list includes Alec Bemis, Ben Smith, Ben Sterling, Cathy Braasch, Damian Da Costa, Dan Amsterdam, David Levine, Emilie Baltz, Gautam Borooah, Gautam Srikanth, Ian Blecher, Kenan Halabi, Liena Zagare, Matt Saunders, and Qasim Naqvi. Still others have accompanied my more recent journeys through finding new formats to create community and connection (+ karaoke!). This work, which will form the basis of my next book, is hinted at here in the interview with Alice Grandoit-Šutka from *Deem Journal*.[112] Other fellow travelers include Alex Provan, Amale Andraos, Ana Paula Cohen, Andrew Sloat, Andros Zins-Browne, Chris Leong, Christie George, Clara Brandt, Dan Wood, Dominic Leong, Fanny Gonella, Gabriel Kahan, George Bermudez, Kalaija Mallery, Kali Nikitas, Kimberly Sutherland, Kristan Kennedy, Julia Kaganskiy, Libertad Guerra, Marcos Lutyens, Mary Ceruti, MENSCHMASCHINE (Stella Friedenberger & Benedikt Rottstegge), Naoco Wowsugi, Natalia Lombardo, Noah Simblist, Paige Emery, Peter Russo, Phillip Niemeyer, Richard D. Bartlett, Sofia Reeser del Rio, Summer Guthery, and Susan Ploetz.

David Reinfurt, whom I've had the good fortune to know since the late-20th century, has been a friend, mentor, reader, and publisher. His enthusiasm for my work throughout its many disparate turns has been essential to continuing. Phillip Niemeyer has played a particularly prominent role as an ambassador to many of my Projects with a capital P.

Thanks to Rebecca Raue for her brilliantly transformative work and openness to connection to the world of spirit in its many forms. Her coaching on the book and my thinking, working, and being has been essential.

And then, coming cautiously closer to the close: my deeply supportive family deserves the greatest note of thanks. My older sister Preethi Krishnamurthy served as my first editor; she is someone from whom I've learned an unquantifiable amount about words and language, arguments and reasoning. Thanks to my brother-in-law Dietmar Detering for his Teutonic clarity and incredible cooking. My wonderful nieces, Ananya & Romy, make a small cameo in this book[113]–the future belongs to them.

Profound thanks are due to my parents, Bala and Ramachandran Krishnamurthy. I could not have done any of this work over the past decades absent their tireless support, love, and understanding for the many things about me that they still don't understand. Without them, there would be no past to speak of.

The final dedication goes to Barbara Novak and Brian O'Doherty, who continuously encouraged my writing. Polymathic Brian in particular exhorted me to move past existing definitions of art, design, language, and life to embrace my own unique way, regardless of whether it made sense to others. I would not have mustered the courage to make a first or second—let alone third!—book without their radiance to illuminate the way.

Beyond them, I would like to thank all of the other incredible artists, curators, designers, writers, and musicians—well, actually, all of the incredible *humans*—whom I've had the privilege to connect and commune with over these brief forty-six years. I learn everything I know from others.

This includes you. Thank you for everything.

With love,
Prem

New York, June 2024

To be continued by the reader …